R D Laing: Contemporary Perspectives

Salman Raschid

(editor)

FA^B

Free Association Books

Published in the United Kingdom 2005
by Free Association Books
57 Warren Street
London W1T 5NR
© Free Association Books

British Library Cataloguing in Publication Data
A catalogue record for this book is available from the British Library

Produced by Bookchase, London
Printed and bound in the EU

ISBN 1853437018

To the memory of **R D LAING** (1927-1989)
Pioneer - Extraordinary

List of Contributors

Daniel Burston is Professor of Psychology at Duquesne University
F A Jenner is Emeritus Professor of Psychiatry at Sheffield University
Eric Matthews is Emeritus Professor of Philosophy at Aberdeen University
The late Roger Poole was Reader in Literary Theory at Nottingham University
Douglas Kirsner is Professor of Philosophy at Deakin University
Louis Sass is Professor of Clinical Psychology at Rutgers University
Francis Huxley is a British Social Anthropologist
Thomas Fuchs is Professor of Psychiatry (and Head of the Psychopathology and Phenomenology Unit) at Heidelberg University
Richard Bentall is Professor of Experimental Clinical Psychology at Manchester University
The late Loren Mosher was Clinical Professor of Psychiatry at the University of California (San Diego)
Luc Ciompi is Emeritus Professor of Psychiatry (and Head of the Academic Social Psychiatry Research Unit) at Bern University
The late Robin Cooper was a Psychotherapist based at the Philadelphia Association
John Heaton is a Psychotherapist and Philosopher based at the Philadelphia Association
Salman Raschid is a Psychiatrist and student of philosophy

Copyright acknowledgments

The editor gratefully acknowledges permission to reproduce the following items:
1. R.D. Laing – Review of Karl Jaspers *International Journal of Psychoanalysis* 45: 1964 (590-3).
2. Luc Ciompi's chapter in this book is a revised version of a special lecture given at the 93rd Annual Meeting of the Japanese Society of Psychiatry and Neurology (Tokyo, May 29, 1997); now published here with the permission of the author.
3. J.R. Bola and L. Mosher *Journal of Nervous and Mental Disease* 2003 191:4 (219-229)
4. Frontispiece photograph of R.D. Laing: the Editor is grateful to Jutta Laing for obtaining it from the photographer Dorothy von Greiff.

R D Laing: Contemporary Perspectives
Contents

part one
introduction

"The present condition of European sciences necessitates radical investigations of sense. At bottom these sciences have lost their great belief in themselves, in their absolute significance. The modern man of today, *unlike the "modern" man of the Enlightenment,* does not behold in science, and in the new culture formed by means of science, the self-objectivation of human reason or the universal activity mankind has devised for itself in order to make possible a truly satisfying life; an individual and social life of practical reason. *The belief that science leads to wisdom* — to an actually rational self-cognition and cognition of the world and God, and, by means of such cognition, to a life somehow to be shaped closer to perfection, a life truly worth living, a life of "happiness", contentment, well-being, or the like - t*his great belief, once the substitute for religious belief, has (at least in wide circles) lost its force. Thus men live entirely in a world that has become unintelligible,* in which they ask in vain for the wherefore, *the sense,* which was once so doubtless and accepted by the understanding, as well as by the will.

Now, however critical and skeptical our attitude toward our scientific culture as it has developed historically, we cannot simply abandon it, with no more reason than that we lack an ultimate understanding of it and are unable to manage it by virtue of such an understanding because, in other words, we are unable to explicate its sense rationally, to determine the true range of its sense, the range within which we can self-responsibly justify the sense of our culture and, with our continued labor, make this sense actual. If we are not satisfied by the joy of creating a theoretical technique, or contriving theories with which one can do so much that is useful and win the admiration of the world — if we cannot separate genuine humanity and living with radical self-responsibility, and therefore cannot separate scientific self-responsibility from the whole complex of responsibilities belonging to human life as such — then *we must place ourselves above this whole life and all this cultural tradition and, by radical sense-investigations,* seek for ourselves singly and in common the ultimate possibilities and necessities, on the basis of which we can take our position toward actualities in judging, valuing and acting."

Edmund Husserl - Formal and Transcendental Logic (1927)

"In the perspective of the Analytic of Da-Sein, all conventional, objectifying representations of a capsule-like psyche, subject, person, ego, or consciousness in psychology and psychopathology must be abandoned in favour of an entirely different understanding. This new view of the basic constitution of human existence maybe called *Da-Sein*, or being-in-the-world. Of course, in this context the *Da* of Da-sein certainly does not mean what it does in the ordinary sense — a location near an observer. Rather, to exist as Da-Sein means to hold open a domain through its capacity to receive-perceive the significance of the things that are given to it [Da-sein] and that address it [Da-sein] by virtue of its own "clearing" [*Gelichtetheit*]. Human Da-sein as a domain with the capacity for receiving-perceiving *is* never merely an object present-at-hand. On the contrary, it is not something which is objectified at all under any circumstances."

Martin Heidegger
Zollikon Seminars (2001)

1: Editorial Introduction

Salman Raschid

In considering the complex nature of R.D. Laing's legacy, and its continuing intellectual vitality and relevance, a convenient point of entry is provided by his devastating 1964 review of Karl Jasper's *General Psychopathology* (*International Journal of Psychoanalysis* 45: 1964 590-3). I am therefore reproducing the review in full:

R D Laing on Karl Jaspers

General Psychopathology. By Karl Jaspers. (Manchester Univ. Press, 1963. Pp.922. 75s)

This book is already regarded by many eminent psychiatrists as a major psychiatric classic. Jaspers is also regarded by many as a great philosopher, and this book can be seen as the golden touch on psychiatry of the finger of a master European thinker. Despite the fact that a number of people whom I respect hold Jaspers in high regard as a philosopher and as a psychologist, in my view there is a radical lack of discrimination on the highest level if Jaspers is classed among the great thinkers of recent European history. As a philosopher, Jaspers has produced an amalgam of the work of others, mainly of Kant, Hegel, Kierkegaard, Nietzsche, Max Weber – in a way that Sartre has called 'soft and underhand'.

As a psychopathologist, I find Jaspers even less satisfactory than Sartre finds him as a philosopher. For here, his grasp of large tracts of the subject is not merely undistinguished, it is inadequate. I refer the reader to his sections on dreams and his remarks on transference, repression, conflict, childhood, for instance.

Consider dreams. His account of the phenomena of dreams (pp. 144-145), based on Hacker, does not begin to grapple with the subject. In his section on dream contents and their interpretation (pp. 372-376), not only does he not give evidence of a first-hand knowledge of the stuff of dreams, he virtually limits his account of dream interpretation to the work of Silberer, and he appears to have no understanding of the different functions that dreams may have in a person's life. When, here as frequently elsewhere, he calls on his own resources, one sees both the lack of quality in his own thinking and the lack of instinct for empirical discovery.

'Taking it all in all, I think that some truth is to be found in the principles of dream-interpretation. My objection is not raised against its correctness (though it provides an endless field for fantasy and mock-performance) but rather against the importance attached to it. Once the main principles are learnt, and tested out on certain cases, there is little else to learn. The dream is a remarkable phenomenon, but after the first flush of enthusiasm to investigate it we are soon disillusioned. So far as any knowledge of psychic life is concerned, the information we gain in this way is of the slightest' (p.376.)

Perhaps one should judge this book as of historical interest only. But this is not Jaspers' view of it.

'The aim', he states, in his preface to the 1959 edition, 'has been to work through all the available empirical knowledge critically, by reflecting on the methods whereby it was gained, and then give it a general presentation'. Although he admits that he has not kept up with everything in the two decades 1939-1959, he states that it 'does not seem to be out of date'.

Not only is virtually all the vast non-German European literature ignored, but the whole American experience is totally neglected. Jaspers' views on psycho-analysis are well known, but his presentation of the psycho-analytic position in its empirical aspects must be regarded as simply incompetent. Similarly, his account of Jung's work is such that no reader could infer from Jaspers' pages what Jung's contributions to psychopathology actually were. The many experiences with the psychotherapy of schizophrenia that seriously challenge Jaspers' concept of process are not even mentioned. Any student of psychiatry who took Jaspers' own estimate of the book on trust could not fail to be seriously misled.

Considered in terms of its first edition, Jaspers' book had in some respects a salutary effect on psychiatry. This effect can be understood only in terms of the theoretical and practical falsity and philistinism that had overtaken psychiatry by the early years of this century. Jaspers had to caution against the incautious espousal of total theories of man, masquerading as science. At best he reports competently the work of others he is not biased against. His critical examination of rash over-generalizations and inadequate methods is a useful corrective to those who are over-hasty in turning a hypothesis into a fact, and a theory into an ideology. Not a few psychiatrists have undoubtedly been making fools of themselves in this way for years. Unfortunately, Jaspers does not have much to say about the somatic therapies that have been in and out of fashion in the last fifty years.

We owe Jaspers credit for elbowing into psychiatry the relevance of 'the subjective experience' of the patient, even now not fully accepted as the hard stuff of science. He called this division of psychopathology phenomenology. Although the term was not new, Jaspers was the first to introduce it into psychiatry. For Jaspers, phenomenology was the study of the subjective experiences of the patient, as we intuitively realize or represent them to ourselves through our capacity for empathy. We make present the patient's experience to ourselves, through the study of his spoken and/or written testimony, his gestures, expressive movements, and actions generally. Jaspers, in the study, contrasts phenomenology particularly with psychological methods that study the external signs of illness, or measure 'objective' performances of the patient (e.g. intelligence tests), but he also restricts it to the task of the careful description of experience while maintaining, in parentheses as it were, one's possible genetic dynamic understanding of this experience.

An example of Jaspers' phenomenological method is his work on delusions. By questioning, by attention to the patient's own verbal testimony and by the examination of written documents, Jaspers was led to the view that some delusions are preceded by a subtle but decisive and extensive change in the patient's whole experience of himself and his world. A delusion may be preceded by a diffuse mood of delusion: an indescribably obscure experience, permeated with dread, charged with the threat of impending catastrophe. The world is vaguely menacing: chaos is possible. There is a sense of something somewhere that is horrible and unspeakable. In such a case, the delusion is an end-product, a crystallization of this pre-delusional experiential change.

His use of the term should not be confused with its general current usage, which refers to a comprehensive approach to all the data of psychiatry, and which sees the whole of psychopathology as the product of one stance among others that one may adopt towards oneself and the other as patient.

For Jaspers, 'the basic problem of psychopathology' is the issue: personality development or process? This issue, as Jaspers expounds it, is hedged around with so many misconceptions that it is impossible to grapple with it within the scope of a review. It has at least served to make articulate what many psychiatrists think they have in mind when they regard someone as psychotic.

Jaspers' application of this concept can be illustrated by many examples, but the following is particularly valuable because of the exceptional quality of the autobiographical fragment that he quotes. Jaspers states that 'much can be learnt from patients' own interpretations, when they are trying to understand themselves' (p.417). One patient had the recklessness apparently to 'interpret his illness as a whole', and thereby he unified into a single meaning everything that the psychiatrist saw as the sequence of the process:

'I believe I caused the illness myself. In my attempt to penetrate the other world I met its natural guardians, the embodiment of my own weaknesses and faults. I first thought these demons were lowly inhabitants of the other world who could play me like a ball because I went into those regions unprepared and lost my way. Later I thought they were split-off parts of my own mind (passions) which existed near me in free space and thrived on my feelings. I believed everyone else had these too but did not perceive them, thanks to the protective and successful deceit of the feeling of personal existence. I thought the latter was an artefact of memory, thought-complexes, etc., a doll that was nice enough to look at from outside but nothing real inside it.

In my case the personal self had grown porous because of my dimmed consciousness. Through it I wanted to bring myself closer to the higher sources of life. I should have prepared myself for this over a long period by invoking in my omission a higher, impersonal self, since "nectar" is not for mortal lips. It acted destructively on the animal-human self, split it up into its parts. These gradually disintegrated, the doll was really broken and the body damaged. I had forced untimely access to the "source of life", the curse of the "gods" descended on me. I recognized too late that murky elements had taken a hand. I got to know them after they had already too much power. There was no way back. I now had the world of spirits I had wanted to see. The demons came up from the abyss, as guardian Cerberi, denying admission to the unauthorized. I decided to die, since I had to put aside everything that maintained the enemy, but this was also everything that maintained life. I wanted to enter death without going mad and stood before the Sphinx: either thou into the abyss or I!

Then came illumination. I fasted and so penetrated into the true nature of my seducers. They were pimps and deceivers of my dear personal self which seemed as much a thing of naught as they. A larger and more comprehensive self emerged and I could abandon the previous personality with its entire entourage. I saw this earlier personality could never enter transcendental realms. I felt as a result a terrible pain, like an annihilating blow, but I was rescued, the demons shrivelled, vanished and perished. New life began for me and from now on I felt different from other people. A self that consisted of conventional lies, shams, self-deceptions, memory-images, a self just like that of other people, grew in me again, but behind and above it stood a greater and more comprehensive self which impressed me with something of what is eternal, unchanging, immortal and inviolable, and which ever since that time has been my protector and refuge. I believe it would be good for many if they were acquainted with such a higher self and that there are people who have attained this goal in fact by kinder means. (Pp. 417-418.)

This patient's experiences are subject, of course, to psycho-analytic interpretation if one chooses, just as is any experience or behaviour. That is not the important issue at the moment. This is that they seem in no way alien to me. The inner world reaches through domains of experience (imagination, reverie, dreams, fantasy, visions...) into realms that we are *only beginning* to discover. It seems as reasonable to me that man should wish to climb the Mystic Mountain as Mount Everest. It is as understandable to me that a man should undertake a journey into his own mind, and get confused and lost, as that he should discover a new ocean or explore a continent.

I wish to state that I hope if I ever lose my way in my travels on the same path as this patient, I have the courage to endure, the luck to get back, and the grace to express myself with such lucidity, insight and humility.

Here are Jaspers' comments.

Such self-interpretations are obviously made under the influence of delusion-like tendencies and deep psychic forces. They originate from profound experiences and the wealth of such schizophrenic experience calls on the observer as well as on the reflective patient not to take all this merely as a chaotic jumble of contents. Mind and spirit are present in the morbid psychic life as well as in the healthy. But interpretations of this sort must be divested of any causal importance. All they can do is to throw light on content and bring it into some sort of context. (Op. cit. p.418.)

It could be argued that Jaspers was addressing such philistines among his psychiatric colleagues that even this statement, or his assertion elsewhere that a spiritual cosmos which is closed to most sane men may be opened to the psychotic, is revolutionary. This is only too true. But Jaspers at least deserves to be judged by the highest standards, and even in 1913 he was writing with Kierkegaard, Rimbaud, Dostoevsky, Nietzsche and others to guide him.

He had a great opportunity to grasp for the modern world in the modern idiom the meaning of clinical madness within a contemporary world gone mad, as the tragic outcome of a drama raging between protagonists spiritual and mundane, internal and external, and highly paradoxical and ambiguous. He muffed his chance. This task remains unaccomplished. His attempt to combine the clinical stance of a psycho-pathologist with loyalty to the insights of this élite is already a hopeless compromise.

When I read Jaspers' pathographies of Van Gogh, Hölderlin and Strindberg, I thought that here was a betrayal by a philosopher of the artist and poet. Instead of a compassionate understanding of the all-too-human risks involved in the exploration of reaches of reality that transcend those that a learned pedant will ever wish to know at first hand, Jaspers is no longer with them when they go too far.

Later, I have come to the opinion that Jaspers was not even in a position to betray. To betray, one must have some understanding of what one is betraying.

Jaspers' use of process indicates that he fails to understand the dialectic of the person's life before the supposed alien, meaningless intrusion occurs. It is because he has lost track long before, that the person's experience finally loses all meaning to Jaspers, and process is then invented. I devoted a book (*The Divided Self*) largely to demonstrating that the way from apparent sanity to apparent madness could be understood well past the point where Jaspers tells us to give up.

Jaspers tells us;

When a few decades ago I studied Freud thoroughly I only saw the non-existential, nihilistic principle of his work which seemed to me destructive both of science and philosophy. Later I have only sampled his work and that of his followers and this has confirmed me in my opinion. Yet it is difficult to convince others in respect of these deeper judgments. Anyone who can see the point at all will see it in a flash. (Op.cit. p. 775.)

There is a destructive principle at work in Jaspers. It is present in his dismissive attitude to dreams, and his application of his concept of process, to give only two specific examples that I have singled out for brief illustration. Certainly, I can see more than a 'non-existential, nihilistic principle' in him. But it is there also in full measure in this would-be Faust without Mephistopheles.

Ronald D. Laing

Whilst acknowledging that 'we owe Jaspers credit for elbowing into psychiatry the relevance of 'the subjective experience of the patient' (and calling this new division of psychopathology 'phenomenology') Laing makes it quite plain that he finds Jaspers unsatisfactory both as a philosopher and as a psychopathologist.

On the Jasperian view the central problem of psychopathology is the issue of *personality development versus organic (i.e. disease) process*. Although Laing finds Jaspers' discussion of this and kindred issues deeply faulty he does recognise that Jaspers' assertion that a spiritual cosmos, closed to most sane people, may be open to the psychotic, is revolutionary. Nevertheless "Jaspers at least deserves to be judged by the highest standards, and even in 1913 he was writing with Kierkegaard, Rimbaud, Dostoevsky, Nietzsche and others to guide him. He had a great opportunity to grasp for the modern world in the modern idiom the meaning of clinical madness...He muffed his chance. This task remains unaccomplished."

Laing's perusal of Jaspers' pathographies of Van Gogh, Hölderlin and Strindberg led him to the conclusion that "Jaspers' use of process indicates that he fails to understand the dialectic of the person's life before the supposed alien, meaningless intrusion occurs. It is because he has lost track long before, that the person's experience finally loses all meaning to Jaspers, and process is then invented. I devoted a book (*The Divided Self*) largely to demonstrating that the way from apparent sanity to apparent madness could be understood well past the point where Jaspers tells us to give up."

These preliminary considerations bring us to the conceptual heart of this whole problematic: the crucial issue of 'social intelligibility' versus 'organic process'.

In an illuminating paper Douglas Kirsner (*Journal of the British Society for Phenomenology* 21:3 October 1990, 209-215) has explored the alleged Jasperian 'abyss of difference' between normal and psychotic persons in terms of the philosophy of Jean-Paul Sartre, which had been a major, and decisive, influence on R.D. Laing's thinking. However, wider and deeper issues, in both conceptual and historical senses, are implicated in this discourse.

The Nature of Madness

The term 'madness' carries a powerful historical and emotional charge — as exemplified dramatically in the English title of Foucault's seminal work on the history of insanity *Madness and Civilization.* However the medicalisation of madness by the late nineteenth-century German pioneers of modern clinical psychiatry (notably Emil Kraepelin b. 1856 and Eugen Bleuler b. 1857) has proved, in the long-term (Laingian) perspective, to be an unmitigated disaster.

Quite apart from the critical revisions of the standard account of 'schizophrenia' by radical psychiatrists such as Thomas Szasz (USA), Felix Guattari (France) and R.D. Laing (UK), there have been noteworthy sceptical/critical views expressed by leading mainstream psychiatrists such as Manfred Bleuler (see his contribution in *Psychiatrists on Psychiatry* edited by M. Shepherd Cambridge Unversity Press 1975) and Luc Ciompi (Is there really a Schizophrenia? *British Journal of Psychiatry* vol. 145:636-640, 1984). Powerful arguments against narrowly, or exclusively, medically-based theories have also been advanced by such notable pioneers of clinical psychology as Gordon Claridge (*British Journal of Psychiatry* 151 (1987) 735-743 "The Schizophrenias as Nervous Types Revisited"), Richard Bentall. (*Madness Explained* London 2003), and Louis Sass (*Madness and Modernism* Harvard 1992)

Although there have been various confused, and confusing, attempts, notably by Siegler, Osmond and Mann (*British Journal of Psychiatry* vol. 115: 525, 1969) to read specific 'models of madness' (such as 'conspiratorial', 'psychoanalytic' etc.) into Laing's work, it needs to be carefully noted that Laing himself did not propose any model of 'schizophrenia':

> "We do not accept schizophrenia as being a biochemical, neurophysiological, psychological fact, and we regard it as a palpable error, in the present state of the evidence, to take it to be fact. Nor do we assume its existence. Nor do we adopt it as a hypothesis. We propose no model for it." (*Sanity, Madness and the Family:* preface to the second edition, London 1970 p.12).

Entirely consistently with the 1964 statement he told his biographer Bob Mullan:

> "I have never come out with a general theory of schizophrenia because I've said that the whole category and whole thing is so corrupt in its intellectual first principles and in terms of the design and application of anything to test it, that it is

undiscussable really. (*Mad to be Normal*: Conversations with R.D. Laing. London 1995 p.375.)

Note, in this particular context, that Karl Jaspers' shrewd observations of 1913 now, in 2004, appear prophetic:

> If the reader tries to get a precise hold on the entity involved, he will find it melts away from him even as he looks at it. The question as to what underlies all phenomena in general used to be answered in the old days by the notion of evil spirits. These later turned into disease-entities which could be found by empirical investigation. They have proved themselves however to be mere ideas. (*General Psychopathology* Manchester 1963 p. 570).

The philosophical significance of R.D. Laing's theoretical formulations turns on the fundamental issue of whether psychosis is to be *understood* as a disorder of the *person*, or explained as the manifestation of a diseased *biological organism*. (Raschid, M.S. Psychiatry and Philosophy – *Psychiatric Bulletin* (1992: 16, 727; 1993: 17, 693-4); Psychiatric Pioneers – *The Times Literary Supplement April 7 2000 p.21 (letter); The Philosophical Significance of R.D. Laing* 6th International Conference of Psychiatry and Philosophy, Florence, August 2000; *The Human Being as 'Person' and as 'Organism'* 7th International Conference of Psychiatry and Philosophy, Heidelberg, September 2004.) It should be noted that current genetic studies do *not* support the traditional medical view of a specific brain-based disease entity, and are indeed fully compatible with a person-based revision of the standard view (as envisaged by Laing). See Murray R. "New ways of thinking about and treating psychosis" *Progress in Neurology and Psychiatry* Vol.8 Oct.2004 20-26.

On the conceptual issues implicated here see the two recent reports by Peter McGuffin and his colleagues. (Rutter M. and McGuffin P.: The Social Genetic and Developmental Psychiatry Centre: *Psychological Medicine* 2004, 34, 933-947; McGuffin P. and Plomin R. A Decade of the Social, Genetic and Developmental Psychiatry Centre: *British Journal of Psychiatry* 2004, 185, 280-282.)

I turn now to the distinct, but related, issues of *schizogenesis* and *social intelligibility*. Laing's fundamental contribution was the central, and all-important, one of demonstrating that the seemingly bizarre and 'abnormal' manifestations of psychosis were intelligible when seen in a micro-social context (and the designated patient's family was used by Laing and Esterson as the locus of their ground-breaking study *Sanity, Madness and the Family*, London 1964). This was widely misconstrued as a claim along the lines that, to put it bluntly, 'families cause schizophrenia'. The distinction is crucial: to show that psychotic symptoms can be made sense of within the complex constellation of family dynamics does *not* imply that they have been *caused* by specific, or non-specific, interpersonal transactions within the family network. In some cases, such causation is conceptually conceivable and much circumstantial evidence does indeed point in such a direction. However firm claims cannot be made in the absence of much more detailed and methodologically sophisticated research work. Be that as it may, the concept of *psychogenic psychosis* is a well-established one (see Faergeman P., *Psychogenic Psychoses* London 1963).

The deeper conceptual issue in this discourse is that Laing has opened up a *wholly new mode of understanding madness* — focussing on the *person* (who cannot be understood/explained by the application of a purely biological conceptual matrix). Major theoretical issues are implicated here - they bear not only on the immediate issue of understanding madness but also on the all-important matter of *therapy*. Underlying all such considerations is the profound and complex matter of the nature, status and prestige of the natural sciences in modern culture i.e. since the 'scientific revolution' (See A.R. Hall *The Revolution in Science*, London 1983) of the seventeenth century. Hence the widespread use of such unexamined terms as 'the scientific approach', 'the scientific worldview': terms which are either ideological or pseudo-philosophical. As John Macmurray noted in his Gifford Lectures of 1954 (*Persons in Relation* London 1961 p41/2):

> We not only objectify science as an entity but personify it, endowing it with personal attributes. 'Science', we say 'has proved this', or 'has discovered that', or 'has shown that religion rests on a mistake'. Now strictly - and in this context strictness is essential - there is no such thing as 'science' and what is sometimes referred to as the scientific view of the world is either a pure fiction of the imagination, or else a half-baked philosophy which many scientists would reject, and which no scientist, *qua* scientist, is competent to judge.

Beginning with the Romantic movement (of the 17th and 18th centuries) there has been mounting scepticism and/or criticism of the larger claims made on behalf of the natural sciences. One important instance is the contemporary modern criticism of scientific intellectual culture in certain forms, or schools, of depth psychology: notably that of Carl Jung (see the eloquent account by Philip Rieff in his important book *The Triumph of the Therapeutic*, London 1973, especially pages 114-120).

The Continuing Counter-Revolution of Science

F.A. Hayek's *The Counter-Revolution of Science*, London 1964, is a major landmark in the twentieth-century discussion of 'scientism'. He claimed that he had given the term a precise meaning (in *Economica* in 1942). On account of its obvious importance I give the *Economica* text in full (as quoted by Hayek himself in The *Times Literary Supplement* (letter 21.5.1970):

> Wherever we are concerned, not with the general spirit of disinterested inquiry but with slavish imitation of the method and language of Science [the capital "S" indicating that I was speaking of natural science] – we should speak of "scientism" or the "scientistic prejudice". Although these terms are not completely unknown in English, they are actually borrowed from the French, where in recent years they have come to be generally used in very much the same sense in which they will be used here. It should be noted that, in the sense in which we shall use these terms, they describe, of course, an attitude which is decidedly unscientific in the true sense of the word, since it involves a mechanical and uncritical application of habits of thought to fields different from those in which they have been formed. The scientistic as distinguished from the scientific view is not an unprejudiced but a very prejudiced approach which, before it has considered its subject, claims to know what is the most appropriate way of investigating it.

Hayek (p.120) attributes the origin of the designation 'The Counter-Revolution of Science' to an author named Bonald, and he dates it rather dramatically to Saint-Simon's Swiss visit of 1803 to Voltaire ...'the father of the cult of Newton... carried to ridiculous heights by Saint-Simon'.

Saint-Simon had claimed a sort of divine dispensation: his utterances were, according to Hayek, "the outpouring of a megalomaniac visionary who spouts half-digested ideas".

The new 'religion' was *"physicalism"* and the eventual programme formulated by the mathematician Comte as the "positive hierarchy" of the sciences; represented as a single linear order of reducing generality (but increasing complexity). Mathematics was the highest level and 'social physics' (sociology) at the bottom of the hierarchy.

The counter-revolution of science has continued apace - with deleterious, and potentially dangerous, consequences. Consider one or two examples. The current edition of one standard British psychiatric text-book (*The Shorter Oxford Textbook of Psychiatry*, M.Gelder, P. Mayou, P. Cowen Oxford 2001) widely studied by trainees, has a full chapter on EBM (*Evidence-Based Medicine*: Chapter 6, Evidence-Based Approaches to Psychiatry), without showing any awareness of the wider conceptual issues implicated in such approaches. In fact there is no discussion at all of conceptual/philosophical issues — which should, properly speaking, be an integral part of the introductory chapter. EBM does *NOT* make the theory and/or the practice of psychiatry scientific, any more than does the application of sophisticated statistical techniques to clinical research. The practice of psychiatry is, and will always necessarily remain, an art, although it may be based on a variety of natural scientific and social/ humanistic scientific disciplines. At the present time the practice of clinical psychiatry is based, firmly and soundly, on clinical experience and intuition, i.e. the relevant evidence is almost entirely of an empirically and anecdotally-based variety. In the absence of sufficiently sophisticated conceptual matrices, with a precise delineation of such fundamental categories as 'illness' and 'disease', the current vogue for EBM can only lead to a reinforcement, or possibly a refinement, of existing clinical practices.

Interrogation and Phenomenology

Douglas Kirsner has made the original observation that throughout his career Laing was engaged in the range of philosophical problems initially posed by Kant (see Kirsner's chapter in this book). Kirsner refers at this point to 'the *interrogatory* nature of his endeavours which question fundamental assumptions in our attitudes...' (my emphasis). Edmund Husserl, the founder of phenomenology (who regarded philosophy as "an infinite meditation") was the philosophical interrogator *par excellence* (see Merleau-Ponty's essay *Philosophy as Interrogation* Chapter 10 in *Themes from the Lectures at the College de France 1952-1960* Northwestern University Press, Evanston 1970).

Laing has been quite explicit about his indebtedness to the philosophical tradition of existential phenomenology — see Burston D. *The Wing of Madness* Harvard 1996 (Chapter 9: Philosophical Anthropology); Laing R.D. *The Divided Self* London 1960; Mullan B. *Mad to Be Normal* London 1995 (Chapter 2: Influences). The Laingian scepticism about the exaggerated claims made by scientists, as well as his adumbration of a possible theoretical basis for understanding persons (or developing a 'science of persons') was inspired by, and rooted in, this particular tradition. It would therefore be appropriate to sketch out, in brief and schematic fashion, some salient features of the powerful critiques of modern scientific culture developed by the founding father of this movement (Edmund Husserl 1859-1938) and to indicate how this led to the radical new departure initiated by Husserl's most famous student Martin Heidegger (1889-1976).

The issue of *intelligibility* is a central *leitmotif* running through the massive and complex corpus of Husserl's philosophical writings. The title of the very second section of his last, and arguably his greatest, work is *The positivistic reduction of the idea of science to mere factual science. The "crisis" of science as the loss of its meaning for life* (Part I: Section 2 p.5.), *The Crisis of European Sciences and Transcendental Phenomenology, Northwestern University Press Evanston 1970*: henceforth The Crisis.

This theme is developed in the whole of Part I (Sections 1 to 7 – pp.3-18) of *The Crisis* text in the form of a spirited historical polemic. Husserl begins with a consideration of the manner in which the significance of science ("the positive sciences") for human existence, and consequently "the total world-view of modern man", underwent a radical change in the late nineteenth century. Writing in the period between the two world wars

Husserl was concerned that "this science has nothing to say to us. It excludes in principle precisely the questions which man, given over in our unhappy times to the most portentous upheavals, finds the most burning: questions of the meaning or meaninglessness of the whole of this human existence" (p.6). But, Husserl asks, can the world, and human existence in it, have a meaning if the sciences recognize truth only in what can be objectively established in their own sphere?

Husserl argues that the European Renaissance witnessed a revolutionary transformation of the initial conception of Greek philosophy ('this renewed 'Platonism' p.8). This would involve not only a fundamental ethical change in human beings but, more comprehensively, "the whole human surrounding world, the political and social existence of mankind, must be fashioned anew" through the establishment of a new universal philosophy. We can therefore see that the modern concept of science has somehow dropped all the questions earlier covered by the rubric of metaphysics. Therefore "positivism, in a manner of speaking, decapitates philosophy" (p.9).

In fact Renaissance philosophy had taken up the ancient Greek conception of metaphysics, honoured as the queen of the sciences, and aspired to develop it into a systematic *philosophia perennis*. This indeed was the hallmark of the eighteenth century (which called itself the philosophical century, and which we now remember as the Age of Enlightenment).

However "the new humanity, animated and blessed with such an exalted spirit" (p.10) soon lost its belief in the ideal of a universal philosophy. Successful accomplishments were confined to the positive sciences, but in the area of metaphysics a long succession of philosophers, from Hume and Kant right up to the time of Husserl's reflections, engaged in a "passionate struggle for a clear, reflective understanding of the true reasons for this centuries-old failure".

The collapse of the ideal of a universal philosophy meant a functional crisis of all modern sciences "with regard to the meaning of their original founding as branches of philosophy". Since the new philosophy was an endeavour to renew European humanity radically this crisis implied a crisis of European humanity itself "in respect to the total meaningfulness of its cultural life".

"…the fate of the philosophical modern age" is "the reestablishment of philosophy with a new universal task," with the dual aim of achieving both a renaissance of ancient philosophy, as well as a "universal transformation of meaning". Modern scepticism amounts to a collapse of the belief in reason which, Husserl argues, "ultimately gives meaning to everything". Reason is related to truth and correlatively to the term "what is". Husserl, arguably the greatest *rationalist* philosopher of the modern period, characterizes this momentous decline in the philosophical destiny of the West as follows:

> "Along with this falls the faith in 'absolute' reason, through which the world has its meaning, the faith in the meaning of history, of humanity, the faith in man's freedom, that is, his capacity to secure rational meaning for his individual and common human existence" (p. 13).

The renewal of philosophy in the modern age must first recognize "the *telos* which was inborn in European humanity at the birth of Greek philosophy — that of humanity which seeks to exist, and is only possible, through philosophical reason, moving endlessly from latent to manifest reason and forever seeking its own norms through this, its truth and genuine human nature" (p.15).

The new ('metaphysical') theories about the natural world are labeled by Husserl as 'Objectivism' and/or 'Naturalism' — roughly speaking the notion that the world that we know is simply the actual, solid world studied by the natural sciences (later re-described by Merleau-Ponty as 'le prejuge du monde'). This view is profoundly naïve, i.e. philosophically unclarified: it is completely oblivious of the fact that, and the precise manner in which, such 'natural knowledge' is based upon, and rooted in, the massive and complex *pre-given* 'structure' of the world of ordinary, daily, common experience i.e. the *lebenswelt* (the life-world). The 'uncovering' of the life-world is itself to be achieved by means of a further 'transcendental reduction' — when it is seen as an *accomplishment* of *transcendental* (as distinct from *empirical*) consciousness (*bewusstseinleistung*). In *The Crisis* text Husserl defines 'transcendental' as:

> "the motif of inquiring back into the ultimate source of all the formations of knowledge, the motif of the knower's reflecting

upon himself and his knowing life in which all the scientific structures that are valid for him occur purposefully, are stored up as acquisitions, and have become and continue to become freely available. Working itself out radically, it is the motif of a universal philosophy which is grounded purely in this source and thus ultimately grounded. This source bears the title *I-myself*, with all of my actual and possible knowing life and, ultimately, my concrete life in general. The whole transcendental set of problems circles around the relation of *this*, my 'I' – the 'ego' – to what it is at first taken for granted to be – my soul – and, again, around the relation of this ego and my conscious life to the *world* of which I am conscious and whose true being I know through my own cognitive structures."(p.97/8)

The emergence of the completely, and radically, new theory of the life-world represents the heroic culmination of Husserl's entire philosophical career. Note Maurice Natanson's astute comment: "...we must say that philosophy is implicit within mundane existence, that common sense may itself be considered as potentially the richest of objects for philosophical inspection. Indeed, this was the insight which led Edmund Husserl, in the last phase of his thought, to the discovery of the concept of the *Lebenswelt*..." (*Psychiatry and Philosophy* Ed. M. Natanson New York 1969 p. 91/2). Husserl was actually ailing, and in his late seventies, when he was working on the (unfinished) text of *The Crisis*. There was also the additional, and very major, burden of being constrained to live under the severe restrictions imposed upon a man of Jewish origin by the Nazi regime.

Maurice Merleau-Ponty's great work *The Phenomenology of Perception* (London, 1962) is firmly based upon specific ideas and insights developed in Edmund Husserl's *Crisis*. With reference to Martin Heidegger's seminal work *Being and Time*, Merleau-Ponty noted in the famous Preface that "the whole of *Sein und Zeit* springs from an indication given by Husserl and amounts to no more than an explicit account of the '*natürlicher Weltbegriff*' or the '*Lebenswelt*'."(p.vii).

Thus, quite apart from its intrinsic importance, the *lifeworld* concept forms a conceptual bridge between the foundational work of Husserl and the two major subsequent elaborations of some of its central themes: in the divergent 'fundamental ontology' of the early Heidegger and the 'existential phenomenology' of Merleau-Ponty.

What is a Human Being?

R.D. Laing's Heideggerian-sounding formulation of this problem has already been noted (*Kirsner interview*: as quoted in the opening section of his contribution to this volume *Laing and Philosophy*).

Martin Heidegger's entire philosophical career was devoted to the sole, and colossal, task of exploring and expounding a fresh understanding of the notion of 'Being' – the correct (historically pre-Socratic) understanding having been 'covered up' by an initial process of obfuscation which began with the philosophy of Plato (428-348 BC). Heidegger is therefore committed to the extraordinary "Task of Destroying the History of Ontology" (*Being and Time* London 1962: section 6 p.41) i.e. of demonstrating how the issue of the meaning of Being has been radically misconceived/misinterpreted by the philosophical tradition which dates from Plato. As Heidegger's own bold declamation states:

> "by taking *the question of Being as our clue*, we are to *destroy* the traditional content of ancient ontology until we arrive at those primordial experiences in which we achieved our first ways of determining the nature of Being – the ways which have guided us ever since" (*Being and Time*, p.44)

Two entirely original themes are introduced by Heidegger in this programme: firstly, his own concept of 'time' and, particularly, the intuition that time is "the horizon for the understanding of Being" (*Being and Time* p.39). The second major innovation is his radical departure from Husserl's conception of phenomenology.

A most learned disquisition about the terms '*phenomenon*' and '*logos*' prefaces Heidegger's statement of "The Preliminary Conception of Phenomenology" (*Being and Time* p.11).

Heidegger's subsequent account/analysis of the concept of the 'person' *under the radically revised notion of Dasein* forms the formidable Part One of *Being and Time* – in two divisions; Division Three and the projected Part Two (in three divisions) did not appear at all. However it is the view of leading Heidegger scholars (e.g. Albert Hofstadter: Translator's Introduction to Heidegger's *The Basic Problems of Phenomenology* Indiana University Press 1982 p.xvii) that if we take the following two Heidegger volumes (*The Basic Problems* volume just noted and *Kant and the Problem of Metaphysics* 5th edition Indiana U.P. 1997) in conjunction with the (incomplete) published text of *Being and Time*, then this composite work actually constitutes what Heidegger had initially envisaged as the whole project of *Being and Time*.

The Zollikon Seminars

As perhaps the last major academic exercise of his long career, Martin Heidegger gave a special series of seminars at the mountain retreat (Zollikon) of the distinguished German Swiss psychotherapist Medard Boss — addressing fifty to seventy psychiatrists and psychiatric trainees (1959-1969; the German protocols have been available since 1987 but the English translation did not appear until 2001 — *Zollikon Seminars*: M. Heidegger Edited by M. Boss: Northwestern U.P.). Heidegger was addressing professionals with a medical-scientific training but with no background in philosophy. The Zollikon Seminars constitute an exceptionally remarkable document, in which some of Heidegger's central doctrines have been expounded by the maestro himself with consummate clarity. They may be read as a most reliable introductory guide to his philosophy — tough, but deeply rewarding reading.

A Note on Therapy

R.D. Laing termed the spontaneous process of psychosis-resolution *metanoia* (see the Karl Jaspers review reproduced above). He attributed the first use of the term to Carl Jung (see the Mullan biography '*Mad to be Normal*' London 1995 p. 104). Contrary to widespread belief Laing was *not* opposed to the therapeutic use of antipsychotic medication: however, an important proviso was that the use of high doses of such medication would block the deeper healing process described by the term *metanoia*.

This *metanoia* concept, and kindred notions, provided the theoretical background to the major therapeutic 'experiment' conducted by Laing in London (1965-1969): the Kingsley Hall community project. Similar work was done under N.H.S. auspices by Laing's colleague Dr. David Cooper (see 'Results of family-orientated therapy with hospitalized schizophrenics' *British Medical Journal*, 18 December 1965 (2), 1462-5). American work on similar lines, by now extensively published, carried out by Dr. Loren Mosher was directly inspired by, and based upon, Laing's work in London. Professor Luc Ciompi's 'Soteria Bern' project was directly based on Mosher's work, and therefore indirectly on Laing's work in London (Luc Ciompi: personal communication 1991; see the contributions by both Mosher and Ciompi to this volume: Chapters 12 & 13). See also the important overall report — by Ciompi and Hoffmann — presented to the twentieth anniversary meeting of the Soteria Project held at Bern University in 2004 and published as a *Special Article* in *World Psychiatry* (Ciompi L. and Hoffmann H. Soteria Berne 3:3 October 2004 140-146).

The composition of this volume

The chapters by Daniel Burston, Lui Ciompi, Robin Cooper, Thomas Fuchs, John Heaton, Francis Huxley and Roger Poole originated in papers from the first and second R.D. Laing conferences (held under the auspices of the Philosophy Special Interest Group of the Royal College of Psychiatrists, in February 1999 and October 2000). The remaining chapters, with two exceptions (Chapter 12 by Loren Mosher and Chapter 2 by Daniel Burston), were specially commissioned for this volume.

I shall not attempt the customary, and often misleading, editorial practice of providing very brief summaries of the individual chapters. The material is far too complex to allow any such oversimplification: the names of the individual authors taken together with their respective chapter headings should suffice to give a clear indication of their content.

2: R. D. Laing: A Biographical Sketch

Daniel Burston

R. D. Laing: A Biographical Sketch

Daniel Burston

Ronald David Laing was born on October 7, 1927 on 26 Ardbeg St. in the Govanhill district of Glasgow, the only child of David and Amelia Laing. David Laing started his career as an engineer and ordnance man in the Royal Tank Corps and Royal Air Corps, and became a civil engineer for the Corporation of Glasgow. He was principal baritone for the Glasgow University Chapel choir, and enjoyed musical passtimes exceedingly. Amelia, his wife, had a reputation as a secretive, suspicious and eccentric person, who — as her son later recalled — drove David's musical friends and collaborators away from their apartment through her hostile and duplicitous behavior (Laing 1985).

The Laing flat stood opposite a public library, and young Ronald, being bookish, resolved to read everything in the non-fiction section from A-Z at the age of 14. This was how he first encountered Kierkegaard and Nietzsche, Marx and Freud, at around the age of 15. Like his father, Ronald was exceedingly musical, and received a Licentiate in music from the Royal Academy of Music at age 16 — a rare distinction, even today. At seventeen, Laing enrolled in Glasgow University, and at eighteen, decided to specialize in medicine. He also helped found the Socratic Club, a debating society that still exists, whose patron was Bertrand Russell (Laing 1994). However, Laing's own tastes in philosophy were more continental, and by 22, he was working his way diligently through Hegel, Husserl, Heidegger, Sartre, Merleau-Ponty, Jaspers, Wittgenstein and Camus (Mullan 1995).

Laing had hoped that when he finished his MD he could study existential psychiatry with Karl Jaspers in Basel. However, military service was mandatory then, and so in 1949, Laing did basic training. After a brief apprenticeship in neurosurgery at Killearn in 1950, Laing spent 1951-1953 as an army psychiatrist, whose task was to differentiate soldiers who were truly disturbed from malingerers. Despite rigid prohibitions on communicating with patients, Laing found ways of developing a rapport with deeply disturbed inmates by sitting quietly in their padded cells, often for hours at a time; a move construed by his superiors as a dedicated research effort (Laing 1985). And in a sense, of course, it was. Unlike his peers and superiors, who either avoided their charges or addressed them in military fashion, Laing demanded nothing of these lost souls, neither silence nor speech. He allowed them to open up at their own pace, because he was anxious to discover how these miserable, frightened and deeply confused people experienced the world, and how they would respond given the chance to communicate without external constraints.

In 1952, now a captain, Laing was placed in charge of the Army hospital in Catterick, in Yorkshire, where he met and married his first wife, Anne Hearne. Soon thereafter, he left the Army for the Royal Gartnavel Hospital and Southern General Hospital in Glasgow, where he worked under Dr. Angus McNiven and his superior, Dr. Ferguson Rodger (Laing 1994). In 1954, Rodger brought Laing to the attention of Dr. J.D. Sutherland, then the Director of the Tavistock Clinic in London. With the help of Sutherland, and his successor, John Bowlby, Laing, his wife and their four children came to London in 1956 so that Laing could train as a psychoanalyst. His training analyst was Charles Rycroft, and his clinical supervisors were Donald Winnicott and Marion Milner (Burston 1996).

As odd as it sounds, in retrospect, the fact remains that when Laing arrived in London he was considered a very *conservative* psychiatrist, because like Angus McNiven at Gartnavel, and Donald Winnicott in London, Laing was inexorably opposed to electroshock. Remember, these were the days when psychiatry went in for "heroic" measures (Valenstein 1986), and Laing's reluctance to use patients as guinea pigs was more characteristic of the older generation, who were nearing retirement, than younger and middle aged psychiatrists who saw themselves as more "progressive."

Laing's first four years in London were very turbulent at times. After his fifth child was born, his marriage began to unravel, his best friend, Douglas Hutchison, died in a tragic accident, and he became extremely ill. To make matters worse, Laing offended the Kleinian faction at the Institute for Psychoanalysis, who pressed vigorously for his immediate disqualification (Mullan 1995). Fortunately, Rycroft, Winnicot and Milner were equally vigorous in their defence of Laing, and he squeezed through as a fully qualified psychoanalyst in 1960 (Burston 1996). During this time, Laing worked as the Registrar of the Adult Services Section at the Tavistock Clinic, and completed *The Divided Self*, a classic in the literature on existential psychotherapy (Laing 1960). His second book, *Self And Others,* appeared in 1961 (Laing 1961). In 1964, Laing and another Glaswegian psychiatrist, Aaron Esterson, published a brilliant and disturbing book entitled *Sanity, Madness & The Family* (Laing 1964). That same year, Laing also published *Reason & Violence: A Decade of Sartre's Philosophy* with South African psychiatrist Dr. David Cooper (Laing 1964).

In 1965, Laing separated from his first wife, who returned (with their five children) to Glasgow. That same year, Laing, Esterson, Cooper and friends founded the Philadelphia Association, a charitable foundation devoted to the creation of therapeutic communities for people suffering from mental and emotional crises (Clay 1996). The Philadelphia Association was committed to the idea that a psychotic breakdown is not a symptom of genetic abnormality or neurological disorder per se, but is an *existential* crisis, and therefore an attempt to reconstitute the self in a more authentic and integrated way. Professional and patient roles, as implemented and understood in mainstream psychiatry, usually preclude a genuine understanding of the psychotic as a person, and are not conducive to the process of cure. To remedy this situation, Laing and associates set up therapeutic households to provide genuine asylum from the world outside, free from the stigma and coercion entailed in "normal" psychiatric treatment.

In February of 1967, Laing published *The Politics of Experience*, which became a runaway best-seller. Though not his most memorable book, at least to discerning readers, it is the one he is most remembered by, and because of its massive sales, the one which left an indelible imprint on Western intellectual life (Laing 1967). Laing's frame of mind when he wrote *The Politics of Experience* was somewhat akin to Freud's when he wrote *Civilization and Its Discontents* (Freud 1930). As the winds of war gathered, Freud used his book to alert humanity of the danger of self-annihilation posed by the inexorable advance of technological weaponry. In a similar spirit, Laing warned readers that a nuclear holocaust resulting in planetary death (as well as the extinction of our own species) was a real and ever-present possibility in a world polarized between the Soviet and American camps — adding that, whether we were aware of it or not, we would have first laid waste to our own sanity before actually destroying the planet.

In 1968, Laing was approached by Phyllis Webb of the Canadian Broadcasting Corporation to do the Massey Lectures for CBC radio, on a program entitled *Ideas* . The Massey Lectures – five in all – were broadcast nationally, and then published by the CBC under the title of *The Politics of the Family*, and re-issued two years later by Pantheon Press under the same name (Laing 1971). This was followed by *Knots*, which became another huge best-seller (Laing 1970). It was his last big publishing success.

In 1970, Laing left London for an 18 month interlude of meditation and study in Sri Lanka and India, accompanied by his partner, Jutta Werner, and their two children. When he returned to London in 1972 Laing embarked on a whirlwind speaking tour of the USA and Europe that lasted many months. While in the United States, he witnessed the "rebirthing" therapy practised by mid-wife Elizabeth Fehr, and began to integrate her approach to treatment with ideas gleaned from the earlier work of Francis Mott (Laing 1976; Laing 1994).All through that decade, Laing became engrossed with the politics of birth, and of the impact of "pre-birth experience" on adult patients; a fact attested to by *The Facts of Life*, a series of reflections on "intrauterine experience", his own memories of childhood, and the grotesque inhumanity of mainstream psychiatric theory and practice (Laing 1976). The book sold poorly. In 1982, he published *The Voice of Experience*, a more cautious and coherent meditation on many of the same themes, but it sold poorly too (Laing 1982).

While Laing maintained that his interests in "intra-uterine" experience were completely consistent with his earlier work, many members of the Philadelphia Association felt that he had strayed rather far from his original orientation. As tensions in the Philadelphia Association grew, Laing resigned his post as Chair, separated from Jutta and their three children, and began work on a new organization — the St. Oran's Trust — which expired in 1985. Meanwhile, however, he published *Wisdom, Madness and Folly: The Making of a Psychiatrist*, a memoir that chronicled his development from conception to age 26, when he began work on *The Divided Self*. Given how turbulent and unsettled his life was at the time, it was a remarkably lucid statement (Laing 1985).

In 1986, Laing and his third wife, Marguerita Romayn Kendon, embarked on a period of extensive travel, and eventually settled in the town of Kitzhubel in the Austrian Tyrol. From then till his death in August of 1989, Laing fathered another child, Charles, and worked on two (unfinished) manuscripts — a biography of C.G.Jung, co-authored with Eugene Nemeshe, and a book in progress called *The Lies of Love* .

Laing's legacy to the mental health professions is rich and ambiguous. Laing hoped to liberate the mad, or elicit greater awareness of their plight. But by depicting psychotics as rebels against oppressive families, and psychiatrists as the "mind-police" who — wittingly or unwittingly — enforce the rules of expectations of the family and the culture at large (Laing 1967; Laing 1971), Laing helped to provoke a massive backlash against the movement that David Cooper called "anti-psychiatry" (Cooper 1967). Laing eschewed the anti-psychiatry label, but friends and critics alike thought of him as one of the movement's leaders (Laing 1994; Burston 1996). Stung to the quick, aggrieved parents and hyper-defensive psychiatrists joined forces to create powerful organizations and political lobbies which are now lavishly funded by the large pharmaceutical companies. As a result, in psychiatric circles, any idea or initiative labeled "Laingian" nowadays is usually dismissed as irrelevant, silly or faintly sinister, and unlikely to get anything remotely resembling a fair hearing (Burston 2000).

Another, closely related problem for contemporary readers is that Laing was a somewhat restless and dynamic thinker who was not keen on synthesis or systematization. Once he had explored or addressed a certain issue to his own satisfaction, he would move on, and leave it to others to reconcile the disparate threads and phases of his work. As a result, given the prevailing animus against him, the real problems in Laing's sprawling body of work seldom surface for careful analysis and reflection in the secondary literature, because others read him chiefly as a psychiatrist or psychoanalyst, ignoring his immersion in existential phenomenology (Burston 2000), with its emphasis on the primacy of experience and the interpersonal dimension, and the Scottish intellectual tradition, with its humane skepticism and emphasis on the relationship between sociability and reason (Miller 2004). Nevertheless, if we can excuse — or better yet, wrestle with — his internal contradictions, the fact remains that Laing at his best was a lucid and compassionate theorist of human suffering, a genius of our time, whose work repays close and continuing study.

Nevertheless, Laing's legacy still lingers on the margins on the mental health professions, and in the minds of many advocates and activists in the mental health field who still honor his work and memory.

references

Burston, D. (1996). *The Wing of Madness: The Life and Work of R.D. Laing*. Cambridge, MA, Harvard University Press.

Burston, D. (2000). *The Crucible of Experience: R.D. Laing and the Crisis of Psychotherapy*. Cambridge, MA, Harvard University Press.

Clay, J. (1996). *R.D. Laing: A Divided Self*. London, Hodder & Stoughton.

Cooper, D. (1967). *Psychiatry and Anti-Psychiatry*. London, Tavistock Publications.

Freud, S. (1930). *Civilization and Its Discontents*. London, Hogarth Press.

Laing, A. (1994). *R.D.Laing: A Biography*. London, Peter Owen.

Laing, R. D. (1960). *The Divided Self*. London, Tavistock Publications.

Laing, R. D. (1961). *Self and Others*. London, Tavistock Publications.

Laing, R. D. (1967). *The Politics of Experience and The Bird of Paradise*. New York, Pantheon.

Laing, R. D. (1970). *Knots*. New York, Pantheon.

Laing, R. D. (1971). *The Politics of the Family and Other Essays*. New York, Pantheon.

Laing, R. D. (1976). *The Facts of Life*. New York, Pantheon.

Laing, R. D. (1982). *The Voice of Experience*. New York, Pantheon.

Laing, R. D. (1985). *Wisdom, Madness & Folly: The Making of a Psychiatrist*. New York, McGraw Hill.

Laing, R. D. a. C., D. (1964). *Reason and Violence: A Decade of Sartre's Philosophy*. New York, Pantheon.

Laing, R. D. a. E., A. (1964). *Sanity, Madness and the Family*. London, Tavistock Publications.

Miller, G. (2004). *R.D.Laing*. Edinburgh, Edinburgh Review.

Mullan, B., Ed. (1995). *Mad to Be Normal: Conversations with R.D. Laing*. London, Free Association Books.

Valenstein, E. (1986). *Great and Desperate Cures: The Rise and Decline of Psychosurgery and Other Radical Treatments for Mental Illness*. New York, Basic Books.

Appendix (to the biography)

R. D. Laing and The Politics of Diagnosis

We live in curious times. Before Sigmund Freud and Carl Jung, no educated person would have regarded a specialist in the mysteries of mental disorder as a preceptor to humanity at large. As the 19th century drew to a close, however, it slowly dawned on some people that the malaise experienced by mad and acutely neurotic individuals was different in degree, rather than in kind, from the suffering of relatively normal people struggling with the constraints and injustices of civilized life. Philosophy, art, literature and drama all contributed to this emergent cultural awareness. Indeed, they created the climate of opinion that enabled Freud and Jung to become cultural icons.

Many objected strenuously to this fashionable new trend. Many still do. Some cling to an outdated rationalism that attempts to expunge irrationality in all its forms from our concept of the human. Others insist that the boundaries between normals and neurotics are not permeable, but distinct and intelligible to any clear-headed individual, although the authors of the DSM IV freely concede that it is often difficult to impossible to distinguish a disorder from a "non-disorder."

In any case, Freud and Jung heralded the emergence of a new cultural form at the turn of the century; the alienist or "head shrinker" as public intellectual. Although Adler and Rank tried, no doubt, no one else in the mental health professions achieved comparable public stature until the cold war era, when Bruno Bettelheim, Erik Erikson, Erich Fromm, and R. D. Laing became the pre-eminent examples of this new cultural trend. Indeed, by 1970, their fame rivaled or exceeded that of Freud and Jung because they spoke to issues, experiences, and ideals with which young people could readily identify in those turbulent times. Laing's place in this group is quite distinctive, however.

Freud said that neurosis and normality exist on a continuum, and therefore, that normal people succumb to acute neurotic conflict in certain circumstances. This assertion strikes many of us as self-evident, but was once considered a very radical idea. But like his contemporaries, and most of us, Freud thought of *psychotics* as having a very different existence from normals and neurotics, or "normal neurotics", as some prefer to call them. Unlike their more adapted contemporaries, said Freud, psychotics are not amenable to psychoanalysis because they cannot form a "transference", and by implication, a working alliance, with the therapist. Freud was not alone in this respect. Eugen Bleuler, who coined the term "schizophrenia", once remarked that when all was said and done, his patients were stranger to him than the birds in his garden. And in a similar vein, Karl Jaspers argued that an abyss of understanding separates the schizophrenic from the non-schizophrenic. Echoing Freud, Bleuler and Jaspers, Carl Rogers said that schizophrenics are utterly incapable of forming meaningful human relationships, hinting that they were not merely deficient in this respect, but that they actively repudiate the bonds of human fellowship.

C.G. Jung, a student of both Bleuler and Freud, disagreed. Indeed, his differences with Freud on this point played a small but significant role in the controversies that precipitated Jung's resignation from the Presidency of the International Psychoanalytic Association, and the emergence in Zurich of Analytical Psychology (Hogenson, 1984). Jung believed that psychotherapy with psychotics is not always doomed to failure, and that psychosis represents an existential crisis, an attempt at a radical inner transformation which he termed *metanoia,* a term he borrowed from the New Testament, which is usually translated as "repentance." Being Jewish, and an atheist as well, Freud probably found this usage a bit distasteful, but conceded that the delusions and hallucinations of psychotics often symbolize an abortive attempt at self-cure in "Psychoanalytical Notes Upon An Autobiographical Account of A Case of Paranoia" (1911). But he remained thoroughly skeptical about the prospects of analyzing psychotics successfully, in principle, if not always in practice (Roazen, 2000).

Undeterred by Freud's pessimism, in the 1920s several psychiatrists began to explore the psychotherapy of schizophrenia here in the United States. Adolph Meyer, Richard Kempf, Harry Stack Sullivan, and later, Marguerite Sechehaye and Frieda-Fromm Reichmann, were the most celebrated and successful. Despite minor differences in theoretical orientation, Sullivan and Fromm-Reichmann both stressed that, to do effective therapy with psychotics, the therapist must be able to empathize with their states of mind by drawing on their own "psychotic potential".

That means, in effect, that they must be in touch with their own psychotic core, while remaining firmly anchored in reality. This is arduous work at the best of times, and well beyond the capacity of the average psychiatrist or psychoanalyst. Coping with anguish, confusion and despair that intense, that annihilating, and doing it routinely, is more than most people, and most therapists, however dedicated and well-intentioned, can bear.

Ronald David Laing was cut from the same cloth as Sullivan, Sechehaye and Fromm-Reichmann. Born in 1927, he was raised and educated in Glasgow, and apprenticed in psychiatry in the British Army during the Korean War. In 1951, while stationed at the Royal Victoria Hospital at Netley, Laing read Sullivan, Fromm-Reichmann and Sechehaye with keen interest. There, and again at Catterick Military Hospital (Yorkshire), where he was stationed from 1952 to 1953, Laing spent as much time as possible in padded cells with the men placed in his custody. This kind of intensive immersion in the schizophrenic life-world was unheard of at the time. He found that with enough patience and persistence, he could eventually get on their wave length and make sense of the peculiar speech and gestures that his colleagues found completely unintelligible (Laing, 1985).

When Laing left the British Army in 1953, he conducted similar experiments in civilian hospitals at Gartnavel and the Southern General Hospital in Scotland, where his patients were generally women, for almost three years. Then in 1956, he set out for London, where he worked as a Registrar at the Tavistock Clinic, and trained at The Institute for Psychoanalysis. Charles Rycroft was his training analyst, while D.W. Winnicott and Marion Milner were his clinical supervisors (Burston, 1996, chapter 3). Significantly, however, Laing was profoundly disenchanted with most analysts' closed-minded and dogmatic world-views, and their derogatory attitude toward psychotics (Burston, 1996, 2000). The Freudians and Kleinians in London, for their part, did not trust Laing because he committed the cardinal sin of taking Jung's notion of *metanoia* seriously. This was not yet evident in 1960, when he published *The Divided Self*. But it was vividly apparent in *The Politics of Experience*, published in 1967.

According to some critics, *The Divided Self* is Laing's best book. It attempted to make the process of going mad intelligible to ordinary people. Although couched in the idioms of existential phenomenology, and quite critical of psychiatry and psychoanalysis, *The Divided Self* was relatively "low-key" in its criticism of mainstream society and politics. By contrast, *The Politics of Experience*, written in the midst of the Vietnam War, bristled with angry denunciations of psychiatry and psychoanalysis, of capitalism and imperialism, of family piety, schools and universities, and so on.

In between *The Divided Self* and *The Politics of Experience*, Laing published *Sanity, Madness and the Family* with Aaron Esterson (1964), *Reason and Violence* with David Cooper (1964) and *Interpersonal Perception* with Phillipson and Lee (1966). Along with Esterson, Cooper and various friends and co-workers, Laing founded the Philadelphia Association, which he chaired from 1965 till 1982. The Philadelphia Association is chiefly a psychotherapy training organization now, but its original mandate was primarily the creation of therapeutic households or "safe houses" where disturbed individuals could undergo a metanoic journey free from the useless labels and coercive practices of mainstream psychiatry (Burston, 1996, chapter 4). Their most famous experiment, Kingsley Hall, ran from 1964 till 1970.

Nestled in the heart of London's east end, Kingsley Hall was a meeting place whose function and leadership were seldom clearly defined. It hosted training seminars, fundraising events and informal meetings with luminaries from the mental health field, new-left activists, rock stars, artists, writers and others. Some people reveled in the alternating currents of carnival and of deep anger and confusion that animated the place; others were shocked and dismayed. Other therapeutic households that followed it were less chaotic, and less accessible to the avid crowds of hippies, thrill seekers and celebrities who thronged to Kingsley Hall. As places of healing, they actually fared better, as a rule (Burston, 2000, chapter 4).

In any case, by 1969, Kingsley Hall and *The Politics of Experience* had gleaned so much media attention that they transformed Laing from a medium-size British celebrity, and the darling of the British left and artistic avant garde, into an international celebrity on a par with Sartre or Marshall McLuhan. It also conveyed the mistaken impression that Laing was positioning himself to assume some sort of leadership role in the anti-Vietnam, pro-disarmament, and counter-cultural movements, or indeed, had already done so.

This was not the case, however. In 1968 Laing became deeply disenchanted with leftist politics, and began divesting himself of political commitments and affiliations, turning inward to yoga and meditation, and fostering the proliferating network of therapeutic households the Philadelphia Association had by now created. Nevertheless, *The Politics of Experience* continued to sell, conveying to the world an image of an angry, politicized Laing that was already somewhat discrepant with the mellower, more retiring and essentially apolitical person he was trying to become.

Fed up with the limelight, in 1970, Laing left for India and Ceylon, where he studied Buddhist mediation and Shiviite Yoga for 18 months. He returned a changed man. Unlike his former, angrier, radical self, the new R.D. Laing now enjoined a kind of gentle, Buddhist austerity as the best path to liberation, and expressed a great skepticism about the left's agenda and methods (Burston, 1996, chapter 5). Moreover, he no longer condemned the nuclear family or the use of psychotropic medication as a treatment of last resort, provided these drugs were taken voluntarily, with the patient's informed consent. He remained categorically opposed to electroshock and involuntary psychiatric treatment, and eager to explore alternatives to psychiatry. But he now rejected the "anti-psychiatry" label that others had placed on him, and made several conciliatory gestures toward his estranged psychiatric colleagues.

But Laing was not the only one who changed. In his absence, the world had changed too. When Laing returned from India, the Philadelphia Association was in turmoil, and many former colleagues who left the organization, like David Cooper, Aaron Esterson, Morton Schatzman and Joseph Berke, had published books and acquired followings of their own. Moreover, many old allies on the left who were wounded or puzzled by his retreat to Asian mysticism now turned on him. In the mental health field, for example, Peter Sedgwick, Joel Kovel, Giles Deleuze and Felix Guattari vigorously denounced him. And they were joined by a growing chorus of ambivalent appraisals and abrupt dismissals by prominent feminists like Juliett Mitchell, Phyllis Chesler, Elaine Showalter, and others.

Despite the boos and brickbats of the early and mid-seventies, Laing retained some of his old cache, and could still draw a crowd almost anywhere he chose. But his creativity faltered, and his main book in the seventies, *The Facts of Life*, was a disappointing flop, commercially speaking, that alienated even many loyal fans. By the late seventies, the Left had truly and completely taken its leave of him, and the universities of the Anglo-American world were inundated by the wave of new French theory embodied in the works of Bachelard, Baudrillard, Deleuze and Guattari, Derrida, Foucault, Jacques Lacan, Lyotard, as well as feminist-Freudians (and anti-Freudians) like Kristeva, Cixous and Irigeray, and so on. They buried Laing — in the universities, at any rate. And curiously enough, Laing played a significant role in facilitating the move of this new trend to the English-speaking world.

In 1961, with the help of David Cooper, Laing edited the first English translation of Foucault's *Madness and Civilization* in a Tavistock series entitled "Studies and Existentialism and Phenomenology." Foucault had divorced himself from phenomenology some five years earlier, but Laing stubbornly insisted on regarding him as a phenomenologist (e.g. Laing, 1985, 1987). Laing's regard for Foucault never wavered (Laing, A., 1994). Indeed, Laing wept openly at the news of his death (see Hanja Kochansky, in Mullan, 1997).

Unfortunately, Laing's esteem for Foucault was never quite reciprocated. In 1975, when they finally met, Foucault's courtesy toward Laing was strained and ironic, and he seemed to regard Laing as an irrelevant has-been. That is certainly how most of his compatriots viewed him. Laing was no longer fashionable, and he knew it. And in all likelihood, though he seldom said so, he probably suffered from nagging doubts about the viability of the therapeutic communities he founded with the Philadelphia Association. Some were singular successes. But many floundered or folded, leaving a legacy of bitterness and disillusionment behind them.

In any case, in the late seventies, Laing entered what might be construed as a protracted mid-life crisis. He second marriage had deteriorated, he suffered from chronic writer's block, and almost abandoned his once flourishing private practice in favour of group marathons based on improbable ideas about birth traumas and intrauterine experience. Meanwhile, every rumour and breath of scandal that emanated from his circle and his increasingly turbulent life was circulating freely — including the deathless rumour that he had finally "flipped out." As it happens, he did not, though his personal conduct and public appearances became more volatile and erratic, and many people had more trouble distinguishing between Laing the skeptic, scholar and psychotherapist and Laing the cynic, sybarite and publicity hound. His attempts at re-packaging himself as a lay preacher, poet, and producer of movies and musicals during the late 70's only deepened that confusion. Worse still, his frequent lapses into silliness, sadism and self-aggrandizement shortly before and after his second divorce in 1984 were used to discredit the ideas and causes he championed (Burston, 1996, chapter 6).

In the books and papers that appeared between 1976 and his untimely death in 1989, one sometimes saw flashes of the old brilliance. But by the time he recovered his footing, more or less, his health was failing fast. Shortly before Laing's death, Andrew Feldmar and Kirk Tougas in Vancouver released a video entitled "Did You Used to Be R. D. Laing?" documenting a group co-run by Laing and Feldmar in the spring of '87. The title of the video was culled from a question addressed to Laing by someone vaguely familiar with his work or reputation who probably thought he was already dead — another widespread rumour at the time.

Although nonsensical on the face of it, the question "Did you used to be R.D. Laing?" can be construed as a covert statement. In effect, the questioner was saying: "I suspect that you are someone who used to *be* somebody." In other words: "Hey man, you're history!" And indeed he was, in most people's estimation. Mention Laing nowadays and most people can dimly conjure up a flamboyant rebel of the psychedelic era, a chum of Tim Leary, Ram Dass, and Allen Ginsburg — which he was, of course, off and on. But press them to describe what he stood for, what he actually thought or said, and you'll only elicit a trickle of platitudinous sound bites, proving that serious reflection on his work has virtually halted. The lasting fame that Freud and Jung achieved, and that some predicted for Laing, eluded him, and the recent stream of books about him, (my own included), have done nothing to change that.

My first book on Laing, *The Wing of Madness*, appeared in 1996, and since then many people have asked me why Laing's credibility declined so dramatically over the years. By way of a reply I generally rattle on about his internal contradictions, his inability to follow through and finish his various projects, his flamboyant and provocative gestures, and so on. All true, up to a point. Laing must shoulder some of the responsibility for his current neglect — something he was apparently unwilling or unable to do. But on further reflection, the reasons for his brief fame and rapid decline are much more complex and have less to do with his enigmatic personality than with changing climates of opinion. Let me explain.

The Divided Self was published in 1960. At the time, and for another decade afterwards, psychiatry had little evidence to support — much less prove — the view that schizophrenia is basically a neurological disorder. Indeed, many critics — including many psychiatrists — freely concede that the extant theories of schizophrenia (and evidence in their support) were astonishingly flimsy at the time. That being so, Laing's eloquent appeal to treat the schizophrenic as an anguished, despairing person, rather than a bundle of irksome neuropathology, struck a deep and responsive chord in and out of the mental health field, particularly in view of the coercive atmosphere and the pervasive apathy, anonymity and indifference of most mental hospitals, and the horrifying side-effects of drugs, lobotomy and electroshock.

Since the mid-seventies, however, numerous breakthroughs in the brain-imaging field demonstrate that there are significant correlations between certain varieties of brain disorders and certain schizophrenic symptoms. A clear cut etiology for any single form of schizophrenia is still quite elusive, but the newer drugs and psychosurgical techniques are more effective and less disabling or disfiguring than their predecessors. So there is progress of a sort going on here.

But even now, despite manifold improvements, compliance rates among diagnosed schizophrenics in the United States are still quite low — as low as 20%, by some estimates. That means that about 80% of mental patients do not take their medication as prescribed; some take it episodically, and some not at all. This says something about the culture of psychiatry, and the pervasive mistrust that has grown up among psychiatric patients (and ex-patients). Beyond the self-serving rejoinder that patients mistrust psychiatrists (and therefore do not comply) because they are "ill" or "incompetent," what else may account for this striking climate of non-compliance, psychologically speaking?

This brings us to a very peculiar problem. For reasons that are not yet clear, some people are actually quite relieved when they are told that their anguish, confusion and despair, their sense of helplessness, futility and self-loathing, and so on, are simply the by-products of neurological dysfunction. This verdict gives them palpable hope for improvement, and they are only too glad to tinker with dosages and to try new medications till the right one materializes, eventually. For these people, the loss of dignity, of self-command and of hope that they suffer while symptomatic are viewed as temporary setbacks, to be conveniently erased when their neurological integrity is restored, more or less. Patients like this are a boon to biological psychiatry — their greatest, most grateful and most loyal fans, who are not easily disappointed or deterred by mishaps or mistreatment of one sort or another.

Other patients are averse to this whole approach. They feel that this way of construing things trivializes and demeans them, that it defines and deforms their experience in ways that are at variance with their deepest, though often groping and inarticulate sense of who they *really* are. Whether they know it or not, people like these are often looking for something akin to a religious experience as a solution to their difficulties — a new experience or a fresh perspective that will elicit or confer deeper meaning on their suffering, giving it some ennobling *raison d'être*, assuring them it is actually *in aid of* something. It doesn't take much insight to see why. They feel that their lives have been hijacked or derailed somehow. They don't just want their suffering to *stop*, or to see some light at the end of the tunnel. They desperately want that tunnel to be a necessary rite of passage to a new and better place than the one they left behind, one which they are loathe to return to.

In addition to patients (or prospective patients) like these, there are people who shun conventional psychiatric remedies because they feel shattered by the blows of life, and look to the psychotherapist to address their deep sense of victimization at the hands of others, to enable them to clarify and cope with it more satisfactorily than they can at present. If the psychiatrist isn't listening, or isn't helpful in this respect, they will not stay the course.

Finally, many candidates for a psychiatric diagnosis have *both of* the aforementioned tendencies in extremely pronounced form. Being told that what they feel or experience is purely the result of a disordered brain is quite distressing for them, and prompts deeper self-doubt and/or distrust of others. In Laing's terminology, they feel "invalidated" by a summary appraisal like this, and fear that their mental-health worker is colluding with all the others who neglect or oppress them, despite their overt or conscious intentions. Rightly or wrongly, then, they are likely to experience the standard treatment approach as disrespectful and coercive, and they've had quite enough of that already, thank you very much. As a result, they are far more likely to go astray with conventional psychiatric treatment. And their numbers are legion.

Laing drew attention to these and other features of work-a-day psychiatry long ago, but many things have changed since *The Politics of Experience* created such a sensation. The general public isn't as moved by the plight of these people as it was in Laing's day. And though Laing was far more effective with people like these than the average clinician in a one-on-one setting, he never developed a workable alternative to the conventional mental hospital. In the absence of such an alternative, people in distress are inclined to rely on the devil they know. Besides, really good psychotherapy is time and labor intensive. It requires a substantial emotional investment from the therapist as well as the patient. It is not cheap and not fast, and in the recent climate of fiscal restraint we want a quick fix: something clean and cost-effective, not messy and time consuming.

OK. But let's not kid ourselves. These new drug treatments do not work for everyone, not even those who *do* comply with their physician's advice. And while drug companies minimize their side-effects — they always do — their long term repercussions may come back to haunt those whose treatment was "successful" in the first instance.

Another reason Laing is neglected now is that we are weary of the culture of victimization. And rightly so. We are all so frightfully fed up with people making lurid careers of their victimization that we try to ignore them, and in our state of numbed inattention, we need to be reminded of how nauseated we actually are by this cultural state of affairs. Only a lucid appreciation of our impatience and disgust enables us to distance ourselves from these almost reflexive feelings sufficiently so that we may remember that many mental patients really *are* profoundly victimized by those who claim to be their nearest and dearest, and that they often have no form of redress, and no way of explaining or calling attention to themselves. Even when they do have the means, they often lack the ability to make themselves heard, because life has robbed them of the confidence and clarity they need to address us on *our* terms, and in a language *we* readily understand. The most that many of them can manage, finally, is to let their symptoms do the talking, and hope vainly that someone, somewhere, will "hear" their strange, disembodied voices.

This is a hard nut to swallow. Most mental health professionals are trained to believe that diagnosis entails the accurate identification of a disease entity or some discrete form of psychopathology situated in the body, brain or unconscious of the patient/client. The corollary assumption at work here is that until the disorder in question is correctly diagnosed, an appropriate treatment cannot be prescribed. However, Laing argued that labeling the individual often has little to do with accurate assessment of the patient's real problems, and that the remedial interventions mandated by a specific diagnosis often serve complex *social* functions by equilibrating extant social systems, i.e. maintaining the status quo. In short, clinicians frequently locate the cause of the disturbance in individuals to divert attention from the processes that actually engendered their disturbed behavior. If they did not, they would often construe the "signs and symptoms" of these diagnostic entities as intelligible responses to what Laing termed "unlivable situations" — ones which the patient can neither understand, nor tolerate, nor change effectively.

Laing often told a story about a weeping mother who came to inquire about her teenage son, "Julian," who had just been diagnosed schizophrenic. She would spare no expense to avoid the standard psychiatric zombification doled out to troubled teenagers like him. When asked about the initial onset of Julian's problems, she said that some months previously, he started to insist that the man his mother married was not his real father. That was only the beginning, unfortunately. Soon, other delusional fantasies, charges of conspiracy and deception, appeared. But this was the central or core complaint, which he never relinquished, and which was driving her and her husband to distraction.

After seeing the boy once, Laing informed the mother that he might be able to help her son if she would level with him.

Was her husband truly the boy's father? After beating around the bush, the mother finally confessed that he wasn't. In fact, Julian was conceived during a premarital fling she had hidden from her husband all these years. Laing then informed the mother that he could not help her or her son unless she was honest with herself and her husband about his real paternity. So long as she and her husband construed his suspicions as delusional, Laing noted, the psychiatrists she engaged to treat Julian would act as unwitting but thoroughly obliging accomplices to a sustained family cover-up. At some cost to herself, no doubt, the mother eventually leveled with her son and her husband, and in a few months, the boy was back to normal.

Cases like these, which were not uncommon in Laing's practice, suggest that there is often much literal as well as symbolic truth in the (real or alleged) delusions of schizophrenics, and that an honest attempt to discern and to validate those truths may be indispensable, therapeutically speaking. It also indicates that people who are deeply disturbed and disturbing to others need not be suffering from brain damage or the ravages of repression, regression and/or other specifically internal disturbances. They may be reeling from the effects of what Laing termed *interpersonal defences*, which are subtle, silent and usually unconscious tactics designed to silence and/or discredit a prospective patient who may very well recover his or her sanity when these collective defences are exposed. Far from being an act or expression of medical *gnosis* — or of "knowledge," as the Greek roots suggest — the act of diagnosing may be the perfect cover for ignorance, perhaps willful ignorance: a way of *not* knowing the patient, as Laing would say.

In such circumstances, the treatment patients receive, however well intended, often compounds the damage they've suffered, rather than reversing it. And this is especially so when the diagnosis of schizophrenia — or some other grave mental disorder — is rendered in ignorance of the deeper levels of the patient's experience and social surround.

references

Burston, D. 1996, *The Wing of Madness: The Life and Work of R.D.Laing*, Cambridge: Harvard University Press.

Burston, D. 2000, *The Crucible of Experience: R.D. Laing & The Crisis of Psychotherapy*, Cambridge: Harvard University Press.

Foucault, M. 1967. *Madness & Civilization*, London: Tavistock Publications

Laing, A., 1994. *R.D. Laing: A biography*, London: Peter Owen.

Laing, R.D. 1960, *The Divided Self*, London, Tavistock Publications.

Laing. R.D. & Esterson, A. 1964. *Sanity, Madness & The Family*, London: Tavistock Publications.

Laing, R. D. 1967, *The Politics of Experience and the Bird of Paradise*, New York: Pantheon.

Laing, R.D. 1969, *The Politics of the Family*, Toronto: CBC Publications.

Laing, R.D. 1976. *The Facts of Life*, New York: Pantheon.

Laing, R. D. 1982, *The Voice of Experience*, New York: Pantheon.

Laing, R.D. 1985, *Wisdom, Madness and Folly: The Making of A Psychiatrist*, New York: McGraw Hill.

Laing, R.D., 1987. "Laing's Understanding of Interpersonal Experience" in *The Oxford Companion to the Mind*, ed. Richard Gregory, New York: Oxford University Press.

Mullan, B. 1997, *R. D. Laing: Creative Destroyer*, London, Cassell.

3: Conversations With R.D. Laing

F. A. Jenner

Conversations with R.D. Laing

F. A. Jenner

It is flattering to be asked to report on my interactions with R.D. Laing, because although they did influence me considerably, they were only sporadic and very occasional contacts. Further, what I can write now depends on an old and flagging memory. The quotations cannot be reliably what was actually said. Nevertheless, Laing has been reported as saying that I was the only classical psychiatrist with whom he felt able to have a profitable discussion. It is also true that he said things on such occasions which seemed to me to be more open minded about physical and chemical studies than would have been anticipated by most people. Of course there were the occasional pieces of outrageous behaviour which it is fairly necessary to put largely on one side here, except perhaps to see them as illustrating the personal struggles, and impulsive outbursts from which he himself presumably had to suffer. Perhaps they give great clues about how it was that he had his remarkable understanding of other troubled and rebelliously independent souls? He did, I think, have to have made great efforts to tolerate the conventional mundane common sense civility and so-called morality of a real, rather than of some romanticized and probably impossible, society.

On one occasion Ronny had asked Dr. Dimitri Vlissides, another member of our department, and myself to London to dine with him and Francis Huxley. We were to discuss establishing a house in Sheffield. It was to be linked with the university department and to be so structured as to gather information on relative effectiveness. He had previously sounded very enthusiastic, but during the dinner he would not discuss it. After eating he chose to play the piano and sing and he said, "Fuck the house in Sheffield!" We returned disappointed, but in fact the house would not have materialized anyway as money we had already been promised locally was subsequently not forthcoming. We were all anyway aware that one could only hope to enrich the debate by such a project and not totally answer very fundamental questions, but was he frightened of even that? I do not know. I was certainly very irritated but it did not damage our relationship, and it was never even mentioned again.

Why then did we manage to have interesting discourse? For me it was great to speak with such a famous person. I suspected that my position as a Professor of Psychiatry and as an Honorary Director of a Medical Research Council Unit influenced him; I may have seemed to have the respectability he ambivalently shunned. That would be strange if it was so, as he was well known throughout the world, in a way quite beyond any recognition I attained. On the other hand, he was to a degree ridiculed by most in important positions in psychiatry, while I did at least listen to him. I was so flattered to know him and did not mind it that much when he was rude and indifferent. Francis Huxley, who was much closer to Ronnie than I was, referred to Laing's changes in behaviour as central among the reasons why he was the best and worst asset that the Philadelphia Association had. Subsequently Laing and the Association he had set up went their own separate ways.

Perhaps our relationship was helped by the fact that we had in common the same year of birth. He strangely made much of the few months seniority, six in fact, that I suffered. He gave me the impression of having a very conscious fear of death, and he spoke about anticipating my prior demise! One felt that there was an underlying acceptance of, or influence by the Heideggerian only certainty in life.

We both also had puritan Scottish mothers. His, however, forever warned him about the menace of eating the wrong and dangerous foods. Mine, a humble but literally *nouveau riche* lady, celebrated our rise from comparative penury by plying everyone with everything she could so munificently give them to eat. Hence he declared, my waistline compared to his waistline, and my complicit conventionality contrasted with his, he said, taciturn tendencies. He poignantly, and probably correctly, suggested that I had suffered insufficiently to acquire understanding.

In a friendly way when I told him about a patient whom I had taken to my own home; with whom I had shared many trips (along with others) to pubs theatres, walks etc., without any progress being achieved, he rightly laughed at me. He knew that I had been in the Royal Navy, and he said "you are like an Admiral covered in gold braid saying to an Able-Bodied Seaman in bell bottoms, 'have a cigarette, and let us talk man to man'. Wasn't that fraudulent?" This was a poignant comment on me, it was independently repeated in a similar form by one of my best Ph.D. students. He said you take them home and give them dinner, which they do enjoy, but the next day is like all the previous days, what has changed? Laing, when I told him that, said candidly "you want success and admiration on the cheap just as I do." That was perhaps one of the most profound and true comments in our discussions. It led to questioning the meaning of *should*.

Should, we began to agree, should be followed by for whom. and that was all that could be sought. With my more thorough going agnosticism, I felt happy to leave the human predicament and moral issues there. He, however, as though playing chess, saw the dangerous possible gambit I had made towards his greater openness to a spiritual outlook. He felt that great art and morality could, just like the material world, be perceived: "what better empirical evidence of realities can we have?" He tried to develop a position much nearer Heidegger's (1978) than Sartre's (1956). This was especially clear in his toying with schizophrenia as a mystical voyage. For reasons which may be clearer later he saw me as seeing through much of pseudo statistical and probabilistic mathematical technology in psychiatry but as still seeing, with Pythagoras, God as a mathematician.

Our friendly relationship was somewhat cemented when I arranged, on his advice, to appoint for a brief period Francis Huxley, one of Laing's really close associates, as a short term lecturer in the Department of Psychiatry in Sheffield. This was in order to give the medical students at least some contact with outlooks which had so influenced Faculties of Art and radicals throughout the Western world. Similarly, Laing very much approved of it when we had Mary Barnes (1971) to talk to, and freely discuss with the students, her "Journey through Madness". Laing knew that my outlook had been far nearer to "it is all biochemistry really" than to Sartre, Heidegger, Foucault, Binswanger, Boss and all the other existentialist writers. I had said to him that I wanted to understand them better, especially the existentialism of Laing himself.

In fact I was still fascinated by the studies of so called Periodic Catatonia[1] which had not quite disappeared as a condition, and he knew a great deal about this story, now strangely lost in time. Related to that for me was an enquiry into other predictably recurring psychotic and non-psychotic mental phenomena. When I started, the periodically predictable patients were people easy to study, very difficult to treat, and with them of course I was looking at very easily recorded responses to psychopharmacological agents. Laing said that that was all very fine and interesting. He conceded that the research technique was impressive and could possibly produce striking results. However it was only justifiable in as far as I accepted that my ideas were at best just hypotheses. When I agreed but retorted, turning the tables on him, by saying that his concepts too were no securer, he said that he was influenced by existentialist concepts and an intellectual domain in which one sought to grasp what it was like to *Be* like that. One can know what is so and correct in the way one can when playing music. He did not deny the relevance of cerebral functioning to mental states as in dementia for example, but he repudiated the over powering mathematicalization so influential in the taxonomic and other psychiatric studies of the period. He liked my banal statement that I agreed, and that was why I had made intense studies on individuals (see Jenner 1983), "Statistical methods cannot classify anything objectively, they only function to help achieve a categorization according to what you declare that you want the taxonomy for. In that sense it is never totally objective." This is much better appreciated now than it was then. At that period many had made their names famous at the very highest echelons of psychiatry by pseudo objective statistically based classificatory methods. They tended to be more respected than critically questioned. It was however for some, such as Rolv Gjessing (1976), who influenced me, a reason for studying periodic catatonia, that is, individuals who seemed to change predictably and without any apparently similarly timed recurring environmental factors. If one could find the biochemical clock or pendulum or negative feed back circuit the further steps for psychiatry would be obvious. That clock, if it existed, controlled aspects of human behaviour. Laing was pleased though to realize that I was aware that I had picked a field of enquiry likely to reveal solutions close to a biochemist's heart. Such choices by research workers guarantee, that, in as far as they will get results, that they will be consistent with their own philosophy. Those eschewing philosophy are the blindest to their own axioms. The politics of where and at what to look, he said was not what Husserl (1970) would have termed without presumptions or just looking at a thing itself. Of course he was right. He appeared though, surprised, if very appreciative, of my suspicion that even the phenomenon of periodicity could be analogous to the pitch of a violin string (Jenner and Damas Mora (1983)), that is, due to the tension it experienced on it from outside forces. Perhaps in recent years the conditions for such gross stresses of asylum life have almost disappeared because the mental hospitals have changed. In fact now they have generally been closed. Then they were already being much improved. But perhaps the story came to an end with the advent too of the phenothiazines, and then Lithium etc.? Periodic catatonia remained commoner longer in The Third World. One needs to be fairly old to grasp the historical significance of much of this, and to realise that even the most trenchant, critical grey eminence, and acerbic psychiatric writer as Sir Aubrey Lewis[2] had accepted periodic catatonia as one form of schizophrenia already shown to have a biochemical basis.

Laing was very generous to me in praise of all the work I had done. Of course, like me, he was intrigued about why mental conditions change with time. He added, schizophrenia, asthenia and hysteria aren't what they used to be, are they fashions? Crazes are pervasive, but could Periodic Catatonia have been like Encephalicitis Lethargica and also have a microbial basis?

Laing was most delighted when I confessed that my curiosity about him and his work came from, or was at least much enhanced by, patients telling me that he understood them and I did not. One of them gave me "The Divided Self" (1965) for my edification, as a Christmas present! Another later gave me "One Flew over the Cuckoo's Nest"!

I had become a professor of psychiatry in the nineteen sixties, in the era of Laing's persisting and quite staggering international fame. When I first invited him to lecture in the University so many people came that the local fire brigade was called and asked us, for reasons of safety, to reduce the numbers in the largest theatre in the medical school. However, few psychiatrists were there!

The period was perhaps best typified by the slogan that "One should not change one's mind as there is a fault in reality." In the turbulent period of student revolts and protests in France, Germany, some parts of Britain and the USA etc, nothing very much happened in a city like Sheffield, and especially not within medicine. Few medically trained persons quite understood what was being implied. After all, reality is reality, how could there be a fault in it? Clearly for Laing and many others the reality which matters is that of human despair, loneliness, insecurity and the fear of others. There was the eternally necessary, even if romantic and passionate, belief too that it could all be different, and the almost certainty that much of the problem lay in conventional bourgeois life with its rules about Ought and Ought Not to do. They included so much related to sex, drugs and the family. Further, the internationally important French academic world of Sartre had influenced Laing. Sartre was himself a reaction to the Second World War and the degradation of European culture that it had displayed. He saw each human individual as doomed to be free and left to create his own values, but, despite that, it was false not to be able to see what was so despicable. Laing, unlike Sartre, did try to find spiritual guidance but both did seem to grasp the tragically possible loneliness of an isolated individual. Both understood Kierkegaard's "Sickness until Death" and the awesome reality we avoid or hide by the trivialities of ordinary life.

Before personally meeting Laing, his book "The Divided Self" had intrigued me. It did not completely convert me, as I did find it to be a very curious work, one requiring a paradigm change I have never been able to totally make. The three Ms of a past of Methodism, Marxism and Materialism have left indelible stains, as does childhood and background on everyone's mental health and sickness.

Laing's best work starts with a very insightful satirical parody of Emil Kraepelin's outlook. Kraepelin's careful studies and his ultimate self-critical reflections had always impressed me. They still do, especially following the opportunity I have had to actually read his meticulously beautifully handwritten case reports, and then his own self criticism and willingness to see the limitations of his own life's work. However, the opening of the "Divided Self" very brilliantly makes what Kraepelin saw as utterly bizarre in the assertions of a patient quite understandable. The poor man was on show in an enormous lecture theatre as a clinical exhibit of madness. There was little evidence that anyone realised the nature of such an experience for the man himself. I was certainly concerned, as I had been involved in somewhat similar shows. At first, as the new Professor, and not without my own anxieties, when I presented people to professional audiences I was probably as interested in my own performance as I was in their feelings!

Laing's lesson was very discomforting. It taught me about myself and Kraepelin without completely demolishing Kraepelin's studies. It struck me later as strange then that Laing said he so wanted to work with Karl Jaspers, the recognised authority on the fact that the schizophrenic is pathognomonically beyond ordinary human comprehension. That is, of course, not to say he has no feelings as perhaps we almost thought. To be beyond everyday understanding was essential to Jaspers for the very diagnosis itself. Laing however had a great respect for the existential position that Jaspers also later held within philosophy, and he felt that in the passing years Jaspers may have changed his attitude to schizophrenia from what he had written in his influential masterpiece, the "General Psychopathology". In addition Laing saw *General Psychopathology* as one of the greatest texts in psychiatry. One which had medical and philosophical erudition and that was why he wanted to work with Jaspers, although he never did do so.

Jaspers in his *General Psychopathology* would have agreed with Laing who urged in *The Divided Self* that it is not possible to see a person as a set of symptoms. Jaspers did not do so, he even said about the schizophrenic person that unlike the demented person he can surprise the observer with apt, indeed shrewd philosophical comments. So perhaps both would have agreed that one must struggle to discern the individual's existential position as someone relating to a human and social and meaningful environment. In his writing, but less in talking with me, Laing however tended to neglect a possible genetic constitutional, or other physical factors, which Jaspers thought was probably central. Both were being critical of Freud in different ways, in relation to the unconscious mind. Jaspers felt that psychoanalysis was far too speculative and so not testable. Laing was more critical of a need for an unconscious mind but, like Binswanger and Boss, was indebted to Freud for his psychologizing the field of enquiry, but denying, as did Jung, the centrality of the sexual.

Laing was very aware of his debt to Martin Büber (1937), the Jewish theologian, who made so much of the necessary distinction between *I, Thou* and *It*. Classical medical science Laing felt can only deal with *It*. Nevertheless I did show Laing some striking results I had obtained using Lithium Carbonate in Manic Depressive patients; he was genuinely so very impressed by them that he subsequently telephoned me and asked me whether I would accept someone very close to him for such treatment. The person never actually came, I think they were cross with him, but Laing did say that there were situations when that treatment was clearly highly appropriate. He added that he never stopped his clients from taking the drugs they wished, prescribed or not. The problem he felt was the gross tendency to believe most human ills could be adequately treated in that sort of way, when so much was obviously, in fact, given for the advantage of some over others, often in a covert power struggle. Often drugs reduced protest. Such a discussion did have a significant impact on my outlook. In particular it reinforced an influential assertion of Wittgenstein (1949) "You cannot open a window without holding the hinges still". So much does depend on what is in our background and our views depend upon that. Laing was anxious to also stress that few professionals are consistent; the explanations of behaviour in the clinic are not always the same as at home. The whole problem of morality and the distinction of bad and mad for him raised issues about thing or person. I think he said that "You can neither live without concepts of good and bad, nor ugly or beautiful, dismissal of such notions is only possible for analytical philosophers away from the family" that was, at least approximately, a repeated refrain. It had much to do with Sartre's *engagement* and the falsity of neutrality and objectivity in relation to realities which matter.

Laing was eager to suggest that the schizophrenic had already tried to solve his own problems by erecting a barrier around himself, long before the psychiatrist sees him. He had made himself an *It*, and you the therapist, had to get beyond that barrier which he had erected and defends. So you must try to allow him to be *Thou* (modern English does not do justice with Thou for the friendly affectionate German Du, and Romance languages' Tu, but we understand what is being said here). To a degree modern medicine leads the medic to discourse about It, with the nurse and now the therapist considering Thou.

We discussed whether the strangeness of complementarity and quantum mechanics gave us some route away from the deterministic aspects of earlier science, in particular from the Laplacian position that if a super intelligence knew the position, speed of direction of all particles at one moment he would know the whole future and past. We agreed that something analogous survives in some who call themselves scientists. We hoped modern physics might help us to escape from what classical physics had taught us. It might, but, while seeing how counterintuitive it all seems, neither felt competent to confidently take the escape route it might offer. Laing felt that any overwhelming rejection of our potential to change is inauthentic, it is far too great a leap to look to physics to help in fields like psychodynamics or, for example, politics. One has to consider the meaning of the word fundamental, and fundamental for whom or what? Desire and subjectivity underlie much in language.

To be a human being is to have possibilities until death, for while there is life there is hope. The trouble for many people was their ideological brainwashed opposition to their own possibilities. Their ontological insecurity gave them no safe ground on which to build their lives. I seem to think that he said that they were like painters with brushes and paint but no canvas. By that he meant no self.

The above led to my revealing my obsession with David Hume's views and so to putting forward the question he posed of the illusion of a self. "I never catch myself, only myself doing something." What self was there then to be divided, true or false? My destructive ploy was to ask what was the analogous *It* in, "It is raining." This was probably quite rightly and sharply put on one side. It was declared to be a scholastic and academic negation of the obviously meaningful. It had as a thought a place but only in a different universe of conversation   Laing seemed to take the view that it all depended on which language one wanted to use, and which game you wanted to play. Hume's, would be a useless ploy in psychotherapy, it would sound schizophrenic to imply that you do not exist. There was little opportunity to ask whether Buddha might have agreed with Hume and so found and offered relief and enlightenment in grasping illusions. In that our changed roles in the discussion would have been too great. Laing was aware of Hume's own realisation of the pointlessness of philosophy. Certainly, as Hume himself practised it, he was very logical and destructive by analysing language rather than persons. There was as well Hume's own advice that one should be a philosopher, if one wished, but one should first be a man. Moreover Hume was candidly conscious that he wrote his *Treatise on Human Nature*, in the search for fame and a reputation for himself. Laing won the round with his query "for which self?"

Philosophy for Laing was not the logical analysis of language but the search for wisdom about the reality of human existence and experience. Hume after all had a clear and apparently very satisfying concept of himself, and he toiled hard to embellish it in others' eyes. Why deride others' need of a self they could polish, accept and live with?

With a somewhat prosaic sixth former's scientific-cum-technician's outlook, the poetical and creative lateral thinking in Laing's writings and language was and is always difficult for me. When he asserted that a man who said he was dead was telling us his truth, my style of converse asserted that I could not understand him, after all he clearly was not dead, he was alive. Why not speak clearly? Obviously for Laing my ontological security was involved and I was perhaps too able to trust words as well as other people. There was an additional lack of awareness of the potential disintegration of the self and the gross inability to interact successfully with others.

For Laing there are two ways of dealing with ontological insecurity; the feeling that the self will be submerged and unable to avoid the engulfment by others. So one either retracts into a cocoon by oneself, or simply submits completely to being swallowed up by another person and so, in either case, one loses one's own self as an entity. The problems get worse when the stratagems fail, when one of the twins gets married etc. Then the "schizophrenia" or so-called death becomes more obvious. For Laing there is no need for a Freudian concept of the unconscious Id taking over the ego, nor of sexual desires causing the anxiety as in classical psychoanalysis. These people simply desired to be, and that desire is not difficult to understand. To do so does not stand in need of a self-contradicting concept of an unconscious mind. The desires are obvious at least to existential analysts like Binswanger, Boss and Laing et al.

To some extent that led us on to considering social and political issues. I did not dare to ask whether he had, as the Basaglias thought and had told me, rejected the publication of an English edition of *"L'instituzzione negata. Rapporto da un espedale psichiatrico" We* did however broach that topic in terms of political involvement and contracting out. Laing had already supported my initiation of a psychiatric protest against psychiatric abuse in the Soviet Union. He told me rather proudly though, that Jock Sutherland, his senior at the Tavistock Clinic, had advised him to remain within the National Health Service. He was warned that leaving would result in his subsequent loss of support and to his own obscurity. He was full of pride that that had not happened, and somehow he had not got the personality to just be one of the tribe. Notwithstanding that he did declare his amazement at his own sudden rise to fame, comparable to that of the less academic Beatles. In a way he bemoaned notoriety's tempting and destructive intrusiveness. There was something about him which struggled for validity, enlightenment, and at times he seemed to believe that understanding is really possible for creatures as strange as we are. Surely, he strangely urged, we can understand ourselves? Can we? Hence his passage from Presbyterianism to the army and psychiatry then anthropology and India and back? He was very aware of Heidegger's view that we must all spend much of our time inauthentically living our daily lives and obscuring and avoiding the need, in fact to search for understanding of Being. For Heidegger, that was the *raison d'être* for philosophy. Laing was conscious that his greater hero, Sartre, so influenced by Heidegger, rejected that possibility, favouring an emphasis on our freedom in creating meaningfulness as well as morality almost as an aesthetic product. Laing did not think as Heidegger did that Sartre had failed to understand what Heidegger intended. He did not accept that Sartre had so misled the Western world about Heidegger, because English was the international language, and the English speaking and reading world were so much more influenced by the salons of Paris and French rather than German thought. Laing himself certainly appeared to be more familiar with French than German. Nevertheless he told me that he was writing an important book on Nietzsche that would make many issues such as we had discussed clearer and that would take all my thinking much much further forward. No one else to whom I have spoken seems to have heard anything about this intention.

Laing's intentions were not philosophical but in a way *psychiatric* or more accurately *quasi psycho-analytical* in the sense related to the ideas of Binswanger and Boss. He saw the child's need to be noticed and taken seriously in order to be. Mary Barnes, for example, said her parents were good but always distant from her, hence she and her brother became schizophrenics. Despite her very strenuous efforts he unfortunately remained unwell. Such past realities led to the development of a false self akin to Sartre's view of bad faith, in his "Being and Nothingness" and perhaps even more so to Heidegger's concept of lack of "authenticity" in face of our knowledge of death in his "Being and Time." I was anxious to convert the debate into a consideration of compliance and complicity as possible strategies with some emphasis and personal taste for complicity. The latter has the connotation of a degree of collusion, in this case as the ticket to becoming a member of an inevitably real rather than an impossible ideal society. The truth of situations requires one to negotiate, in doing so there is difficulty in perceiving our own true or false self. Underneath thorough going compliance, there can be a rebellious and offended person displaying a very false self who really brooks no compromise. Perhaps when such underlying rebelliousness of the false self breaks out, it is seen as a strange madness beyond comprehension. Binswanger saw the compliant self as accepting only either / or, in fact victory or defeat.

Laing's analysis was by D.W. Winnicott who also had a theory of true and false self, and as I have previously written the realisation of this is among factors which place Laing in a historical position and movement. There are few isolated geniuses and iconoclasts springing as it were from outer space with totally new ideas. It is more the case that historians, and the public find it simpler to write history in terms of strides taken by individuals. Of course I was very impressed and influenced by Laing, so it would be unfair to underrate his importance, but it would demonstrate lack of authenticity to succumb to one person's views, especially since, in a way, he implied that that is to have a type of false self.

Kingsley Hall and other houses were the result of the valiant attempts of Laing to give so-called schizophrenic persons the space to become themselves. Unfortunately successes like that achieved with Mary Barnes were not everyday events. Nor was it completely demonstrated that psychiatry was as he thought mainly more harmful than successful. He of course with others made the important attempts to help and further develop and test existential methods of therapy. Many others based their struggles upon his.

Because I favour complicity, I find myself still feeling that Bassaglia did achieve more for the mentally ill than Laing. He too was but one of a crowd who saw the pernicious nature of life in the asylums, and with many others humanized the regimes offered to people now more often in the community. Basaglia made life more tolerable and the persons more tolerated because he also worked on the community which had to accept the distressed. He and his wife were involved in politics with inevitably somewhat soiled hands or at least subterfuges and compromises in order to achieve human changes.

Laing's intellectual challenge was the more thought-provoking, but for me also confusing. Frequently returning to the "Divided Self" left me very challenged but still confused and uncertain, open to the possibilities and need for a less medical and more humanistic approach. I had however lived through the advent and introduction of chlorpromazine to the asylums and I had seen the changes so often explained away by other theorists. But there was also the *Camisol chemique*[3] reality and the powerful halo effect of a degree of success. It was difficult to feel that Laing's clinical successes were more than the actually very limited clinical achievements even of Freud, with neurosis. Perhaps neither believed in cures?

For all manner of reasons, do what we may, schizophrenia as a concept evades our explanations at almost every level. Its homogeneity is largely linguistic, and we might do well to follow Wittgenstein's more general advice not to ask what things are but rather enquire about how the word is used and by whom and for which reason. Science might then be, as Popper would have it, merely knowledge which is difficult to deny for the time being in the light of the evidence available, and expressed in the language we are using and thinking in. Religion would be in line with its joint etymological origins with ligament knowledge: some are bound irrespective of evidence or their own doubts to accept. Philosophy then becomes a tiresome pretence of being especially able to discover truth without extra empirical evidence. To a degree Laing did very much agree with this position, but, as ever, with the caveat that the empirical must not deny the subjective observations and experiences of being human. Of course, he concurred, every new technique of non-intrusively studying brains or anything else should be used to acquire knowledge, but the history of the enthusiasms that the latest physical techniques have brought us near to the real truth about schizophrenia must also beckon caution. Still in almost every moment in life, we can be aware of our own emotional instability, or more academically reflecting, note on what rests our own ontological security, and even that of the sciences in general. We of course need our acceptable and accepted niches, both intellectually and humanly, but always in relation to others, unless we wish to be hermits living with fantasies. A problem for others was put well by Laing himself:

> "If a violinist in an orchestra is out of tune and does not hear it, and does not believe it, and will not retire and insists on taking his seat and playing at all rehearsals and concerts and ruining the music, what can be done? If all persuasions fails, is there anything else to do than to have him or her removed by physical force, against his or her will?"

My own failure to know why some of my patients got better, and my disappointment that few when asked were able or wished to tell me, did limit what I could learn from their experiences.

I still realise my simplicity in at one time thinking that perhaps just "offering a place at the table with us would cure the isolated person". However it is still not obvious what more we can do beyond occasionally and reluctantly medicating, clearly accepting and making space at the table and elsewhere, and not below the salt, for them.

Kraepelin (1904), Bleuler (1911) Schneider (1959) and Jaspers (1963) et al really worked in eras when effective therapy seemed a fairly distant hope. However they did try to state how they used the word schizophrenia (or dementia praecox). They said less about why they did. Their outlooks hinged on the underlying assumption they had uncritically accepted. Many difficult states of mind and behaviour that the man in the street had already defined as highly undesirable were, they thought, appropriate concerns for medical management. Of course there were political manoeuvres to gain control too. This was not so difficult with a problem with which, initially, few wished to be landed. Subsequently great vested interests have arisen in the production of drugs which *treat* or *control* human beings. That has increased in the light of success in producing and discovering such chemicals. There had been a history of the psychopharmacology and medicine of the mind from Greek times. So medicine, which is partly a trade union, remained in a strong position (especially when united). Psychiatry remains powerful despite the development of Social Work, nursing and Psychology as challenging professions. Historically the challenge had been limited in Europe even if there had been some deviation of the thought, especially in the Middle Ages, into demonology, witches and theology. Nevertheless, it seemed, and still seems, common sense to most that something is very wrong, not just ordinarily undesirable. So Sedgewick, a very sympathetic radical whom I also knew, insisted, "mental illnesses are illnesses". But what is illness but an undesirable state? Laing certainly raised the issue for me as to why what is called schizophrenia is so much more appropriately to be considered a medical problem than for example most states of jealousy. He stimulated me at least to hesitate in my confidence, and he did so in a way more generous to the sufferers than Szasz. Szasz would send many sufferers to prison, not a Kingsley Hall House, in order to defend the nature of the American constitution and its guarantee of civil liberty.

With Socrates, I feel I am left only knowing that I don't know.

references

Avenarius. R (1979) "Emil Kraepelin, seine Persönlichkeit und Konzeption In Psychopathologie als Grundlagen Wissenschaft" Enke Stuttgart

Binswanger L "Being in the World" translated by Jacob Needleman Souvenir Press London.

Bleuler E (1911) "Dementia Praecox or the group of Schizophrenias" translated by A.A. Brill International University Press New York

Boss M. (1983) "Existential basis of Medicine and Psychology." Jason Arason New York.

Büber M. (1937) "I and Thou" translated by W. Kaufman, Clark Edinburgh.

Foucault M. "The Birth of the Clinic. An Archeology of Medical Perception." Translated by A. Sheridan, Vintage Books New York

Gjessing R. (1976) "Contributions to the Somatology of Periodic Catatonia." Translated and edited by L.Gjessing and F.A. Jenner, Pergamon Press Oxford

Heidegger M. (1927) "Being and Time" translated by J. Macquarrie and E. Robinson, Blackwell Oxford 1962

Husserl E. (1970) Logical Investigations" Translated by J.N.Findlay, Routledge Kegan Paul London.

Jaspers, K. (1962) The General Psychopathology" Manchester University Press. Manchester

Jenner F.A. and Damas Mora J. (1983) Philosophical and Neurobiological studies of some Periodic Psychoses" Igaku-Shoin, Tokyo

Kierkegaard S. "The Sickness unto Death!" translated by H.V.Hong and E.H.Hong. Princeton University Press New Jersey.

Kraeplin E. (1904) "Clinical Psychiatry - a textbook for students and physicians" translated by A.R. Diefendof, Macmillan New York

Laing R.D. (1965) The Divided Self" Penguin, Harmondsworth

Laing R.D. (1986) "Wisdom, Madness and Folly" Macmillan London

Sartre J.P. (1957) "Being and Nothingness" translated by E. Barnes, Methuen London

Schneider K (1959) "Clinical Psychopathology" Grune and Stratton New York.

Szasz T (1976) "Schizophrenia, the sacred cow of psychiatry" Oxford University Press Oxford

Wiittgenstein, L. (1949) "Philosophical Investigations" translated by G.E. Anscombe, Blackwell Oxford

notes

[1] Periodic Catatonia was a condition hardly ever seen now but in a way described by Kraepelin but more precisely by Gjessing. It wasn't that uncommon in the earlier years of the twentieth century and it referred to patients who became recurrently psychotic to a time. It was thought to be due to retention of a nitrogen containing compound(s) which affected the brain and the regulation of the levels of which for some reason oscillated. The evidence was that large doses of thyroxine seemed at the time to lead to remission —see Gjessing, R. (1976)

[2] See early editions of Price's Textbook of Medicine" Oxford University Press

[3] Camisol chemique a term introduced by the French pharmacologists who had developed chlorpromazine, the first of the major tranquillizers. They meant that the drug can be seen as being a chemical strait-jacket.

part two

ideas

4: Laing and Merleau-Ponty

Eric Matthews

Laing and Merleau-Ponty

Eric Matthews

I

Laing had a profound interest in philosophy, particularly of the existential-phenomenological tradition, and saw it as directly relevant to his clinical practice. His writings clearly show that this interest was based on genuine understanding. Nevertheless, he was not a professional philosopher, and did not approach philosophical propositions in the way that a professional philosopher would. Quite reasonably from his own point of view, he was interested, not so much in the arguments which were intended to justify these propositions, or in their place in a wider systematic context, as in the use which he could make of them in dealing with his patients in a more humane and sensitive way. This was refreshing in many ways, but it had its downside. The failure to make fully explicit the rational philosophical basis for his approach laid him open to unnecessary and unjustified charges of pursuing a purely personal agenda, motivated by sentimentality about mental disorder, and made it easier for his opponents to present themselves as defenders of hard science against merely subjective opinion.

I will attempt in this essay to make good as far as I can this philosophical deficit. I shall seek to do so by, first, outlining the philosophical framework which Laing himself presents, and in the terms which he himself uses, in his major work *The Divided Self*; and then presenting an account of some of the relevant thinking of the French philosopher Maurice Merleau-Ponty (1908-1961), in which I shall explore, in a more systematic philosophical way, the underpinnings of Laing's approach. I have chosen Merleau-Ponty for a number of reasons. First, because, although Laing does not include his name in the list of existential philosophers he cites in the "Preface to the Original Edition" of *The Divided Self* (Laing 1965, p.9), it is clear from the "References" given at the end of the same work that Laing had read Merleau-Ponty's major works; and indeed he makes a point derived from Merleau-Ponty's *Structure of Behaviour* in the text (Laing 1965, p.31). Sartre and Heidegger seem to have been much more influential in forming Laing's thinking, but Merleau-Ponty played at least some role. Secondly, and more importantly,

Merleau-Ponty devoted more attention to, and showed greater knowledge of, psychology and psychiatry than most other existential philosophers of equal stature, and certainly more than Sartre or Heidegger. His account therefore, I believe, provides a richer basis for justifying Laing's approach than theirs. (A more complete exposition of Merleau-Ponty's philosophy as a whole can be found in my book *The Philosophy of Merleau-Ponty* (Matthews 2002), or, much more briefly, in Matthews 2004).

II

The first task is to present Laing's own views on the relevance of an existential-phenomenological approach to psychiatric practice, in particular in relation to schizophrenia. The basic purpose of *The Divided Self* is, Laing declares in the Preface to the original edition, "to make madness, and the process of going mad, comprehensible" (Laing 1965, p. 9). In the Preface to the Pelican edition, he says, more modestly, "I wanted to convey above all that it was far more possible than is generally supposed, to understand people diagnosed as psychotic" (Laing 1965, p.11). One might well think this was the purpose of any psychiatric writing about schizophrenia, or any other mental disorder, but it is the *kind* of comprehension at which Laing aims which distinguishes his approach as "existential-phenomenological". In order to elucidate this point, we need to say something about the work of a number of 19th century German philosophers, notably Dilthey, Rickert and Max Weber, who distinguished between two ways of making sense of, or comprehending, something. The one kind, which they called "explanation" (in German *Erklären*), was claimed to be characteristic of the natural sciences, physics, chemistry, neurophysiology and so on. The other kind, called "understanding" (in German *Verstehen*) was peculiar to the *Geisteswissenschaften* or "human sciences": Dilthey was mainly concerned with history, but this description also included such disciplines as sociology, economics, political science, literary studies and other forms of systematic study of human beings as cultural, rather than simply biological, entities.

"Explanation", in their sense, is equivalent to what is usually called "causal" explanation. It operates by showing that one event is the result of another, antecedent, event, and is justified by deducing the particular statement of a causal relation from a well-established general law linking events of the one type (the "causes") with events of the other type (the "effects"). For instance, we might explain why my pen falls to the floor when I let go of it by reference to the general law that unsupported bodies of any kind (on earth) fall towards the centre of the earth, which is a special case of Newton's law of gravitational attraction. Causal explanation is our way of making sense of things by seeing how they come about; what processes in nature bring about other processes. It involves no reference to purposes or reasons: clearly, my pen has no *purpose* in falling to the ground, it simply does so once support has been withdrawn, and it does so in the way that any other object of the same mass would in the same circumstances. "Understanding", on the other hand, is making sense of something precisely in terms of its purpose or intention, and so can obviously be applied only to something to which purpose or intention can meaningfully be attributed. My pen's falling to the ground cannot be understood in this way; but if I deliberately dropped my pen, it could. Others could ask me, "Why did you drop your pen?"; and my answer might be something like, "Because I wanted to attract your attention", or "Because I wanted to express my frustration – my pen ran out just as I was finishing my letter" or perhaps simply "Because I wanted to illustrate a philosophical point about ways of making sense of things". "Understanding" in other words is making sense by saying *why* someone did something: it does not presuppose any general laws, since the reason why person *A* did action *X* is not necessarily the same as the reason why other people do the same action in broadly similar circumstances.

When Laing talks of making madness comprehensible, it seems clear from the general tenor of his writings that it is comprehension in the sense of "understanding" that he has in mind, rather than in the sense of "(causal) explanation". It is his opponents who want to make sense of madness by giving a causal explanation of it, on the assumption that madness is essentially a neurophysiological phenomenon like, for example, Korsakoff amnesia. For them, schizophrenia is a form of brain disease, to be treated in exactly the same way as any other disturbance of nervous functioning. Laing, however, wants to contrast his approach with that of "formal clinical psychiatry and psychopathology" (Laing 1965, p.17). This is where existential phenomenology comes in. As Laing correctly, if rather vaguely, expresses it (*ibid.*) "Existential psychology attempts to characterize the nature of a person's experience of his world and himself". That is, its starting-point is subjective experience rather than objective nervous or other physical processes. Without denying (as we shall see later) that human beings are biological organisms, it takes as central to their humanity, not their biological character, but the way in which they think and feel about the world, their intentions and actions towards the world and the meaning which they find in things around them.

From this point of view, a mental disorder like schizophrenia, whether or not it involves disturbances to brain processes or biochemistry, is primarily a disorder in a subject's way of experiencing his or her world. Thus, Laing defines the term "schizoid" by saying it "refers to an individual the totality of whose experience is split in two main ways: in the first place, there is a rent in his relation with his world and, in the second, there is a disruption of his relation with himself" (Laing 1965, p. 17). Schizophrenia is therefore seen as a disorder of *persons*, not of *brains*: something, as he says on the next page, to be "lived out" by the individuals concerned, and so something of "human relevance and significance", not a medical condition which they passively suffer. Because it has human significance, it can and must be understood, not simply causally explained. Indeed, Laing even claims that the current methods of clinical psychiatry are incapable of grasping the essential nature of the symptoms presented by schizoid and schizophrenic people.

Why is this? Laing suggests that the very terms in which clinical psychiatry expresses itself are inappropriate to understanding schizophrenia as a human problem. The terminology of psychiatric theory, he claims, splits human beings in much the same way that schizophrenia does: it divides one human being from another, and destroys the internal integrity of human beings. Human problems can be understood, he says, only if we regard human beings as both necessarily related to other human beings, and unitary wholes within themselves. Both their relations to others and their inner wholeness depend on a subjective sense of themselves as related and as whole, and the breakdown of relatedness and wholeness occurs when that subjective sense is disturbed. So the task of understanding the problems depends on taking seriously the person's own expression of that subjective sense: psychiatrists must listen to their patients, not simply treat them as "cases". That means, Laing contends, an existential-phenomenological insight into how their problems feel for them, not a quasi-scientific explanation of their behaviour from the outside.

The vocabulary in which the problems are described is relevant to this task. Current clinical terminology, as stated earlier, militates, in Laing's opinion, against seeing patients as human beings with human problems, and encourages the detached view of them as cases. Given the time at which he was writing, Laing's examples of clinical terminology are naturally taken from Freudian psychoanalysis: the psychiatrist, he says, does not see his or her own relation to the patient as a human relationship, a matter of "I" and "You", but looks on the patient in a detached way as a kind of specimen to be analysed in terms of discrete aspects, "the ego", "the superego" and the "id". But we could update Laing's remarks by reference to the terminology of clinical neuropsychiatry, analysing patients in terms of various types of brain functioning — speech, movement, affect, thought, and so, each localized in particular areas of the brain. Freudians think of the relation of analyst to analysand as, in Laing's words, "the interaction of one mental apparatus with another" (Laing 1965, p.19); neuropsychiatrists might be said to regard the relationship of psychiatrist to patient as the interaction of one brain and central nervous system with another. But neither thinks of the patient as a human being to whom they, another human being, stand in a certain human relation. (This is not intended as a reflection on the moral attitudes of psychiatrists of either school. Both may well seek to be as humane as possible in their dealings with patients. It is rather an attempt to express the implications of the philosophical position inherent in their theoretical terminology, which, if Laing is right, conflicts with any desire they have to be truly humane to their patients).

Laing similarly uses a phenomenological method to expose the origins of this philosophical position. He draws on the phenomenological conception of the "intentionality of consciousness" to do this. This concept was originally used by some medieval philosophers, but was revived by the Austrian philosopher Franz Brentano (1838-1917). Brentano made "intentionality" the distinguishing mark of the mental. In a lecture which he gave in 1889 on *The Origin of our Knowledge of Right and Wrong* he asserted:

> "The common feature of everything psychological, often referred to, unfortunately, by the misleading term 'consciousness', consists in a relation that we bear to an object. The relation has been called *intentional*; it is a relation to something which may not be actual but which is presented as an object. There is no hearing unless something is heard, no believing unless something is believed; there is no hoping unless something is hoped for" (Brentano, 1969, p.14).

Mental or psychological activities, in other words, are characterised not by their inner content, but by a relation in which they stand to something outside themselves, to an "object". This object is referred to as an "intentional object" to indicate that, as Brentano says, it "may not be actual". We can, for instance, be afraid of ghosts, whether or not ghosts actually exist; but we cannot be afraid without being afraid *of* something or other; we can hope for a win on the Lottery whether or not our hopes are ever realised, but we can't hope without hoping *for* something. The intentional relation is thus different from e.g. spatial relations: my hand can't be to the left of my telephone, for instance, unless both hand and telephone actually exist. And "psychological" acts and states are defined as what they are, and distinguished from each other, in terms of the nature of their intentional objects and the way in which they relate to them: thus, hope is distinguished from fear because hope relates to something desired, while fear relates to something to be avoided.

It is this last-mentioned feature of intentionality that Laing draws on to make one of his most important points. He distinguishes "persons" from "organisms" as "the object of different intentional acts" (Laing 1965, p.21). We *relate* differently, he says, to organisms and to persons: we see an organism as "a complex physico-chemical system", but we see a person "as another person like myself" (*ibid.*). For example, we can relate to another human being who is talking by studying the sounds she produces as the outcome of certain neural processes, or by attempting to understand the meaning of what she is saying. The former is relating to her as an organism, the latter is relating to her as a person. A science of persons will correspondingly differ from a science of human organisms, without any implication that the persons we know are not also human organisms. A science of persons will take seriously the meanings which persons attach to their own behaviour, and will not simply see them as bits of neural machinery, whose behaviour consists simply of certain physical movements to be explained entirely by internal neurophysiological processes.

This is directly relevant to the way in which Laing wants to approach psychiatry. He wants it to be based on a science of persons in this sense. That is, he wants psychiatrists to treat their patients as persons to be understood in terms of their own conceptions of their situation, their motives and reasons for behaving as they do. Correspondingly, he wants the aim of psychiatric treatment to be, not the improved functioning of neurophysiological mechanisms, but helping patients to achieve genuine freedom and growth. He says in the Preface to the Pelican edition of *The Divided Self* that "Psychiatry could be, and some psychiatrists are [he clearly would want to include himself in that number] on the side of transcendence, of genuine freedom, and of true human growth", contrasting that with psychiatry seen as "a technique of brainwashing, of inducing behaviour that is adjusted, by (preferably) non-injurious torture" (Laing, 1965, p.12). To see psychiatry in this way is to see mental disorder as something different from "brain disease", mechanical failure in the brain, comparable to "liver disease" or failure in the functioning of the liver, and to be treated, like the latter, by drugs, surgery and the like. It is to see mental disorder as consisting of problems in personal life, to be treated by understanding the sufferer's own experience of them and offering human help in finding solutions to them.

But there is a difficulty here, especially if we concentrate on psychosis, as Laing explicitly declares he is going to do. Laing says in chapter 1 of *The Divided Self*:

> "In the following pages, we shall be concerned specifically with people who experience themselves as automata, as robots, as bits of machinery, or even as animals. *Such persons are rightly regarded as crazy* [my italics]" (Laing 1965, p.23).

To be "crazy" (Laing's word, not mine) must surely mean something different from having problems in one's personal life. A friend may have problems in his personal life and may turn to me for help. Perhaps he is experiencing difficulties in his marriage: to help him, I must use whatever resources I can muster to understand what those difficulties are. I can do so because they are the kind of difficulties which I can imagine having (or may even have had) myself. Using that shared experience, I can perhaps suggest some things he might do to resolve the problems. But if I am confronted with someone who believes himself to be an automaton and acts accordingly, I cannot draw on such resources. This is a belief which is so far outside the normal range of human experience that it is scarcely possible for me to have myself, or even to imagine myself having, at least as a *serious* belief. How can I even begin to understand it? And if I can't understand it, I can't help the person who has it.

Psychotic experience, in other words, is not within the boundaries of personal experience: it is not another kind of problem in personal experience, like marital difficulties. Laing himself describes it as "a quite specifically personal form of depersonalization and disintegration" (Laing 1965, p.23). But can we really account for the breakdown of the personal in terms appropriate to the understanding of personal experience in its fully integrated form? Isn't the phrase "a personal form of depersonalization" something of an oxymoron? It is one of the weaknesses of Laing's position that he fails to do justice to this. It leads him into unwise attempts to blur the distinction between the "sane" and the "insane", as in this passage from chapter 2 of *The Divided Self*.

> "When I certify someone insane, I am not equivocating when I write that he is of unsound mind, may be dangerous to himself and to others, and requires care and attention in a mental hospital. However, at the same time, I am also aware that, in my opinion, there are other people who are regarded as sane, whose minds are as radically unsound, who may be equally or more dangerous to themselves and others and whom society does not regard as psychotic and fit persons to be in a madhouse. I am aware that the man who is said to be deluded may be in his delusion telling me the truth, and this in no equivocal or metaphorical sense, but quite literally, and that the cracked mind of the schizophrenic may *let in* light which does not enter the intact minds of many sane people whose minds are closed" (Laing 1965, p. 27).

This picture of the schizophrenic as someone who is at least no more deluded than many people described as "sane", and who may even possess special prophetic insight (Laing quotes Jaspers' opinion that Ezekiel was a schizophrenic) is unsatisfactory from several points of view. First, it diminishes the seriousness of the schizophrenic's experience of inner depersonalization by equating it with the deluded beliefs of sane people with closed minds. Secondly, it is inconsistent to say both that schizophrenics are of "unsound mind" and that they have ascended to the level of prophetic insight. Thirdly, if they have indeed *already* achieved transcendence and genuine freedom, why do they need the help of a psychiatrist at all? There is a deep confusion in Laing's thinking here which makes it all too easy for his critics to dismiss his position as a mere expression of personal idiosyncrasy or even sentimentality.

III

Can we rescue what is truly valuable about Laing's view of psychiatry from such charges, perhaps by using the philosophical framework provided by Merleau-Ponty? I think we can, and shall attempt to show this in what remains of this essay. I shall begin with the most central element of that philosophical framework: like Laing, Merleau-Ponty is an existential phenomenologist. But Merleau-Ponty provides a much clearer and more detailed account than Laing does of what existential phenomenology entails. Although phenomenology as a philosophical movement has many sources – indeed, as Merleau-Ponty says, "it merges into the general effort of modern thought" (Merleau-Ponty 1962, p. xxi) – its most systematic presentation is to be found in the work of Edmund Husserl (1859-1938). Nevertheless, in Merleau-Ponty's view, we shall not understand what the phenomenological approach consists of by simply piecing together texts from Husserl and other philosophers. We need to discover the true meaning of phenomenology, and we shall find it "in ourselves" to determine and express in concrete form

> "this *phenomenology for ourselves* which has given a number of present-day readers the impression, on reading Husserl or Heidegger, not so much of encountering a new philosophy as of recognizing what they had been waiting for" (Merleau-Ponty 1962, p. viii).

We "recognize what we had been waiting for" in phenomenology, in that it gives us the possibility of creating a concrete philosophy, one which responds to our need to understand our lives and ourselves rather than being an abstract theoretical system. Phenomenological philosophy starts from the recognition that

"All my knowledge of the world, even my scientific knowledge, is gained from my own particular point of view, or from some experience of the world without which the symbols of science would be meaningless" (Merleau-Ponty 1962, p. viii).

Being a phenomenologist is accepting that in *this* sense (and only in this sense) we are the "absolute source": the whole picture of the world which we have depends for its meaning on the direct contact which we have with the world in our pre-theoretical experience. If so, then we cannot regard ourselves as experiencing subjects as just another object in the world to be explained by science, since the scientific picture of the world and science's ways of explaining the behaviour of objects is itself a human construction based on our subjective experience. Just as the camera cannot be part of the picture which it takes (though its reflection in a mirror can), so we as subjects can't consider ourselves as nothing more than one of the objects we try to understand by constructing scientific theories.

The scientific picture of the world which we construct serves a number of very important human purposes, and besides has considerable power in its own right. To go in for science is to seek to transcend the limitations of our own individual subjective viewpoints, to distinguish the world "as it is in itself", or objectively, from the way it merely appears to me or to you from where we happen to be. As the modern American philosopher Thomas Nagel has expressed it, it is an attempt to arrive at "the view from nowhere", a view of how things are, not from this point of view or that, but from no particular position at all. This is the way of thinking which Merleau-Ponty calls "objectivism" — the conception that the ultimate reality of things is how they would look to a being who is not limited to any particular position in space or time. Traditionally, the concept of a being who is not limited in this way is that of God, so that the objectivist view has also been called the "God's eye view". This whole way of thinking, as said above, has enormous psychological power: surely, we feel, the truth *must* lie in what transcends limited human perspectives, and how things really are *must* be different from how they appear? Furthermore it has practical importance: detaching the reality of things from points of view limited by the subjective interests of a particular human being is important if we are to develop technologies for manipulating things. We have to recognize how things actually work, as opposed to how we might like them to be, if we are to make them work for our benefit.

If reality is distinct from subjective appearance, however, this must apply to the reality of *everything*, and hence to the reality of ourselves and other human beings. To understand myself, my existence, my behaviour, correctly, I must transcend the limitations of my own subjective view of myself — how I appear to myself. I must treat myself and my existence as just another object in the world, whose reality is accessible to everyone else in just the same way as it is to me. I must see myself from the outside rather than, as I normally do, from the inside. My experience of the world, and my interactions with the rest of the world, including other human beings, must be understood "objectively". If I want to explain how my car behaves, I do not ask (absurdly) how it feels about the world, or what purposes it is trying to achieve: I simply apply laws of physics and chemistry to explain what causes what in the car's engine, and so results in the car's motion through space. Similarly, on the objectivist view, if I want to understand how I or any other human being behaves, I must be truly scientific about it and explain the behaviour causally, in terms of laws of physics and chemistry, or, more immediately, in terms of laws of neurophysiology and biochemistry which are derivatives of basic physico-chemical principles. Thus, for an objectivist (which means for most people who have considered themselves rational thinkers since the 17th century), it is plain that if you want to explain those deviations from normal behaviour, thought or affect which we call "mental disorders", the only scientifically acceptable way to do so is to refer to changes in the normal pattern of functioning of the brain and central nervous system which cause the change in behaviour, affect or whatever.

Some examples will help to illustrate this way of thinking of mental disorder. Laing cites the case of a young man showing the signs of catatonic excitement who was presented to his students by Kraepelin in 1905 (quoted in Laing 1965, pp.29ff). The man is said by Kraepelin to sit with his eyes shut and to pay no attention to his surroundings, but to answer questions put to him "beginning in a low voice, and gradually screaming louder and louder". The answers he gives to some of these questions are quoted by Kraepelin, and are said to indicate the man's "inaccessibility", in that they are "only a series of disconnected sentences having no relation whatever to the general situation". But even to describe the patient in this way (as "inaccessible") is to take a detached, objective view of him, as one would of, say, a car which was behaving in ways of which one's current knowledge of mechanics could make no sense. (I have this attitude when my computer starts behaving oddly: I can't explain this unusual and irritating behaviour, but I have no doubt that if I knew and understood more about the inner workings of computers in general I could make sense of it). Laing, a page or two earlier, quotes Bleuler's remark about schizophrenics that when all is said and done they were stranger to him than "the birds in his garden". There is, that is to say, no possibility of *understanding* schizophrenic behaviour: we must resort perforce to causal explanation.

Another example may be taken from Merleau-Ponty, who at more than one point in *Phenomenology of Perception* refers to the case of a man called Schneider, who suffered a number of problems after suffering shrapnel injuries to his brain during the First World War. For instance, he was unable to perform "abstract movements" – movements not relevant to any immediate practical situation, such as moving his arms when told to do so by the doctor; but he could perfectly well perform "concrete" movements – movements related to some practical need, such as moving his hand to the place where a mosquito had stung him. This was part of a general detachment from his own body, which had more dramatic expression in sexual and perceptual problems. On an "objectivist" view, as Merleau-Ponty says, it seems natural to find the complete explanation of this strange behaviour in Schneider's occipital injury. Merleau-Ponty is happy to accept that brain injury forms part of the explanation, but he argues that there are features of Schneider's problems which cannot be fully understood in these terms. "Abstract" and "concrete" movements, for instance, are indistinguishable when simply taken as physiological movements of the limbs through space. So their physiological causes must be the same. What differentiates them is not anything physiological, but the *meaning* which they have for Schneider himself. To explain why he can perform one kind of movement but not the other, we must understand that difference in meaning. That is, we must move beyond thinking of Schneider as an object governed by laws of physiology, and see him as a person whose manner of being involves meaningful relations to the objects around him: what Merleau-Ponty (following Heidegger) calls "being-in-the-world".

Cases like this (but also cases of normal human behaviour) indicate the inadequacies of an "objectivist" view. They show that human beings are not detached spectators of the world: they *could* not be, since if we were not part of the world we could have no experience of the world – there would be nothing to "spectate". Experience of the world implies active involvement with our environment, such that we cannot separate our own being from that of the world. This is what Merleau-Ponty means by saying that human being is essentially being-in-the-world (the hyphens are essential to indicate the inseparability of our being and the world which we inhabit). Furthermore, being part of the world implies being essentially *embodied*, since a disembodied pure subject could not interact actively with the world about it. Finally, it also entails that the human body is not *just* a physical object like any other, but a physical object which has a *subjective* relation to the world, since a pure physical object would not have the intentional relation to other objects which is necessary for active interaction, but would simply respond passively to them in accordance with causal laws.

Hence we arrive at Merleau-Ponty's very unCartesian account of minds, bodies and the relation between the mental and the physical:

"Man taken as a concrete being is not a psyche joined to an organism, but the movement to and fro of existence which at one time allows itself to take corporeal form and at others moves towards personal acts" (Merleau-Ponty 1962, p.88).

This is a view which sees a human being as a mind-body unity, not denying all distinctions between the mental and the physical, but seeing them as derived from differences of emphasis rather than of substance. Taking mind-body unity seriously most definitely does not imply any *reduction* of the one to the other: rather, it means that we cannot understand most human bodily movements (other than pure reflexes, if any such exist) fully without understanding the mental intentions which give rise to them, nor equally understand many human intentions fully without seeing them as arising from bodily needs and as necessarily expressed in certain bodily movements. The latter aspect of human embodiment also entails, it is important to note, that obstructions to neuro-physiological functioning may cause problems for the mental activity which that neuro-physiological functioning normally expresses.

This is where the phenomenological method comes in. The objectivist view, as said earlier, holds a very powerful sway on our thinking: it is an assumption to which we are all too prone. Phenomenology, as we have seen, aims to question all such assumptions, to "put them in brackets", in Husserl's phrase, in order to understand better what kind of truth they have by relating them to our basic pre-theoretical experience of the world. "True philosophy", as Merleau-Ponty expresses it, "consists in re-learning to look at the world..." (Merleau-Ponty 1962, p.xx). Our basic, pre-theoretical, experience of the world is that of beings who are-in-the-world in the sense explained below, who are embodied subjects, who do not simply contemplate the world in a detached intellectual way like a Cartesian *cogito*, but actively engage with it. But to actively engage with the world is to see objects as meaningful: because I am a living human organism, with certain characteristic needs, the apple I see on the tree in my garden, for example, is not simply a physical object with a certain mass, a certain chemical composition and a particular geometrical structure, but something to eat, something which exists because I planted a seed there in the past and have since cultivated the tree on which it grows. These "subjective" meanings for me are just as much a part of the reality of the apple as its "objective" physico-chemical and geometrical properties. The purely objectivist picture of the world cannot therefore be the primary account of reality: seeing the world as nothing more than a system of objects distinct from human consciousness, related to each other only in pure space and time, and by external causal connections, must be an abstraction from the world as it presents itself to us in our fundamental experience as beings-in-the-world. We have good reasons, both theoretical and practical, for engaging in this abstraction, but we must recognize it for what it is, an assumption to be understood in terms of these reasons rather than a fundamental account of what reality is like "in-itself".

If this is the case with objects like apples, it is even more obviously the case with human actions, our own and other people's. We cannot look on ourselves from the outside, since the "outside" view has meaning for us only in relation to the view from where we are. There logically cannot be a "view from nowhere", since any view is by definition a view *from somewhere*. What we think of as the view from nowhere is an abstraction, constructed for certain purposes, from all our particular views from where we are – a view from no one place *in particular*, but not from no place at all, which, as said above, would be a contradiction in terms. We cannot think of our own actions in purely "objectivist" terms, since, as argued above, they are distinguished by the subjective meaning which they have for us. And the same applies to the actions of other human beings, since they have a certain meaning for us simply as the actions of other human beings, to whom we can relate in characteristically human ways. Human actions, our own and those of other human beings, must primarily be made sense of in terms of their subjective meaning for the person acting.

Given that our subjectivity is necessarily embodied, however, does not mean that neurophysiology is irrelevant to the understanding of behaviour. Mind-body unity, as argued above, implies that the nature of the neural "machinery" by which we express our intentions has a bearing on the character of, and thus the way we can understand, the actions which result. A distortion or deficit in the normal functioning of that neural machinery can thus mean an abnormality in the resulting action which has to be understood at least in part in terms of that neurological distortion or deficit. This is why Merleau-Ponty, as was stated earlier, is happy to accept (as seems obvious) that Schneider's occipital injury was not simply a chance antecedent of his strange behaviour and affects, but had some explanatory bearing on them.

Similarly, accepting Laing's account of Kraepelin's patient and his catatonic behaviour in terms of his "carrying on a dialogue between his own parodied version of Kraepelin, and his own defiant rebelling self" (Laing 1962, p.30, in other words, in terms of its subjective meaning for the young man himself) need not entail denying that neuro-physiological or biochemical factors may have played a part in the origination of this behaviour. After all, one of the features of the young man's behaviour (as of

Schneider's) which we have to make sense of is its sheer *strangeness*. Bleuler may have been wrong to find the behaviour of schizophrenics as incomprehensible as that of the birds in his garden: but was he wrong to find it strange and so in need of a special kind of explanation? After all, we can *up to a point* understand the behaviour of the birds in the garden: they sing in order to attract a mate, for example, just as we dress up to do so. But that doesn't explain why their mate-attracting behaviour takes the form of singing, rather than dressing up. To make sense of that, we surely need to bring in considerations about the different physiological characters of birds as one species and human beings as another. Similarly, we can (indeed, we need to) understand the behaviour of Kraepelin's patient as part of a rebellious dialogue with a person he saw as his tormentor (Kraepelin). But that will not in itself explain why he saw Kraepelin as a tormentor, rather than someone who was trying to help him, or why he expressed his rebelliousness in this cryptic form rather than more openly. It is surely at least possible that to explain these features of his behaviour might require reference to some neural abnormality (though equally it might require some other kind of causal explanation, such as a story of the Freudian kind about his early life experiences — which one we should choose is an empirical question to which mere philosophical reflection can offer no answer).

IV

If the principal focus of this essay were Merleau-Ponty, much more could be said about his views on mental disorder and psychiatry. But we are here concerned mainly with Laing, and I hope enough has been said about Merleau-Ponty to justify the claim made earlier that his more systematic and philosophically-argued account of existential phenomenology can offer better support for Laing's positions than Laing himself presents. By his more thorough exposition of the phenomenological method, Merleau-Ponty above all shows just why there is no reason to accept the objectivist picture of the world as the only ultimately true account of what reality is like. It is this objectivist picture which presents human behaviour as simply the motions of matter through space - both the externally visible motions of the limbs and other parts of the body involved in our actions and the internal "motions" of neural processes which are causally responsible for the movements of our limbs. This is the picture taken for granted by the kind of neuropsychiatry to which Laing objects. It is taken for granted because it is assumed without question that that is the only scientifically realistic way to describe human behaviour – that any way which takes human action to involve reasons, motives, meanings is a regression to prescientific subjectivism.

Phenomenology requires that we put all our assumptions in brackets and return to the way in which we experience the world before we start theorizing and as a condition of any meaningful theorizing. If we do this in this case, Merleau-Ponty argues, we shall see that we do not experience human behaviour, either our own or that of others, in this way before we begin to try to construct a scientific theory to explain it. To use the example which Laing quotes from Merleau-Ponty (Laing 1965, p.31), what we see on someone's face is a *smile*, something with a human meaning, not "contractions of the circumoral muscles": the latter way of seeing a smile makes sense only as part of a physiological account of the facial movements required to *express* a smile. In other words, the purely physiological description is the result of *limiting* our account for certain specific purposes – in this sense, an abstraction, rather than the ultimate truth which presents itself to us in our experience.

It is such an abstraction, however, only if its limited nature is taken for the whole truth: but it is all the same *part* of the whole. A smile is not only something with human meaning but also a set of contractions of the circumoral muscles. We cannot smile except by contracting these muscles, and if some physiological deficit prevents us from doing so, then we cannot smile (though we can of course express our pleasure or amusement in some other way, verbally for example). Here Merleau-Ponty's more sophisticated grasp and more extensive presentation of the phenomenological method makes it possible to deal with one of the problems which we earlier saw in Laing's account of psychosis. It was said earlier that Laing's exclusive focus on the personal meaningfulness of psychotic behaviour (like that of Kraepelin's patient) does not explain why that behaviour has an *abnormal* meaning for the person in question, or for the resulting, perfectly genuine, difficulty which "normal" people have in understanding it. It blurs the distinction between normal and abnormal and leads Laing into his ill-advised attempts to present normal society as somehow mad and schizophrenics as having special insights into the reality of things.

Where Laing begins to go wrong in this way, I would suggest, is in his misleading presentation of the neuro-physiological and the human-meaning account of human behaviour as mutually exclusive: as if they were like the kind of gestalt-switch involved in taking the ambiguous figure which he refers to either as a vase or as two faces, but never as both (see Laing 1965, pp.20-21). But to distinguish them in this way is a misunderstanding of the phenomenological method. What is wrong with the objectivist picture, what requires it to be put in brackets, is simply that it presents itself as the whole truth, when it is only an aspect of the truth. It follows, however, that it is at least an aspect of the truth. Behaviour, normal or abnormal, can only be fully understood if it is seen as humanly meaningful: but it is also, as Merleau-Ponty's account suggests, a set of physiological movements by which that human meaning is expressed. Abnormal, e.g. psychotic, behaviour is meaningful and can in principle be understood. But understanding it will be considerably more difficult than understanding normal behaviour. Normal behaviour, by definition, conforms to certain shared norms of reasonableness, to which our own behaviour also conforms, which means that we can readily understand the normal actions of another. But abnormal behaviour, equally by definition, deviates from those shared norms, and that is something which requires explanation. If we see all behaviour as part of human embodied subjectivity, as Merleau-Ponty encourages us to do, then it is open to us to accept that the explanation for the deviation may be some abnormality in the brain (and that the most effective treatment for it may involve some attempt to correct that brain abnormality).

Laing's central humanist approach is not affected by this: indeed presenting it in this way reinforces the case for rejecting any approach to psychotic people which sees them simply as machines which have gone wrong. Psychosis is indeed, as Laing sees, a *human*, not a purely *mechanical*, problem, even if mechanical problems may be a part of what gives rise to that human problem. Psychiatrists who see psychosis in an "objectivist" way, however good their intentions, are more liable to dehumanize their patients and to ignore what is central to the difficulties which they have in living. But we can accept this without accepting Laing's more dubious claims about the madness of society at large.

references

Brentano 1969: Brentano, Franz, *The Origin of our Knowledge of Right and Wrong*, transl. R.M.Chisholm and E.H. Schneewind, London, Routledge & Kegan Paul.
Laing 1965: Laing, R.D., *The Divided Self*, Pelican Books edition, London, Penguin Books Ltd.
Matthews 2002: Matthews, E., *The Philosophy of Merleau-Ponty*, Chesham, Bucks., Acumen Publishing.
Matthews 2004: Matthews, E., "Merleau-Ponty, Maurice", in Murray, Chris (ed.), *Companion to Modern French Thought*, New York and London, Routledge.
Merleau-Ponty 1962: *Phenomenology of Perception*, transl. Colin Smith, London, Routledge and Kegan Paul.

5: R.D. Laing's Reading of Kierkegaard

Roger Poole

R.D. Laing's Reading of Kierkegaard

Roger Poole

"An adolescent Kierkegaard played by Danny Kaye". This description of his patient David in *The Divided Self* turned me into a devotee of the Laing throwaway charm. A dozen things shot into my mind: Danny Kaye as Hans Christian Andersen singing 'Wonderful, wonderful Copenhagen'; Danny Kaye as hopelessly retarded eternal adolescent; Kierkegaard as hopelessly retarded eternal adolescent − the phrase was pure poetry, it was Shakespearean in its reach and remit, it described the case exactly, the case being − well − that under the gloriously extravagant figures of Kierkegaard, Hans Andersen and Danny Kaye the search of an inner guiding 'identity' may come early, may come under embarrassing experimental shapes, but is a problem that is universally human and which contains elements of genius and comedy in all of us.

The phrase has a second usefulness, in that it reflects the earliness of Laing's own first meeting with Kierkegaard. Laing cannot have been very much more than an adolescent himself when he first encountered *Concluding Unscientific Postscript* and was swept up into the Kierkegaardian thought-world in a way that was to be fundamental to his entire later Existential thinking. The story of how the very young (schoolboy)Ronnie Laing first fell under the spell of Kierkegaard is itself semi-magical. In a conversation with Bob Mullan, Laing places the event in the uninspiring space of the Govan Hill Public Library. "Presumably," says Bob Mullan, "it was quite amazing that you were able to read Freud, Nietzsche, Kierkegaard, and so on, in a small public library in the 1940s?"

> "Yes, I suppose it was. There was no one else I knew that had read these things, but nevertheless Govan Hill Public Library had a copy of *Either/Or*. I mean, the first major thing of Kierkegaard that I read was a big book *Concluding Unscientific Postscript* and that was one of the peak experiences of my life. I read that through, without sleeping, over a period of about 34 hours just continually... Well, Kierkegaard was a sort of musical, intellectual Mozart, a combination of Mozart and Chopin. It just absolutely fitted my mind like a glove, my mind,

my sensibility, here was a guy who had *done it*. I felt somehow or another within me, the flowering of one's life. " (1)

Yes, that is the authentic shock-reaction. Anyone who has 'encountered' Kierkegaard will recognise it, will have the same stunned few minutes: But what sort of writing is this? *No-one* is allowed to write like this! He ignores all the conventions. He's speaking to *me*! How dare he be so *free*? I don't know anyone could be *free in that sort of way!*

When Kierkegaard 'strikes' a young impressionable ambitious thinker like this, it comes across as the realisation of a kind of immense inner freedom, a source of energy and thought which is afraid of nothing, a free spirit which has left behind the cautiousness of the professors and the Hegelian 'paragraph communication' equally.

Such an impression from reading Kierkegaard often creates a kind of 'moment of identification', a kind of coming-together of conflicting elements of a personality, a kind of re-ordering of all values along entirely new and unexpected lines. Laing's first two attempts at locating the 'Kierkegaard effect' are with musicians : geniuses of urbanity, sophistication, brilliance and beauty. To compare Kierkegaard with Mozart and Chopin (in spite of the slight breathlessness and incoherence of the text, all those years later) is to acknowledge a debt to a *kind* of inspiration which precedes the act of creation itself.

Reading *The Divided Self* at this distance of time, I am astonished to realise *just how far back* Laing thought he had to go in order to start in on his own theme. Just before he presents his terrifying citation from Kraepelin (a text dated 1905) he writes: "That the classical clinical psychiatric attitude has not changed in principle since Kraepelin can be seen by comparing the following with the similar attitude of any recent British textbook of psychiatry (e.g. Mayer-Gross, Slater and Roth)"(2). "*Any recent* British text book of psychiatry"! Since the first edition of *The Divided Self* appeared in 1960, we are asked to believe that the situation of 1905 is still securely in place in 1960 – that is over a half-century later – and still not challenged in any fundamental way.

So Laing, starting in on his Kierkegaardian-Existential thesis of 1960, takes himself to be opening up an issue that is still firmly in the possession of the physicalists of 1905. Laing has to start right back with fundamental distinctions, like the difference between a person and a thing (p.21). Can any psychiatrist ever have regarded his patient as a thing? It seems incredible. "Seen as an organism, man cannot be anything else but a complex of things, of *its*, and the processes that ultimately comprise an organism are *it*-processes"(p.22). With a patient stripped of humanity, become a thing, an organism, not on any account to be listened to, but studied 'clinically' — *this* far back did Laing have to start. "In man seen as an organism, therefore, there is no place for his desires, fears, hope or despair as such. The ultimates of our explanations are not his intentions to his world, but quanta of energy in an energy system."(p.22)

If Laing, in a revolutionary move, decrees that we must now see the patient as a person, not a thing, he is taking leave of his 'subject' as he inherited it, and substituting a new one. But in order to propose the patient as a subject, as a person, Laing has to make another huge move, right across to — Dilthey! (p.32)

Laing cites Dilthey on 'comprehension' but it is only one paragraph, and in that tiny format, the key 'term of art' does not stand out sufficiently for it to be *perceived as* a key term of art. Laing does not give the German term, (*Verstehen*, with its overlapping cognates *Nacherleben*, *Nachfülhen* and sometimes (though rarely) *Einfühlen* but so foreign is the mere unexplained use of 'comprehension' to the reader of 1960 in an English tradition, that the bearing or significance of it would have been completely missed. Laing was so far out of the Atlantic shipping lanes that an argument based upon the complex and very 'foreign' tradition of German hermeneutics would never have been picked up by an audience still undisturbed by the preconceptions of Mayer-Gross, Slater and Roth.

So, from the temporal point of view, Laing starts very far back in time with Kraepelin in 1905, but then, from the 'geographical' point of view, goes too far out in conceptual space to counter this barbarity, by introducing the tricky world of German hermeneutics — dimly visible through Bultmann's presentation of 1955. Laing's point is thus lost. Laing himself seems to have realised that, and tries to substitute the term "love" for "comprehension" (p.34) but then abandons that effort as well.

I think it is fair to say that Laing simply backs away from the problem by seeing that both 'love' and 'understanding' could, one day, under different conditions, be retrieved by the introduction of the concept of despair, and so, in a footnote that betokens little less than conceptual exhaustion, he hands over to Kierkegaard to hold the pass at Thermopylae.

Laing may have regarded the opening two chapters as a partial (or even a considerable) failure to grapple with the world of Mayer-Gross, Slater and Roth. We can now see it as being that, and yet admire its courage all the more. But, as is evident from the last pages of Chapter 2, the courage to keep believing in his own project came from Kierkegaard.

The Laing of 1960 who writes on 'ontological insecurity', 'the embodied and the unembodied self' and 'the false-self system' and begins to rely heavily on Kierkegaard's *The Sickness unto Death* is however writing at a considerable distance from 'the adolescent Kierkegaard played by Danny Kaye' who first entered into that maelstrom of 34 hours' reading in the Govan Hill Public Library. That early Laing was swept along by the *Concluding Unscientific Postscript*, and for anyone interested in establishing the reality of the patient as subject, the patient as subjectivity, the patient as 'person', then that book is a masterful unfolding of the categories of subjectivity. Perhaps the most surprising aspect of that book is the way it takes the concept of subjectivity absolutely seriously, and has no truck, anywhere, with a desire to please 'objectivity', whatever form it might take.

It is a subjective unraveling of the problem of how an ordinary bourgeois Copenhagener would have to modify his subjectivity, if he were in any way to become open to the 'truth' proposed by the paradox of Christianity. The boot, that is to say, is firmly on the other foot from the beginning. Given that the bourgeois Copenhagener is a rational being, what would have to be done to modify his reason, *his subjectivity*, if he were to be able, one day, to come to believe the totally irrational and indeed paradoxical proposition put forth by Christianity?

To the argument in its strict form, Laing may not have paid very much attention, but to the idea of taking a variety of subjectivities and examining them for their lived presuppositions and human involvements he may very well have reacted, even at that young age, by an experience of exhilaration. *The Divided Self* (even if its overt problematic is despair as treated in *The Sickness unto Death*) could not have got going at all without the absolute seriousness with which the concepts of the person, the individual, the subject, subjectivity itself, are taken in the *Concluding Unscientific Postscript*.

The Divided Self, then, assumes the *Concluding Unscientific Postscript* as founding text. However, *The Concept of Dread*, is the text most helpful to him in getting his own case moving, in particular those pages where Kierkegaard analyses the various forms of despair which take their refuge in silence in a desire not to communicate with anyone in the outer world. Indeed, in considering a patient such as David, Kierkegaard offers him the very tools he needs.

"The 'self' in such a schizoid organization is usually more or less unembodied. It is experienced as a mental entity. It enters the condition called by Kierkegaard 'shut-up-ness' (p.74). The source in *The Concept of Dread* goes as follows: "The demoniacal is *shut-up-ness (det Indesluttede, or Indesluttedhed) unfreely revealed*." (3) This state is called 'demoniacal' because it is a dread of the good. Communication belongs to the public world, to the world of ethics, the world of others. But a refusal to communicate is a desire to have nothing to do with the world, and to retreat into defensive silence. But this turns out to be an impossibility — what the patient desires to occlude will get expression even if involuntarily, and the patient thus betrays himself. Kierkegaard has a wonderful page at this point about the guilty man who will not confess. But if the inquisitor sits there and waits for him to speak, even if it takes 16 hours, he will be successful in the end in wringing out a confession, since, as Kierkegaard says in a line of untypical simplicity, "No man who has a bad conscience can endure silence."(p.111)

But 'shut-up-ness' is what presents when there is despair involved. 'The false self system' (Chapter 6) is based upon *The Sickness unto Death*, a late work written after the dreadful two-year period when Kierkegaard had been ridiculed in the gutter-press and probably more than once faced the thought of suicide. In this work, despair is taken absolutely seriously. The form of the Kierkegaardian work is fiendishly clever, comparing forms of 'the self' for half the book, before suddenly announcing, at the beginning of Part 2, that 'Despair is Sin'. All the apparent difficulties of Part 1 are swept away. Unless Despair is understood as sin there is no help. And that, of course, for the modern reader, is where the difficulties begin. To introduce such an explicitly Christian solution into a volume which appeared refreshingly 'modern' in its treatment of the multiplicity of 'selves' is indeed to throw a spanner in the works. But this does not deter Laing. He now has just what he needs for the analysis of despair, the battle between 'the self' and 'the false self'.

Laing's achievement, in *The Divided Self*, was to adapt a Kierkegaardian form of religious despair to the phenomenology of embodiment: 'ontological insecurity', 'the embodied and unembodied self', 'the inner self in the schizoid condition', 'the false-self system'— this is a whole new vocabulary, which has been chosen to emphasise *the subjectivity of the patient*, not his objective status before the judging psychiatrist. This new vocabulary has been chosen as well to emphasise the fact that *the embodiment of the patient*, that is to say the way that the body of the patient is experienced *by the patient from the inside*, not by someone looking on *from the outside*, can have and does have an absolute importance in the way that the patient relates to himself and relates to others in the 'outer' world.

By suggesting that there is a division between an implied 'true self' (an intelligible self, which is threatened by implosion of other identities and is therefore struggling for survival) and a series of 'false selves', which threaten the true self; and by proposing on top of this that there might be a division between the embodied and the unembodied self, Laing has absorbed the Kierkegaardian insights while moving out beyond them to apply them in modern psychiatric practice.

> "The schizophrenic is desperate, is simply without hope... Schizophrenia cannot be understood without understanding despair. See especially Kierkegaard, *The Sickness unto Death* (p.38)."

This notation comes as early as the end of Chapter 2, and much use will be made of these concepts. And another taboo word, love, is used in the same context:

"I have never known a schizophrenic who could say he was loved, as a man, by God the Father or by the Mother of God or by another man." (p.38)

The distance we have come from Kraepelin is amazing. It is now the embodied individual, deprived of all sense of his own reality, disconfirmed and deprived of the authenticity of his own experience on all sides, who has now taken centre stage. Christian despair as such may not be an issue now, but despair does not go away ever. The human subject, raveled up in despair, refusing to communicate, is exactly the same, in essentials, as he was in 1849. Despair is the result of a lack of love.

In the same year as Laing published *The Divided Self*, Sartre brought out his massive *Critique de la Raison Dialectique*. It seems to have shaken Laing out of his very profitable enquiries into individual or isolated grief into a realisation that much psychic suffering was produced by social groups, and hence, by families.

There can have been very few people in England who read their way through the 755 pages of densely argued and self-contradictory mixture of Karl Marx, Rousseau, Robespierre and the KGB, even fewer perhaps who understood its main contentions, but Laing must have been one of them. Indeed, he must have worried at it, in general and in detail, because in 1964, in collaboration with David Cooper, he published a kind of potted version of its main contentions, called *Reason and Violence*, to which a somewhat puzzled Sartre himself penned an admiring 'Foreword'. Sartre was obviously amazed that two Englishmen could make sense of his work, where so many Frenchmen couldn't, and even more amazed, that they could see some practical use for it.

The basic theory of Sartre in the *Critique* gave hefty intellectual prestige to what Laing, and by now Aaron Esterson, were trying to do, which was to reconceive mental affliction in terms of what a family can do to an individual member of itself. Calling the family a 'group', and attributing to it powers of coercion, blackmail, oppression and 'lynching', in the style of Sartre's 'group', gave to the family 'nexus' a kind of demonic power which was exactly what Laing and Esterson needed to etch out their new theory in shades of deepest black. In their new research, which involved interviewing entire families, separately, in combinations and as a whole, the basic premise was that the family itself produces schizophrenia. *Sanity, Madness and the Family* (1964) was a work of astounding insight, and its convincingness and success were due to this intense reading of Sartre which Laing and Easterson had been doing over the last few years. Indeed, Laing had been reading Sartre for as long as he had been reading Kierkegaard. It was however the secularised epistemology of Existentialism that Laing had always needed, and Kierkegaard had always been read with the aid of a Husserlian *epoche*, in which the religious dimension was systematically discounted.

But the swing from an Existentialism in which the individual is uniquely responsible for his own actions, to an Existentialism where the individual is little more than a helpless creation of a malign family intentionality, may have been too violent a swing. From *total* responsibility, in lonely despair, to a situation in which the individual did not have *any* responsibility was perhaps too radical a theoretical shift. Brilliant as *Families of Schizophrenics* is, indisputably a major advance in our knowledge of how human beings actually behave, it rests upon a premise as one-sided as Kierkegaard's own. In the world of the Churches and the Danzigs, there is visible, yes, of course, a new form of unfreedom which results uniquely from the violence of the group. But the problems of the individual as such now virtually disappear into the praxis of the family nexus. Where have those problems gone? What has happened to *David's* despair?

Laing's solution to this problem seems to me little short of an act of genius. In *Knots* (1970) and in *The Politics of the Family* (1971) he begins to set out a theory of what we might call the 'perspectival world'. Drawing once again on Kierkegaard, this time the opening pages of *The Sickness unto Death*, Laing begins to sketch out diagrams for how people within a family see each other." A person is, in one sense, a set of relations, and relations of and to relations." (4)

The inspiration for this is the complex opening definition in *The Sickness unto Death*:

"The human being is spirit. But what is spirit? Spirit is the self. But what is the self? The self is a relation which relates to itself, or that in the relating which is its relating to itself. The self is not the relation but the relation's relating to itself." (5)

Laing only has to modify this into a form in which a patient observed in the bosom of his family is observed from several viewpoints at once, and he is able to sketch out a remarkable phenomenology of inter-personal perception. By using a kind of Husserlian 'bracket', which ensures that no one view is privileged above any other, Laing devises an elegant shorthand (p55) for the examination of the interpersonal perception of the family as a unit:

"In view of his mother's view of her father, and his mother's view of her mother's view of her husband; and his father's view of his mother, and his father's view of his father's view of his wife, there never had been a real man or woman in the family for four generations. Paul, through his internalisation of this tangled set of relations of relations of relations, is tied in a knot, whereby he is effectively immobilized"(p56).

The Politics of the Family develops a remarkable algebra of 'brackets' for taking account of the lived realities of the perspectival world, the way that perceptions are embedded (bracketed) in other perceptions. The beautiful conceptual layouts of this book are the nearest that any British thinker gets to the later thought of Husserl.

It was Husserl, in The Crisis of European Sciences, who advanced the theory (the painful and expensive abandonment of a lifetime's conviction) that it would only be by studying the relativities and subjective intentionalities of others, that we would ever arrive at any kind of adequate reading of the imbricated perspectival realities of the inter-subjective Mitwelt (6). Perception of the Other, instead of being an awkward solipsistic undertaking as in Cartesian Meditations, would thus become a series of 'brackets' and the study of intentionalities within given cultural spaces .The comprehension of the Other is now proposed as little short of anthropological enquiry, starting from local, embodied and cultural norms. Laing's beautiful diagrams have the same inbuilt hopelessness: if we were capable of combining all the aspects of a family system, with everyone's view understood as well from the point of view of every one else in the system, we are being offered a task so complex that it amounts to little more than a counsel of perfection.

Laing never read Kierkegaard with anything less than absolute respect. There are some handwritten notes on *Training in Christianity* in the Glasgow University Library Special Collections Department (MS Laing K13) on the themes of: suffering; Christendom has done away with Christianity; the God-relationship — not relative, but absolute; Christianity as absolute respect; the possibility of Offence; direct and indirect communication; the sign as sign of contradiction — all the major themes of the very late Kierkegaard. It is clear that Laing is not transcribing these notations in any spirit of antagonism, but in an honest effort to understand. And in my view, Laing never departs very far from the Christian Kierkegaard, even if he may not endorse the doctrine explicitly. It is Kierkegaard's willingness to talk about the absolute that must have impressed him, and the fact that Kierkegaard could be so (in a sense) simple-minded about such complex issues.

It may also have been a respect for the fact, visible everywhere in Kierkegaard's work, that he had suffered intolerably in his childhood and young manhood, and had been on intimate terms with every kind of despair. This led Laing to trust him, to trust his witness. For despair was the theme with which he opened his own authorship in *The Divided Self*, and the battle to the death between what he calls 'the 'inner' secret self and the 'false' self. The whole of *The Divided Self* is a kind of exploration to find that missing term, the one that evaded him at the end of his second chapter — love, understanding or 'comprehension' (in Dilthey's special sense) all (apparently) having failed him. He searches for the word he needs. Wonderful indeed are the technical categories he can invent for analytical purposes, but the central value, the one that one could shore up against one's ruins, the one that would be a genuine answer to despair, he never finds. Perhaps that is inevitable (7). But Kierkegaard's willingness to divide the world into the relative and the absolute must have operated as a kind of endorsing strength as he thought along. It is Kierkegaard's strength, his refusal to be anything other than himself, that Laing must have found guiding him throughout his writing, a kind of gold standard, the authentic, the real thing.

And the answer, in the therapeutic situation, does indeed turn out to be both love and understanding. In Chapter 10 of *The Divided Self*, called 'The self and the false self in a schizophrenic', Laing reverts to his apparently abandoned categories of 'comprehension and 'love': "This provides striking confirmation of Jung's statement that the schizophrenic ceases to be schizophrenic when he meets someone by whom he feels understood. When this happens most of the bizarrerie which is taken as 'signs' of the 'disease' simply evaporates"(p.165). Dilthey's 'Verstehen', then, at last endorsed, if still not defined.

And as for the other term, 'love': "The main agent in uniting the patient, in allowing the pieces to come together and cohere, is the physician's love, a love that recognises the patient's total being, and accepts it, with no strings attached"(p.165).

This is never going to impress Mayer-Gross, Slater and Roth. In fact it is little other than straight Christianity. But who can afford to be a Christian nowadays?

notes

1) Bob Mullan, *Mad to be Normal*, Free Association Books Limited, London, 1995, p.94
2) R.D.Laing, *The Divided Self*, Pelican Books, Harmondsworth, 1965, p.29
3) Soren Kierkegaard, *The Concept of Dread*, translated by Walter Lowrie, Princeton, Princeton University Press, 1957, p. 110
4) R.D.Laing, *The Politics of the Family*, London, Tavistock Publications Limited, 1971, p. 55
5) Soren Kierkegaard, *The Sickness unto Death*, translated Alastair Hannay, Penguin Books, Harmondsworth, 1989, p.43
6) Edmund Husserl, *The Crisis of European Sciences*, translated by David Carr, Northwestern University Press, Evanston,1970. For a clear exposition of Husserl's ideas, and a sharp perception of how radically they depart from everything Husserl had been proposing over a lifetime, see David Bell, *Husserl*, London, Routledge, 1990, Part II, Sections III and IV.
7) Despair is, of course, a lived condition, and the individual can either make an attempt to overcome it, or lapse into apathy. There is a remarkable analysis by David Holbrook, *Gustav Mahler and the Courage*

to Be (Vision Press Limited, 1975) in which he shows how the titanic struggle between the 'inner self' and the' false self' gets expression in the cacophonies and the magisterial resolutions of Mahler's music. Hate and love, despair and hope, are in *constant* struggle, with the blaring brass of *Ach du liebe Augustin* battling against the sublime harmonies of overarching love, often within a chord of each other and interrupting each other. Holbrook's analysis of this in the score in the actual chord-progressions is unique in my reading. Here is a major book which an astute publisher could re-issue.

6: The Separated Self: Schizoid Personality and Modern Life

Louis A. Sass

The Separated Self: Schizoid Personality and Modern Life

Louis A. Sass

There is a potential for estrangement in every act of consciousness. To be aware of something, to know it as an object, is necessarily to become aware of its separateness, its nonidentity with the knowing self that I feel myself to be at that very instant. To perceive something is, *ipso facto*, to cast it outward, into the domain of the not-me that lies at the furthest reaches of the experiential universe. And, since this is an *essential* fact about consciousness, it must surely apply to self-awareness as well: to know my own self is, inevitably, to multiply or fractionate myself. It is to create a division between my knowing consciousness and my existence as a perceivable individual who interacts with others or subsists as a body of flesh and blood.[1]

This, in any case, is one vision of the human condition, a vision rooted in the philosophy of Descartes but whose more extreme implications were not elaborated (or lived out) until the era of modernism, or perhaps just before - a time when engagement in the world can no longer be taken for granted and the mind withdraws, or turns in upon itself.[2] Nowhere is this stated more clearly than in the writings of that scrupulous Cartesian of French modernism, Paul Valery. In "the final analysis." Valery writes, "it is the doubling which is the essential psychological fact." He speaks of a brain "too much occupied internally, [that] deals brutally with external things - rejects them violently, etc., "but also of a brain whose prime function is "to take its [own] acts, its modifications as strange and independent things."[3] Such views are of particular relevance for understanding the so-called "schizoid personality," a character type commonly found in persons who will eventually develop schizophrenic forms of insanity and that seems to have particularly strong affinities with aspects of modern Western civilization.

R. D. Laing's *The Divided Self* is perhaps the most complete and compelling account of the schizoid mode of existence. There Laing describes such persons as experiencing splits of two main kinds: in their relationship with external reality and in their relationship with the self. Instead of feeling at home in the world or together with others, such a person tends to "experience himself in despairing aloneness and isolation; instead of feeling like a complete and integral whole, he feels 'split' in various ways, perhaps as a mind more or less tenuously linked to a body, as two or more selves, and so on". Laing describes a form of existence that lacks a sense of primary ontological security — the "sense of [one's] presence in the world as a real, alive, whole, and, in a temporal sense, a continuous person."[4] To illustrate this problematic mode of being-in-the-world, Laing mentions several 20th century writers and artists, notably Samuel Beckett, Franz Kafka, and the painter Francis Bacon. These, however, are but passing references, the implications of which are not pursued at any length in *The Divided Self*. In the present paper I offer an analysis of schizoid existence that is very much in a Laingian key and that treats a number of his case examples. My purpose, however, is to consider the socio-cultural parallel in greater detail, to explore the nature and implications of the remarkable affinities that exist between schizoid personality and many aspects of modernity and the modernist sensibility.

Schizoid Personality

The term "schizoid" was first used around 1910 by Eugen Bleuler and his colleagues at the Burgholzli Hospital in Switzerland; it served as a way of labeling abnormalities seen in the relatives of schizophrenic patients as well as in the patients themselves prior to their psychotic break. The concept encompasses a congeries of qualities that may not, at least at first, seem to have a great deal in common — including both coldness and hypersensitivity, both obstinacy and vacillation, both rebelliousness and timidity. The most prominent characteristics are an apparent asociality and indifference, often combined with introversion.

Seldom do such people feel in harmony with their bodies or the environment, and typically, their emotions do not flow naturally and spontaneously — instead they seem forced or stiff, and others may find them cold and unfeeling, perhaps overly cerebral or calculating. Often they will seem detached, "as if something unnatural and strange divided them from the world,"[5] and one is liable to sense something not entirely genuine in their behavior and emotional expression. In fact, many schizoids have an "as-if" quality, giving the impression that they are only role-playing — perhaps to caricature themselves, to mock those around them, or else simply to give an appearance of seamless normalcy. But beneath an apparent coldness, these people can be excessively sensitive, thin-skinned, and self-deprecatory, highly vulnerable to slights and criticism. Sometimes they will seem docile, submissive, and awkward, at other times arrogant, superior, rebellious, or extravagant in manner. They have, in any case, an aloof, vaguely mysterious air, suggestive of a realm of experience hidden away from others. Though they may seem circumspect and inordinately controlled, perhaps overly formal or mannered, this can be interrupted by occasional bouts of impulsive or pseudo-impulsive extroversion that smacks of overcompensation — as, for example, when a shy and introverted adolescent suddenly turns bold, propositioning girls he would not have dared approach just a few days earlier.

A similar duality characterizes the schizoid cognitive style, which can encompass both excessive doubting and extreme rigidity and obstinacy, and which can sometimes involve subtle peculiarities of thought or language. Here, as in the emotional sphere, schizoid persons seem out of touch with their fellow human beings: what is practical and obvious to others may be missed entirely. Often they are obsessed with abstract, metaphysical, or technical concerns; bent on independence and originality, they may pursue these in complete indifference to the opinions of others. Most schizoid persons seem to be well aware of their own detachment. "There is a pane of glass between me and mankind," is a typical remark. The playwright August Strindberg, a schizoid man who eventually suffered from a schizophrenic type of psychosis, described people such as himself as seeking loneliness in order to "spin themselves into the silk of their own souls."[6] Their sense of detachment from themselves sometimes gives such people the feeling that they don't fully exist; or that their feelings or actions are somehow unjustified, disruptive, or vaguely incorrect.

Characteristics such as those I have been describing are central to virtually all conceptions of schizoid personality, but two rather different ways of explaining these traits have been proposed. In the first approach, popular in medical-model psychiatry, the schizoid's apparent asociality and emotional flatness is taken more or less at face value, being attributed to some biological predisposition — such as a physiologically based insensitivity, emotional blandness, or imbalance of cognitive and affective functions.[7] Just the opposite tack is taken by psychoanalysts of the British object-relations school. They interpret the apparent insensitivity and asociality as a defence, a way of protecting and masking a deep-lying hypersensitivity and neediness. A richer and more reasonable account, in my view, is offered in a classic work that avoids this polarization of explanatory principles: Ernst Kretschmer's *Physique and Character*, published in 1921.

Like Eugen Bleuler (who had similar, though less elaborated views), Kretschmer distinguished the schizoid or schizothymic person (the latter being a less severe variant) from what could be called the "cycloid" or "syntonic" individual.[8] In contrast with schizoids, syntonic (or cycloid) people are characterized by relaxation and spontaneity and by a harmonious sense of union both with the world and within the self.[9] They tend, in Kretschmer's words, "to throw themselves into the world about them"; they may be sensual enjoyers of life or practical men of action, expansive realists or good-natured humorists,[10] and their dispositions can be predominately happy or sad or, more likely, prone to shifts between the two (hence a propensity for affective illnesses and at the extreme, for manic-depressive psychoses). But in such cases, syntonic or cycloid individuals are quite sociable, immediate, and relatively undivided in their being, tending "to be engrossed in their surrounding and to live in the present."[11] All this is in sharp contrast with the schizoid condition — where "internal multiplicity" and "disharmony" tend to "inhibit a complete, fulfilling, and harmonious devotion to the opportunity of the moment, to a frame of mind, to others, and to the entire world of reality."[12]

In Kretschmer's view, the key to understanding the schizoid temperament is to recognize that most schizoids are, in fact, neither over-sensitive nor cold, but "oversensitive and cold at the same time, and indeed, in quite different relational mixtures"; they are people "full of antitheses, always containing extremes, and only missing out on the means."[13] And for this reason, he argues, one cannot set up too strong an opposition between those schizoid persons whose surface indifference is more active — involving a defensive kind of self-anesthetizing, numbing or cramping — versus those with a more passive or innate insensitivity," an emotional blindness or deadness based on some intrinsic defect (what he calls "affective imbecility"). Indeed, one often observes "within the same schizoid life, how insensitivity turns into coldness, or coldness into insensitivity." "I am as hard as ice, and yet so full of feeling that I am almost sentimental," wrote August Strindberg, thereby capturing the subtle combinations of yearning and indifference, of hypersensitivity and coldness, to be found in personalities of this sort.[14]

Schizoids and schizothymes are best characterized, then, by their propensity to be not at any single point but at both extremes of a dimension indicating degree of sensitivity to the environment.[15] Still, the temperament's centre of gravity and visible manifestation can differ from patient to patient (as it can also from moment to moment within a given patient). For this reason Kretschmer was willing to distinguish two schizoid variants: the (predominantly) "hyperaesthetic" or hypersensitive, and the (predominantly) "anaesthetic" or cold and indifferent subtypes. Whereas the hyperaesthetic subtype may seem "timid, shy, with fine feelings, sensitive, nervous, excitable ... abnormally tender, constantly wounded ... 'all nerves'," the anaesthetic person may seem essentially indifferent, as if there were nothing behind the mask but "a dark, hollow-eyed nothing - affective anaemia ... nothing but ... yawning emotional emptiness, or the cold breath of an arctic soullessness."[16] Yet even with the extreme cases, insists Kretschmer, a closer look nearly always reveals evidence of the other end of the scale.

Traditional Theories, and the Cultural Parallel

Kretschmer, who was particularly interested in the connection between temperament and creativity, believed that neither the schizoid nor the cycloid could be said to be superior in overall creative disposition or ability; each, he claimed, is predisposed toward certain *kinds* of creative activity. The cycloid (or syntonic) individual's acceptance of society and interest in the external world would incline him or her toward realism and good-natured humor in literary production, or, in the sciences, toward careful empirical observation (as examples Kretschmer mentions Zola and Humboldt); whereas the introversion and cerebralism of the schizotype (whether hyperaesthetic or anaesthetic} would generally dispose toward aestheticism and mysticism, or toward more abstract or systematizing efforts. It is therefore understandable that there should be a predominance of people with one or the other of the fundamental temperaments in certain fields, schools of thought, and aesthetic movements, and among those drawn to a particular artistic style. Kretschmer notes the high number of schizothymic individuals to be found in the movements of German idealism and romanticism - such as Kant, Hölderlin, Fichte, and Schiller.

But if the schizothymic disposition has some affinities with romanticism, it would seem to be even more strongly linked with the modernist movements - where romantic individualism and expressivism have been transfigured into a far more radical aesthetic of isolation and detachment. We can see this in the image of the creative personality that has come to dominate our age. In James Joyce's *Portrait of the Artist*, "the bible of modernism in English,"[17] the central character Stephen Daedalus describes the artist as remaining "invisible, refined out of existence, indifferent, paring his fingernails"; Daedalus embraces the artist's destiny as "silence, exile, and cunning" — "not only to be separate from others but to have not even one friend."[18] Such a vision could only have seemed peculiar in the early nineteenth century (a time when Wordsworth could define the poet as "a man speaking to men"),[19] but by the beginning of the twentieth it had come to be a guiding cultural assumption in the West.[20] And it seems likely that this reflects widespread cultural changes, changes extending well beyond the domain of aesthetic attitudes. In this respect we might regard the artist as an emblematic as well as ambivalent figure — his inward turn providing an image of nonconformist escape or of rebellion *against* modem society while at the same time illustrating, in exaggerated form, tendencies widespread in this very same society.

The issue of the affinities between culture and the schizoid attitude has received remarkably little attention in mainstream psychiatry and psychoanalysis. Medical-model psychiatry has focused on cognitive and emotional disorders that are assumed to reflect underlying neurobiological abnormalities; for various reasons these disorders have been conceived largely as defects or deficit states. There has been a tendency to view schizoid conditions as lacking the kind of internal complexity and patterns of intentionality that the parallels with modern culture might suggest.

To generalize about psychoanalytic approaches to schizoid characteristics is difficult, given their heterogeneity and occasional obscurity. It is clear, however, that the most influential authors have relied on versions of the fixation/regression model. Helene Deutsch, for instance, speaks of "a genuine infantilism," with "arrest at a definite stage in the development of the emotional life and character formation" — of instincts that are "crudely primitive" and "untamed," "relationships to objects [that have] remained at the stage of identification," and " a failure to synthesize the various infantile identifications into a single integrated personality."[21] W. R. D. Fairbairn sees the schizoid attitude as largely determined by "fixation in the early oral phase"; [22] his follower Harry Guntrip describes "schizoid withdrawal and regression [as] fundamentally the same phenomenon." The regression, in Guntrip's view, is profound, aimed at the utter dependence and vegetative passivity of the intrauterine state.[23] Another psychoanalytically oriented writer, the social historian Christopher Lasch, writes about possible parallels between modern culture and various pathologies that could be described as schizoid; he speaks of selves "contract[ed] to a defensive core, armed against adversity". But Lasch, too, sees such persons as seeking to return to the very early stage of primary narcissism in order "to annul awareness of separation" — "either by imagining an ecstatic and painless reunion with the mother or, on the other hand, by imagining a state of complete self-sufficiency and by denying any need for objects at all."[24]

I would not deny that fantasies of symbiotic union and primitive instinctual satisfaction may exist on some deep - and thus largely invisible — level of the unconscious of schizoid people (as, no doubt. is the case for many of us). A familiarity with the experiences actually described by schizoid individuals suggests, however, that these psychoanalytic interpretations are, at least, extremely incomplete. To judge by what the patients themselves say, such people seem dominated more by a fundamental awareness of distance, difference, and fragmentation — by forms of "internal multiplicity and disharmony"[25] — than by experiences of boundaryless unity or utter self-sufficiency. And these, the most *distinctive* features of the schizoid lived-world, bear a remarkable resemblance to central elements of the modern or the modernist sensibility.

The relevant aspects of the modern social and cultural framework have by now been described by a small army of sociologists, anthropologists, philosophers, and culture critics of various stripes, writing over the course of the last century or more. Surprisingly enough, there is considerable consensus on certain central points. It seems clear that one of the most distinctive and widely ramifying features of modernity is the intense focus on the self (both as a subject and as an object of experience) and on the value and power of the individual — an emphasis not to be found in the more communal, homogeneous, and organically integrated worlds of contemporary tribal and pre-literate societies or in the culture of pre-modern Europe. The modern cultural constellation obviously has certain strengths, allowing as it does for freedom of movement and thought, and encouraging individual initiative and self-expression. But, of course, it also has a dark side - the forms of alienation summed up in the following list: "isolation, loneliness, a sense of disengagement, a loss of natural vitality and of innocent pleasure in the givenness of the world, and a feeling of burden because reality has no meaning other than what a person chooses to impart to it."[26]

In his classic essay, "The Metropolis and Mental Life" the sociologist Georg Simmel outlines some consequences of the "intensification of nervous stimulation" that he considers a central feature of modern urban existence. Simmel describes a characteristic paradox of detachment and alertness, a heightening of awareness and predominance of intellect, calculation, and abstraction over instinctual and irrational factors. There develops a certain reserve toward others - what Simmel sees as the outer expression of a hardheartedness and indifference that is often accompanied by "a slight aversion, a mutual strangeness and repulsion" between human beings. And along with this heightened impersonality of social relationship arises a highly personal sense of subjectivity and inwardness, together with propensities for certain "tendentious peculiarities" — "extravagances of mannerism, caprice, and preciousness" whose significance rests solely in the form of "being different," standing out and drawing attention to one's uniqueness and one's separateness from the crowd.[27]

Simmel describes the *Angst-* and *spleen-* ridden universe of modernist consciousness, the world evoked by Kafka, Baudelaire, and the other "town criers of inwardness" of modern literature (the phrase is Kierkegaard's). That such a world bears a striking resemblance to the schizoid mode of existence is obvious enough. Still, it is worth considering the parallels in detail. In the next two sections we shall explore aspects of the rift in one's connection to the world; in the following three we shall examine the rift in the self's relationship to itself. As labels for these two forms of separation, I adopt the terminology used by Peter, one of Laing's schizoid patients. "Disconnection" was Peter's way of referring to the sense of separation from the social and external world; "uncoupling" was his term for separation from self.[28]

Disconnection: Interiorizing Trends

The social historian Norbert Elias speaks of "the extraordinary conviction carried in European societies since roughly the Renaissance by the self-perception of human beings in terms of their own isolation, the severance of their own 'inside' from everything 'outside'."[29] This aspect of modern existence is manifest at many levels of cultural reality, not only in the realm of ideas but in characteristic forms of social organization, cultural practices, and the experiential modes of everyday life. For its clearest expression, we might look to the doctrines of the two most influential philosophers of the modern era, Rene Descartes and Immanuel Kant.

Descartes (1596-1650) could be said to have invented the modern concept of mind, or at least to have given it its decisive formulation. It was he who fostered certain dualisms and conceptions of human inwardness that have permeated much of the philosophical, scientific, and ethical thought coming after him. Consciousness in the Cartesian scheme is conceived of as radically distinct from the material plane of extended substances, a plane that includes the body in which this consciousness is mysteriously housed, like a ghost in a machine (in Gilbert Ryle's famous phrase). Further, consciousness is assumed to have direct access not to the external world but only to inner "ideas" that somehow represent this world (it is certain, says Descartes, "that I can have no knowledge of what is outside me except by means of the ideas I have within me").[30] Both these aspects of Cartesianism are by now so deeply embedded in prevailing modes of understanding as to seem self-evident and inevitable; we may need to be reminded that very different visions are quite possible and have in fact prevailed in other cultures and other eras, such as ancient Greece.

The essential implications of Cartesianism for the modern self might be summed up in two words: disengagement and reflexivity. On this account a full realization of one's essential being — which is to say, of one's being as a consciousness — requires detachment from the body and from the passions rooted in it; only in this way can one achieve the self-mastery inherent in recognizing and exercising the capacity for rational self-control. The achievement of certainty in knowledge also requires disengagement; disengagement from naïve acceptance of the existence of the external world in favor of an inspection, by the "Inner Eye" of the Mind, of the "clear and distinct" ideas that can be found within (this is Descartes' famous method of doubt).[31] Going along with this is a reflexive turn, involving recognition of the inevitable participation of one's own mind in every act of awareness (this is the certainty of the *cogito* — *I* think, therefore I am — the essential realization on which all other knowledge will be founded). In this way thought, which had previously been associated with dialogue, begins with Descartes to seem a quintessentially private event; and knowledge, previously conceived as a communal possession, comes to be associated with a "logic of private inquiry."[32]

Kant's philosophy, which was formulated at the end of the 18th century and is sometimes viewed as initiating moder*nist* thought,[33] could be seen as a radicalization of Cartesianism, since it places an even more intense emphasis on reflexivity and disengagement. The *cogito* — the ego's awareness of the fact of its own consciousness — had played a critical role in Descartes' search for certainty in experience; with Kant its role becomes even more crucial. Consciousness for Kant is not just a touchstone of certainty; now its structures — in the form of the (human) categories of time, space, causality, and materiality — are said to constitute, in a sense to create, the world of our experience. Acceptance of this suggestion had the effect (as Hegel put it) of "withdraw[ing] cognition from an interest in its objects and absorption in the study of them, and ... direct[ing] it back upon its self; and so turn[ing] it into a question of form."[34] The Kantian vision also encourages a more radical sense of separation than did Cartesianism. In Descartes' scheme, the ideas we experience were certain inner phenomena, yet they nevertheless were assumed to be linked (albeit uncertainly) to an external world. Kant, by contrast, draws an absolute distinction between the realm of all possible human experience (the "phenomenal" realm, as he called it) and that of ultimate reality (the "noumenal"), thus implying an unbridgeable gap that sunders us eternally from the real, leaving us "lonely and forsaken amidst the world, surrounded everywhere by specters" (Schelling).[35]

As I said earlier, these philosophical conceptions of mind and self are echoed at other, more concrete levels or existence, involving social, political, and economic aspects of modern life. Particularly telling illustrations of a growing self-consciousness and an increasing interiorization and privatization of daily life are offered by the historical sociologist Norbert Elias's vivid studies of the history of manners. Elias describes how eating came to be the object of increasing strictures that had the effect of emphasizing the separation between individual persons, and of disguising, or even denying, their natural or animalistic side. Food, which in the Middle Ages was eaten by dipping hands into a communal bowl or by tearing flesh from a common dish, later had to be ladled out carefully to individual plates, and to be picked up only with certain utensils and at a particular moment in a sequence of courses. Spitting on the table first became taboo; then one could no longer spit on the floor; soon enough it was frowned upon to spit anywhere in public. The new forms of etiquette that were developing required the restraint of emotion and spontaneous impulse by internal controls and an increasing dominance of the cerebral over the affective or instinctual side of life. They also led to an ever-growing self-scrutiny and insistence on self-control, which necessarily lowered the threshold of what was felt to be shameful and offensive. Elias suggests that this necessity to restrain the spontaneous expression of affect and impulse led to a feeling of being separated from the external world by an invisible wall, a "self-perception in terms of one's own isolation" that is expressed in the modern philosophical *leitmotif of homo clausus*, the image of a "self in a case" that is so important in the thought of Descartes, Kant, and many other thinkers.[36]

The spread of literacy may also have contributed to these interiorizing trends. As Walter Ong has pointed out, both writing and reading (especially silent reading, a practice that only gradually came to be the norm) allow - even force - a person to think or to encounter thought alone, with a sense of isolation from the group; and writing especially tends to require and to encourage silent reflection. The written word could also be said to freeze thought, by organizing and reserving it in a visual space; it thereby offers a novel image of an independent mental universe - what Ong describes as a "spectacular ordered environment for thought, free from interference, simply there, unattended and unsupervised by any discernable person." By the 18th century in the West, Ong argues, the commitment of sound to space that is inherent in alphabetical writing had had a noticeable effect on the human sense of the world, gradually making possible what Ong calls a new kind of "schizoid" withdrawal - a remoteness from sensory actuality and social interaction that allowed for escape into something other than violent action or tribal magic: the interior of one's own mind.[37]

Schizoid individuals do seem to have a special affinity for modes of inwardness and withdrawal akin to those of the modern age.[38] Martin, a young artist who experienced his first schizophrenic episode in adolescence, had long had a profound sense of separateness. "I have always found myself thinking and yet my thoughts were an internal reference," he wrote in his diary. Recollecting what it was like to ride in a car as a child, he wrote, "I was at the center of the universe, the 'real world' — the people in the other cars were outside of my inner world." He remembered being very shy when he was young, and often remaining silent, "thus allowing me to listen not only to conversation between people but also to myself." In his relationship both to the external world and his own activity, there was something reminiscent of the Cartesian notion of an Inner Eye that contemplates sensations and actions from a remove: "Hearing a door creak, a calling jay sends a vibration into the receiver of my mind, and I choose from the phenomena an action," he wrote in his diary; and, in a paper for school, "The eye is to watch; the mind watches the eye."

Interestingly enough, Martin felt extremely drawn to Kantian philosophy when he happened to encounter it in a college course, and later he would sometimes insert sentences from Kant into his paintings. Kant's ideas about what Martin termed "the separation we have between the patterns of our thoughts and the existence of the world" were very similar, he explained, to "my own realization of my mind in adolescence". Reading this philosopher calmed him, for, as he explained to me, Kant "has been where I'm going." This provided what Martin described as "security in being in my mind," "the feeling that it was OK to feel what I was feeling." While reading Kant on the nature of judgment, Martin was particularly struck with the uncanny sensation that his own ongoing mental processes, those accompanying the reading itself, were examples of the very thing that he was reading *about* (a realization very much in keeping with the spirit of the Kantian work he was absorbing).

A similar inwardness is described by Jonathan Lang, a patient who developed schizophrenia with paranoid and catatonic trends in his early twenties. When he was in his early thirties, Lang, who had read a great deal of psychology, wrote about his premorbid schizoid traits in an article that was published in the journal *Psychiatry* in 1939. "Even before the development of my psychosis, I can remember the existence of a tendency for ideas to possess a higher affective potential than immediate external stimuli such as persons or things," he says. Apparently he had long felt uncomfortable with emotions and with any kind of direct contact with the outer world, whether through passive perception or active interaction. And for this reason: "[I] trained myself to favor ideation over emotion... to block the affective response from showing any outward sign". He always preferred reading to direct sensory perception,

Lang tells us he viewed the senses "largely as means of obtaining information with which to build ideas". "While I played games during the required physical education period at school, I either thought of something else while I played or tried to govern my playing by verbal ideation rather than direct sensory-motor reaction". And, he insists, his withdrawn concentration on ideas — "ideocentrism," he called it — was "the prime factor influencing the direction and trend along which my psychosis developed."[39]

Disconnection: Loss of Reality

Nietzsche described his own age, and the two centuries to come, as the era of "nihilism" — a term he used, in a complex and rather idiosyncratic way, to refer to various consequences, personal and cultural, of an exaggerated subjectivism. One central element of this nihilism was the disappearance of a sense of external grounding of values (something that occurs with the advent of Cartesianism and the Galilean scientific revolution); another was that devaluation of our experiential world that occurs when it is contrasted with some hypothesized "thing-in-itself" from which we are eternally separated (as in Kant).[40] In Nietzsche's view an important distinction had to be made between two types of nihilism: a passive kind that could be read as a sign of weakness, and more active forms that suggest vitality and will.

A similar critique, also focused on subjectivism, is offered in various works by Martin Heidegger, notably "The Age of the World Picture."[41] It is with Cartesian metaphysics, Heidegger says, that the human subject becomes "that being upon which all that is, is grounded as regards the manner of its Being and its truth." Whereas in the Middle Ages the world was understood to have been brought into being by a Creator-God, now it is "conceived and grasped" as depending in some essential way on the human beings who know it. Here, then, is the essence of the modern age: an "unconditional dominion of subjectivity" whereby the human being sets himself up as the ultimate subject before whom and for whom the world will appear as a kind of "picture."[42] The main problem with this glorification of the knowing subject, according to Heidegger, is that it necessarily brings with it a devaluation of the world, whose ontological status is made to seem secondary, derivative, and somehow vulnerable: "Where anything that is has become the object of representing, it first incurs in a certain manner a loss of Being."[43] For "how can I know," he asks, "that this world is not simply a dream, a shimmering hallucination, a horizon no longer suffused with its own light but with mine?"[44]

Such a loss of the sense of Being seems especially common in persons with schizoid personalities, and for them too it is often accompanied by a heightened awareness of their own role in experience. "Reality recedes from me. Everything I touch, everything I think, everyone I meet, becomes unreal as soon as I approach ..." said James, a severely schizoid patient (verging on psychotic) treated by R. D. Laing.[45] Another patient with a schizophrenia spectrum disorder recalled his premorbid self in the following words:

> I was always a shy, retiring child, not disposed to make myself free with strangers, not much given to prattle ...I was very early in life an observer of my own mental peculiarities ...[there was always] an unsatisfactoriness in my consciousness of what surrounded me. I used to ask myself "Why is it that while I see and hear and feel everything perfectly, it nevertheless does not seem real to me?"[46]

A diary entry from 1921 suggests that Kafka must have had experiences of a very similar kind: "All is imaginary — family, office, friends, the street, all imaginary, far away or close at hand..."[47] These examples illustrate what Nietzsche called *"passive nihilism."* The moods and states of mind which they describe appear to be suffered rather than actively brought about; and they suggest "decline and recession of the power and the spirit,"[48] a sense of being unable to sustain the existence of a world dependent on the self.

Other instances of schizoid derealization are more suggestive of Nietzsche's *"active nihilism."* Here the experience has a far more willful or purposive cast, bolstering a sense of superiority over the world and serving as a "sign of increased power of the spirit."[49] We see this often in the tendency, common in schizoids and many schizophrenics, to be acutely sensitive to the repetitive or hackneyed aspect of what they observe around them, and therefore to react with a certain disdain and a sense of disappointment with the world. Henry, a patient to whom I administered various psychological tests, responded to a series of pictures (the Thematic Apperception Test) by asking if they were "all clichés?" — a term he then defined, most contemptuously, as "an exploited kind of pattern that people consider an aspect of experience."[50]

The sense of pervasive unreality experienced by one young man also suggests this kind of active declaration of superiority and indifference. During a thirteen year period prior to developing schizophrenic delusions, this man maintained an attitude of profound schizoid detachment — declaring that everything he experienced, was, as he put it, merely "hypothetical," and therefore, not worth getting too worked up about. As his analyst, Charles Rycroft, explains,

> ...he had the idea that he attended a Dr. Rycroft for psychoanalytical treatment. It was however, possible that I was not Dr. Rycroft, or that there were two or more Dr. Rycrofts; in any case it didn't really matter whether I was or was not Dr. Rycroft, or whether I was singular or plural. The whole matter was "hypothetical," and no one of the many alternatives was preferable to any other.[51]

This sense of hypotheticalness (which has some affinities with the procedure of phenomenological "bracketing") enabled him to avoid admitting to himself that any aspect of reality could be truly tempting or dangerous, a possible object of painful loss or frightening attack.

Like Martin, the schizophrenic artist mentioned earlier, Rycroft's patient also had an explicit interest in philosophy, and his nihilism (in Nietzsche's sense of the word) emerged most clearly in certain solipsistic claims — as when he stated that his thoughts were the only reality and that his thinking was the world itself in action. As Rycroft remarks, these experiences, fantastical though they were, cannot be considered manifestations of the Freudian primary process for they lacked all signs of instinctual or emotional charge. What this young man seemed to enjoy above all else was the experience of watching his intellectual processes as they "idled in neutral," devoid of affect and severed from all connection to things external to themselves.

Uncoupling: Role Distance

Disconnection is not the only form of separation experienced by the schizoid individual. Typically, such a person's existence is also split in a second major way, along fault lines running through the self rather than between self and world. This is often associated with a second major form of self-consciousness: where consciousness focuses on the self not as a knowing center (a subject ranged against a world that seems remote or unreal) but as an actor in the world and a potential object of awareness for others. The "uncoupling" this entails (in the vocabulary of Laing's patient Peter) can be suffered by the individual or can be intentionally induced. In either case, it sets up a division between two different selves: a hidden, "inner" self that watches or controls, usually associated with the mind, and a public, outer self that is more closely identified with bodily appearance and social role and that tends to be felt as somehow false or unreal.[52] David, another young schizoid man treated by Laing, distinguished between what he called his "own self and his "personality," the latter being what others thought he was or wanted him to be. Within himself his ideal was utter frankness and honesty, but with others he needed to feel he was playing a part, even if this was only the part of himself.

Something like this uncoupling can be present in schizoid individuals with the most diverse patterns of overt behavior. They may, for example, be extremely eccentric or else conventional, rebellious or overtly compliant. They may be highly predictable, perhaps behaving with an excessive formality, or else highly inconsistent, putting on and shedding attitudes, even whole personalities, at a rapid pace.[53] Different as these patterns are in many respects, they do share a false or "as if" quality. David, a sort of dandy with a cloak and a cane, always had a theatrical and contrived quality — as if he were somehow only *playing* at being eccentric.[54] And Kretschmer describes a (predominantly anaesthetic) schizoid man named Ernst Katt who rejected any normal profession or style of life and who would play "the mask of the interesting, bewitched spirit of beauty, which hovers over life"; sometimes he would suddenly say, 'I am a sausage.'"[55]

To the observer, such persons will seem unidentified with or detached from their public performances — uncoupled, if you will — and especially from the inner feelings or qualities of personhood that such roles would normally imply. One may sense an aura of ironic detachment, albeit an ambiguous one, and often an air of mystery suggestive of some hidden intention, or perhaps of an entire private world that is far more significant than anything they reveal. The term "role distance," introduced by the sociologist Erving Goffman, captures this phenomenon — where one scrutinizes and judges one's behavior from within as well as from the standpoint of an imaginary other whose reactions one attempts to anticipate and control. As Goffman points out, role distance is not so much a denial of the role itself as it is a rejection of the "virtual self" that is normally felt to animate or inform one's public performance.

The notion that the individual human being has some kind of inner being or personhood existing apart from or prior to one's actions or social roles, is one of the most fundamental presuppositions of contemporary Western society and thought. Historical and anthropological research suggests, however, that far from being universal, this is actually a most unusual assumption absent not only in traditional societies of the non-Westernized world but also in the West prior to the modern age. In heroic societies such as those of the ancient Greeks or the Vikings, as well as in most so-called "primitive" societies, a human being's identity is inseparable from his social position with all its implied rights and obligations. In such cultures a person knows who he is by understanding his place in the web of social statuses, privileges, and duties; the web itself, the fundamental framework guiding all thought and action, virtually never comes into question. Further, what is required of a person, what counts as virtue and what as vice, is always defined in terms of actions. Visible manifestations of feelings are emphasized. There is little concern with a private psychological domain. Everything that a person is felt, or in all likelihood feels him or herself to be, can therefore be captured in the reports of overt action — as if there simply *were* no hidden depths.[56] Among the Dinka of the southern Sudan, it is said, there appears to be no concept that is even roughly equivalent to "our popular modern conception of the 'mind,' as mediating and, as it were, storing up experiences of the self."[57]

It seems likely that a similar de-emphasis of the concept or experience of an inner self prevailed in European culture until the end of the Middle Ages: it is only in the 16th century that one begins to find literary evidence of a modern awareness of inwardness and role distance; philosophical conceptions of the individual person as independent of roles only come to prominence in the l8th century. Historians and sociologists have viewed the latter as inner, deep-seated changes in the psyche" that betoken "the emergence of modern European and American man."[58] To explain them they point to factors such as the pluralization and segmentation of society — the fact that modern society requires human beings to play a variety of different, even mutually incompatible roles in various reference groups.[59] A related factor is increased social mobility, beginning in the Renaissance and on the increase ever since. This may have encouraged a heightened awareness of the possibility of fashioning human identity in an artful, manipulative way (something that, though common among the elite in the classical world, had been largely absent for a millennium or more).[60]

The polarization of inner from outer or public man has strong evaluative implications, for there is an increasing tendency to value the inner self above its "mere" social roles. We can trace this development in the process whereby the 16th-century ideal of "sincerity" came, by the 19th century, to be replaced by an emphasis on a rival ethic — "authenticity". "Sincerity" — the congruence between actual feeling and avowal — does not imply an overvaluation of the inner: despite the preoccupation with a potential discrepancy between public face and private essence, this ethic nevertheless stresses the honesty and integrity of the performance of public roles. But as Lionel Trilling shows, this concept of virtue has been displaced over the course of the last two hundred years. For some time now we have lived in a post-romantic climate that (at least until very recently) stresses a different virtue: "authenticity" — where the point is not so much to be true to other human beings as to be true to oneself, to fulfill one's own inherent being and potential. Similar developments are suggested by the gradual eclipse of the Renaissance category of "passion" — which implied some overt, often violent accompanying action — by the far more "inner" or "subjective" concept of emotion;[61] it is also apparent in the growing prominence of notions of "dignity" at the expense of the older concept of "honour."[62]

One consequence of this inward turn has been a draining of value from public action, at least when the action accords with conventional expectation, because such action tends increasingly to be seen as irredeemably inauthentic, somehow compromised and contaminated by the demands of conformism and theatricality.[63] More and more the true source of human significance, of what Wordsworth and Rousseau termed "the sentiment of being" is felt to be located not in public action but in the idea of a private or unique self. There seem to be two main ways of responding to this set of cultural attitudes and valuations, the first corresponding to what Kretschmer would call the (predominantly) hyperaesthetic and the second to the (predominantly) anaesthetic kind of schizoid organization.

Uncoupling: Abdication of the Public

The first way of responding to this devaluation of the public self is to attempt to abdicate the public self entirely — either through hermit-like isolation or through refusal to interact in a more than perfunctory way — and this is accompanied by a tendency to locate the source of being in the tremors and yearnings of the inner life. Such an attitude is widespread in modernist culture — one thinks, e.g., of Virginia Woolf and Ford Maddox Ford, among others. Among its most forceful advocates is the contemporary French novelist and essayist Nathalie Sarraute.

Sarraute, a member of the literary school of the *Nouveau Roman*, is a harsh critic of conformity to the "impurities" of social convention and tradition. She associates such conformism with a focus, in novel writing, on "literary types" and "tiresome descriptions" of public events, which she dismisses as but "large empty carcasses" when set beside the "wealth and complexity" of the inner life.[64] Her vision of this inner life recalls Kretschmer's characterization of the exquisitely sensitive hyperaesthetic person: she describes it as a realm of interior stirrings "at once impatient and afraid," of "tiny, evanescent movements" that "blossom out preferably in immobility and withdrawal." Like "little gray insects that hide in damp holes, [these stirrings] are abashed and prudent. The slightest look makes them flee. To blossom out they must have anonymity and impunity. They consequently hardly show themselves in the form of actions." In Sarraute's view, it is the "unceasing play" of inner phenomena — what she elsewhere calls the "sub-conversation" rather than the "conversation" — that constitutes "the invisible woof of all human relationships and the very substance of our lives." An authentic life is one that attends to this inner stuff rather than dissipating itself in the distractions of action and the public life. Extreme dissociation from the outer person exacts its price, however, in the form of painful feelings of fraudulence. "When one has played a part — a false part — all one's life, for I was a sly, artful little liar even in the days of five and six; then one is marked," explains the writer Mary MacLane in an autobiographical book that recounts her markedly schizoid existence. I am "in no small degree, I found, a sham — a player to the gallery," she says; there was always "a spirit of falseness that rose and confronted me and said, "hypocrite,' 'fool'."[65]

Related concerns seem to have been central for another of Laing's schizoid patients: a 28-year old chemist named James who maintained a particularly extreme split between what he considered to be his "true" and false selves. Generally James would try to protect his inner being by appearing like everyone else, by falling in step with them and copying their behaviour. But the result was that nearly everything he did felt inauthentic — only a mimicry of the way "they" thought, perceived, or acted. "If I open the door of the train and allow someone to enter before me," he said, "this is not a way of being considerate, it is simply a means of acting as much as I can as everyone else". Further, the outer self, instead of feeling under his control, came to seem increasingly independent and removed, taking on a mechanical life of its own. If James' wife gave him a cup of milk, he would notice himself responding with an automatic smile and a "Thank you"; immediately he would feel revulsion at what he experienced as mere "social mechanics": "Did *he* want the milk, did *he* feel like smiling, did *he* want to say 'Thank you'? No. Yet he did all these things." Eventually such persons may come to sense that they have no self at all, no weight or substantiality as an independent being: "I am only a response to other people," James said. "I have no identity of my own... no self... I am only a cork floating on the ocean."[66]

Not surprisingly, perhaps, patients such as these will often assume that other people's behavior is just as contrived or mechanical, as devoid of spontaneous involvement, as is their own. Laing's patient David, for example, simply took it for granted that everybody else was also an actor. James, a more extreme case, often perceived the actions of his wife (in fact, a vivacious and lively woman) as those of a kind of robot, an "it" devoid of inner life. When James told her an ordinary joke and she ("it") laughed, this showed no real feeling but only her "conditioned" or mechanical nature.[67] A similar sense of inauthenticity can also occur with frankly psychotic schizophrenic patients — as, for instance, when one patient thought the farmers in the fields looked as if they "were not really working but merely going through the gestures."[68]

Uncoupling: Unconventionality and Inauthenticity

But there are other, more active modes of being that also stem from the modern emphasis on individuality and the separation between inner and public self. Instead of shrinking back from overt action, as from something inevitably contaminating, one may seek instead to display the sovereignty of the inner person or unique self. Usually, this will involve one of two characteristic ways of acting (or both, for they are easily combined): either a radical contrariness, in which one declares one's freedom from social constraint through the unconventionality of one's behavior; or else blatant inauthenticity, in which one flaunts the falseness of one's behavior (which may itself be either conventional or unconventional) as a way of suggesting the existence of a hidden true self - or, at least, of emphasizing the illusory and superficial nature of the self that *is* visible.

Particularly influential statements of this ethic of antinomianism and inauthenticity can be found in the works of Friedrich Nietzsche, that champion of self-invention and the mask. Nietzsche's conception of heroic behavior certainly differs sharply from that of more traditional societies: instead of praising loyalty to one's compatriots and bravery in the service of one's culture, he extols "human beings who are new, unique, incomparable, who give themselves laws, who create themselves"[69] — beings who glory in unconventionality and in their own refusal to be honest or sincere. In *The Will to Power* Nietzsche describes the "Great Man" as

> colder, harder, less hesitating, and without fear of "opinion"; he lacks the virtues that accompany respect and "respectability," and altogether everything that is part of the "virtue of the herd." If he cannot lead, he goes alone; then it can happen that he may snarl at some things he meets on his way. ... he wants no "sympathetic" heart, but servants, tools .... He knows he is incommunicable: he finds it tasteless to be familiar; and when one thinks he is, he usually is not. When not speaking to himself, he wears a mask. He rather lies than tells the truth: it requires more spirit and *will*. There is a solitude within him that is inaccessible to praise or blame, his own justice that is beyond appeal.[70]

But it is in a passage from Hegel's *Phenomenology of Mind* (1807), "The Spirit in self-Estrangement", that we find the clearest analysis of the inner logic of this modern aspiration toward inauthenticity. These pages, an early attack on the ideals of sincerity and integrity, have been called a "paradigm of the modern cultural and spiritual situation" (Lionel Trilling).[71] In them Hegel anatomizes the reasons why sincerity came to be seen as a barrier to self-fulfillment; and why fulfillment would increasingly be sought not only in unconventionality but through strategies of inconsistency, irony, and self-division. Hegel points out that in earlier stages of society (the Middle Ages, for example), people were likely be in a state of unquestioning harmony with the social order, feeling at one with their roles and rendering "obedient service" to an external power for which they felt "inner reverence". But it is of the nature of individual consciousness or Spirit, he argues, to strive toward self-realization, to seek "existence on its own account"; eventually this leads to resentment of any limitation on one's own identity imposed by the social order, whose dictates are now obeyed only "with secret malice and stand[ing] ever ready to burst out in rebellion".

It is through a continual uncoupling from any single identity that one declares one's ultimate freedom and autonomy — and this is why Hegel can speak of the existence of the self "on its own account" as being "strictly speaking, the loss of itself" (i.e., the loss of any *particular* identity). In this case, to negate the self is the only way to find it, the only way to affirm its true (if paradoxical) nature. Thus it is by flaunting the most problematic aspects of the social self — its theatrical self-consciousness, its inconsistency, its separation from the inner life — that one achieves a higher integrity, almost, in fact, a new kind of authenticity. For, as Hegel explains, "...only by self-consciousness being roused to revolt does it know its own peculiar torn and shattered condition; and in its knowing this it has *ipso facto* risen above that condition".[72]

It is significant that Hegel conceives of Spirit as becoming aware, not only of its *self*-estrangement, but of estrangement as a nearly universal factor in all of social existence, whether people recognize it or not. This is why Hegel can refer to the Spirit in self-estrangement as "this self-apprehending vanity of *all* reality": in knowing itself, subjectivity or spirit is at this stage aware of "the contradiction that lies in the heart of the solid elements of reality," the fact that "everything [is] estranged from itself."[73] It follows that for Spirit to "be conscious of its own distraught and torn existence," as Hegel puts it, "and to express itself accordingly — this is to pour scornful laughter on existence, on the confusion pervading the whole and on itself as well."

This kind of scorn is central to the aesthetic stance of Baudelaire, perhaps the greatest of proto-modernists; his notion of the dandy exemplifies this detached and irony-laden stance. But as its credo one might choose the famous assertion by Oscar Wilde: "the first duty in life is to be as artificial as possible" ("What the second duty is no one has yet discovered," he added.)[74] Wilde's flamboyance and cheeky politesse has much in common with the exhibitionistic reticence of Baudelaire's dandy: always polite, reserved, and exquisitely formal in his demeanor, while giving one to feel that this public persona is nevertheless an insult, an exquisite white glove protecting his real self from any contamination by lesser beings.

This is, however, but one of many kinds of behavior that can express this ethic of inauthenticity. Some other possibilities are represented by the raucous outrageousness of Pere Ubu, the mask — half-wildman, half-robot - that the absurdist playwright Alfred Jarry habitually held up between himself and the world; and by the ever-shifting personae of Jacques Vache, a young soldier whose bemusement and flaunted indifference had such a great influence on Andre Breton and the entire surrealist movement. Such an individual may be completely outrageous or studiously conventional, mercurial or eerily consistent and predictable. The one constant is a certain coldness and, along with this, a sense of absence — as if the person did not, actually inhabit his actions but instead stood apart, manipulating like a puppeteer or perhaps only observing from somewhere far above. The uncanny predictability of Andy Warhol represents what is perhaps the zero degree of this way of being. Certainly Warhol was a member of what Baudelaire called "a caste whose very reserve is a provocation" — committed both to causing astonishment and to having "the proud satisfaction of never oneself being astonished."[75] Yet his nearly catatonic demeanor divested him, not only of all outer signs of flamboyant rebellion, but also of any hint of that controlled inner fire that seems to lurk, at least as a potentiality, behind the dandy's haughty reserve. For Warhol came across as infinitely empty — as if the inner self had been rendered content-less and anodyne, reduced to the mere fact of its sense of detachment from the body, the world, and its own bland mask.

This kind of artificiality is common enough among schizoid persons, whose behavior is often characterized by an all-pervasive yet somehow cryptic form of irony. Laing's patient David, for instance, seems to have found a kind of self-protective reassurance in exaggerating his theatricality, in a way that reminded himself and his audience that he transcended whatever part he played. "I could not escape the impression that this young man was *playing* at being eccentric," remarks Laing. "The whole effect was mannered and contrived"; its effect being "to make the split between his own self (which only he knew) and what other people could see of him, as complete as possible." Another of Laing's patients, James, would also exaggerate roles, for example, in mimicking his father's pseudo politeness by asking guests if they'd had enough to eat, and doing this again and again until it was clear he was really offering a satirical comment on his father's veiled aggression.[76]

A similar irony imbued the actions of Philip, a young man whose overt behavior was more flagrantly unconventional. Philip was a markedly schizoid person (of the predominantly anaesthetic type) whom I knew quite well; he developed schizophrenia in his early twenties and committed suicide a few years later. Since early adolescence he had dedicated himself to the heroism of rebellion, and his defiance could reach flamboyant extremes. The quality of both his irony and defiance are very evident in the following passage from a letter, which sarcastically alludes to his father's nagging insistence that he settle on some serious life-goal:

> Speaking of shit, I've finally found a goal (my father has offered to pick a goal for me, again). Have you heard of the refined art of copromancy? copro=shit. I've decided to prophesy my future by careful regulation of my diet. Of course the artistic possibilities are limitless — polka-dots and peppermint swirls, not to speak of medium and method (plop in gelatin — from what height? — up against the wall). And just think, one wrong image in my subconscious and I fuck up the works. The most stringent requirement will be the boredom of eating only slightly varied diets from day to day. (My father said that, for him, the goal was not really satisfactory; but that he would not stop me

from being anything I wanted to be. Of course you must realize that he has always been a man of meager artistic sensibilities... As young Ben Franklin said, "If it's worth doing at all, it's worth doing well.")

Nearly everything in this lengthy letter is reminiscent of Nietzche's vision of the "great man," the one who flaunts his coldness and disdain for "sympathy," haughtily arrogating to himself the right to "make something" of others and living by the ethic of the mask. With cold pride Philip tells of seducing various women in his home town, largely by playing out, in a most calculating manner, roles that either mesmerized them or mollified their fears; and he seems disgusted by the sheer ease of these seductions — which he compares to "shooting swans in cesspools."

Later in his letter Philip speaks of thoughts of having sex with both his parents. He lived in accord with a perverse but unyielding sense of duty, a code that required him to dismantle all conventions, to defy all codes of human conduct, and always to behave as scandalously as he possibly could. An extreme contrariness seemed to steer him unerringly toward the ultimate taboos, making him feel duty-bound to break them:

> I just don't know how I can justify living at home this summer to myself without having slept with either of my parents. There's no question in my mind that they both want it — a little less sublimated in my mother, as is natural — and I suspect I do too, though I never get horny seeing or thinking about them. What's possibly even worse is that I haven't killed either of them. (Typical guilt feelings.) A modern version of the Oedipus myth...

This, it would seem, is a peculiar, and a distinctively modern, form of guilt, a guilt not over feelings of forbidden lust or anger but over the lack of such feelings, and, perhaps, over failing to have transgressed enough of the sacred taboos.

Conclusion: Irony and Inauthenticity in Overt Schizophrenia

We have surveyed the schizoid personality, examining its main subtypes and its characteristic forms of separation from world and from self. Before concluding, it is worth considering the relationship between this mode of being and the overtly schizophrenic condition. This is a controversial issue that brings out one of the fundamental polarities or dilemmas of psychiatric knowledge: the conflict between "disease" and "dimensional" ways of viewing psychopathological conditions, or between explaining an illness as an autonomous "process" versus understanding it as a comprehensible "development" out of a prior personality or form of human existence.

One cannot deny that the onset of schizophrenic psychosis does appear to involve something more than a merely quantitative shift, and also that it *can* develop in the absence of a clearly schizoid predisposition. But, having granted these points, one can hardly fail to recognize the very remarkable similarities that do exist between the two conditions. The most prominent signs of the schizoid personality — an apparent asociality and indifference, and a propensity for introversion — are also characteristic of schizophrenia, where they generally appear in more extreme forms. The psychiatrist H.C. Rumke argued, in fact, that the fundamental phenomenon of schizophrenia is the weakening of the "rapprochement-instinct," the source of normal directedness toward people and the environment.[77] Other writers have emphasized more hyperaesthetic (in Kretschmer's sense) and defensive reasons for the schizophrenic's apparent affectlessness and detachment, such as an exquisite sensitivity and consequent withdrawal — acutely described in just these terms by one such individual: "I can't feel or relate... I used to feel emotions like physical pain and couldn't stand it. So I blocked off. I can't sympathize with people."[78]

As we have seen, schizoid personality seems to be defined by an essential disharmony, a proneness to fragmentation and conflict, both with the world and within the self. Such people tend to feel detached from or somehow at odds with the environment, their own emotional reactions, and their public persona. Similar kinds of disharmony are also central to schizophrenia, a condition that has been described as a form of "intrapsychic ataxia" (a separation of cognition and emotion) and as "a peculiar destruction of the inner cohesiveness of the psychic personality."[79] Here I shall mention but two ways in which disconnection from self and from world can manifest itself in schizophrenia: a propensity for willful unconventionality and flaunted inauthenticity, and a pervasive attitude of ironic detachment.

Rejection of societal norms and conventional roles is common in schizophrenia. Cross-cultural research has shown, in fact, that schizophrenics generally seem to gravitate toward "the path of most resistance," tending to transgress whatever customs and rules happen to be held most sacred in a given society; thus in deeply religious Nigeria they are especially likely to violate religious sanctions, in Japan they frequently assault family members.[80] One is reminded, in fact, of Rilke's line about the modern artist: "This is our fate: to be opposite and nothing else, always opposite." Manfred Bleuler has interpreted this antinomianism as indicating the patient's "ruthless bent to live his life according to his own nature." But our study of schizoid phenomena should alert us to the possibility that the bent toward originality or authenticity may often be a bit more compromised than this reading would suggest. As we know, such behavior can be motivated as much by antagonism as by any simple urge to self-expression; what results can be a form of action by negative reaction, a kind of counter-etiquette riveted on the conventions it is trying to subvert. The focused, oppositional, even tendentious quality of schizophrenic negativism is clear from the following description by Eugen Bleuler:

> In short, [schizophrenic patients may] oppose everyone and everything and, consequently, become exceedingly difficult to handle. They may eat only secretly or at unusual times. They grumble about the food but when asked what they would like to have, their only answer is: "Something else, not what we have."...
> They eat their soup with a fork and their dessert with a soup spoon. They continually sit down in somebody else's place, enter every bed but their own. ...Frequently, a request will be complied with as soon as the proper time for it has gone by.[81]

The unconventionality of such persons does seem too studied or reactionary, too suggestive perhaps of a certain "devious perversity,"[82] to be the natural welling-up of something truly spontaneous, authentic, or original. Indeed, one cannot escape the impression that many such individuals are engaged in a kind of mockery and "chronic 'clowning'."[83] With some schizophrenics, one may even feel that they are *pretending* to be mad (which would not, of course, exclude the possibility that they may in fact also *be* mad.) Eugen Bleuler described patients with a special form of hyperkinetic catatonia who were constantly making disconnected, caricatured grimaces and gestures.

> One has the impression that these patients want to play the buffoon, though they do this in a most awkward and inept fashion. They contrive any number of stupidities and sillinesses, such as beating their own knees, interchanging pillows for blankets when they go to bed, pouring water on the floor instead of into a cup, lifting doors off their hinges. The patients will do all this while they are seemingly well-oriented. ... the "faxen-psychosis" [buffooneries-psychosis] ...usually involves individuals who for some unconscious reason *pretend* to be mentally deranged.[84]

Manfred Bleuler has noted that schizophrenics whom one is concerned about seem to smile in "a soulful, expressive way," their smile telling us something like: "'Dear friend, it's all just an act. Somehow, in some other world, we'll get along with one another.'"[85] Perhaps more common, however, is the sardonic and off-putting yet somehow perplexed irony of patients who feel profoundly alienated from any normal activity of human encounter — who may, for example, shake hands as if they were engaging in some totally absurd and arbitrary action or may respond to questions as if condescending to petty and useless demands. No one who interviewed schizophrenics will have failed, at times, to have the sneaking suspicion that the whole interaction is, to the patient, something of a joke. Often this tone is quite subtle, leaving the interviewer wondering whether the patient is really involved in the conversation or whether he is essentially detached, only watching and mocking the whole event as if from somewhere far above. Harry Stack Sullivan describes the effect of this ambiguous behavior very well: "it looks as if the schizophrenic were laughing at you, and you do not like to be reminded that you might be that humorous; and, anyway, he is too sick to be having such a good time at your expense. Thus the behavior has the effect of separating him from what otherwise might be a slightly reassuring contact that might, in turn, go into more reassuring contact."[86]

Significantly, irony is one of the salient features of modern art and consciousness. Friedrich Schlegel spoke in 1800 of "such a quantity of great and small ironies of different sorts" that seemed to be springing up recently. He warned of the dangers of these tendencies which he saw burgeoning all around him — asking: "What gods will rescue us from all these ironies?"[87] There are, of course, many forms of irony; what seems fairly distinctive about the schizophrenic variety, when it is present, is, first, its totalizing character — like the irony of Marcel Duchamp and Alfred Jarry, it is all-encompassing, not a criticism of one thing in favor of another but a universal mockery — and second, its withholding, confusing, and ultimately off-putting effect.

Given how common this disconcerting and ambiguously ironic posture can be, it may seem surprising that is has not received more attention in the literature on schizophrenia. If one considers the standard models of this illness, however, this seems understandable enough. Irony, after all, is an intensely directed and meaningful mode of consciousness or expression; one can hardly attribute it to an individual without acknowledging a distinct degree of awareness, and particularly of meta-awareness on that person's part. Irony — which is a dominant feature of the modern or modernist sensibility — implies inner distance, an ability to separate from the self; and this is hardly congruent with standard conceptions of cognitive breakdown, instinctual domination, and primary-process thinking.

When schizophrenic irony, mockery, facetiousness, sarcasm, and the like have been considered in the psychiatric and psychoanalytic literature, they have generally been treated as secondary or peripheral features of the illness. The patient's sense of alienation from his own bizarre behavior, for instance, has sometimes been attributed to the survival of an island of normalcy, a fragment of mature "observing ego" that somehow survives amidst the general collapse and regression to which it merely bears witness.[88] The assumption seems to be that, if there is real method in speech or action, then it is not truly madness; thus to *play* at madness, or within one's madness is not to be truly mad. Only in such literary artists as Diderot and Pirandello do we have the suggestion (seldom if ever taken seriously by the mental health establishment) that an authentic madness might, in some essential way, involve just such a playing.

It would be foolish to view schizophrenics as purely volitional and entirely self-aware, or to attempt to reduce madness to the feigning of madness. Still, one must question whether these qualities of alienation, irony, and masquerade are really so peripheral to the schizophrenic condition as is often assumed.

Far from running counter to the general progression of schizophrenic pathology, these schizoid phenomena, in the forms of inauthenticity and self-detachment that they presuppose, may, in fact, be closely bound up with the very essence of the disease.

endnotes

[1] The present paper is based on chapter 3 of my book *Madness and Modernism: Insanity in the Light of Modern Art, Literature, and Thought* (New York: Basic Books, 1992; Harvard University Press paperback, 1994).
[2] I use the term "modernism" to refer to the stylistically innovative forms of art and literature that developed in Western culture in the late nineteenth and early twentieth centuries; see Sass, *Madness and Modernism*, pp. 28-39.
[3] P. Valery, *Cahiers*, vol. 2, ed. J. Robinson (Paris: Galimard, 1974),p. 224; idem, *Monsieur Teste*, trans. J. Matthews (Princeton NJ: Princeton University Press, 1973), p. 107.
[4] R. D. Laing, *The Divided Self* (Harmondsworth, U.K.: Penguin Books, 1965), pp. 17, 39.
[5] S. Arieti, *The Interpretation of Schizophrenia. 2nd ed.* (New York: Basic Books, 1974), p. 110.
[6] See, e.g., T. Millon, *Disorders of Personality, DSM III: Axis II* (New York: John Wiley and Sons, 1981), pp. 273-85, *re* "intrinsic emotional blandness" and a "lack [of] the equipment for experiencing the finer shades of subtleties of emotional life."
[7] "Syntonic" is E. Bleuler's term.
[8] Quotations from E. Kretschmer, *Physique and Character*, trans. W.J. H. Sprott (New York: Harcourt, Brace, and World, 1925), pp. 152, 157.
[9] See E. Essen-Moller, "The concept of schizoidia," *Monatsschrift für Psychiatrie und Neurologie*, 112, 1946, 258-271, p. 260.
Kretschmer notes the stiffness or jerkiness of physical movements in schizoids, in contrast with the smooth mobility of cycloid or hypomanic persons (*Physique and Character*, p. 175).
[10] Kretschmer, *Physique and Character*, p. 260.
[11] E. Kretschmer, *A Textbook of Medical Psychology*, trans. E. B. Strauss (London: Hogarth Press, 1952; originally publ. in English in 1925, in German in 1921), p. 205.
[12] M. Bleuler, *The Schizophrenic Disorders*. trans. S. M. Clemens (New Haven CN: Yale University Press, 1978), p. 498.
[13] Kretschmer, *Physique and Character*. pp. 152, 245.
[14] Kretschmer, *Physique and Character*, pp. 154, 172, 153.
[15] Kretschmer, *Physique and Character*, p. 252.
[16] Kretschmer, *Physique and Character*, pp.151, 152, 157,146.

[17] R. Langbaum, "The theory of the avant-garde: A review," *Boundary 2, I*, 1972, p. 240.

[18] J. Joyce, *A Portrait of the Artist as a Young Man* (New York: Viking, 1964; first publ. 1916), pp. 215, 247. Robert Musil characterized the creative person as "metaphysically restless," "contemptuous of reality," and as appearing to be "asocial," an "unfeeling dreamer" (quoted in D.S. Luft, *Robert Musil and the Crisis of European Culture* [Berkley CA: University of California Press, 1980], p. 161).

[19] W. Wordsworth, "Preface to the second edition of the Lyrical Ballads" (1800), in D. Perkins, ed., *English Romantic Writers* (New York: Harcourt Brace and World, 1967), 320-31, p. 324.

[20] See F. Kermode, *Romantic Image* (London and Glasgow: Fontana Books, 1971).

[21] H. Deutsch. "Some forms of emotional disturbance and their relationship to schizophrenia," *Psychoanalytic Quarterly, 11*, 1942, 301, 21, pp. 310, 314, 308, 316. The "as-if" personality that Deutsch discusses is commonly associated with the schizoid type (see, e.g., Millon, *Disorders of Personality*, pp. 278-80); and Deutsch herself notes that it is a frequent precursor to schizophrenia (p. 319).

[22] W. R. D. Fairbairn, An *Object-Relations Theory of the Personality* (New York: Basic Books, 1954), p. 10, see also pp. 13,25.

[23] H. Guntrip, *Schizoid Phenomena, Object Relations, and the Self* (New York: International Universities Press, 1968), pp. 50, 57, 79.

[24] C. Lasch, *The Minimal Self* (New York: Norton, 1984), pp. 15, 182, 177.

[25] M. Bleuler, *Schizophrenic Disorders*, p. 498.

[26] Y.-F. Tuan, *Segmented Worlds anti Self: Group Life and Individual Consciousness* (Minneapolis, University of Minnesota Press, 1982), p. 139.

[27] G. Simmel, "The Metropolis and Mental Life," in *The Sociology of Georg Simmel*, trans. and ed. Kurt H. Wolff (New York: Free Press, 1950), 409-424, pp. 415-416, 421.

[28] Laing, *Divided Self*, p. 127.

[29] N. Elias, The History of Manners, trans. E. Jephcott (New York: Pantheon Books, 1978), pp. 250-51.

[30] Letter to Gibieuf, 1642, quoted in C. Taylor, *Sources of the Self* (Cambridge MA: Harvard University Press, 1989), p. 144.

[31] See R. Rorty, *Philosophy and the Mirror of Nature* (Princeton NJ: Princeton University Press, 1979), pp. 45ff.

[32] W. Ong, *The Presence of the Word* (Minneapolis MN: University of Minnesota Press, 1981), p. 211.

[33] See, e.g., Clement Greenberg, "Modernist Painting," in G. Battcock, ed., *The New Art: A Critical Anthology* (New York: Dutton, 1966), 100-110.

[34] Quoted in C. L. Griswold, "Plato's metaphilosophy: Why Plato wrote dialogues", in Griswold, ed., *Platonic Readings* (New York: Routledge, 1988), 143-67, p. 150.

[35] Schelling on Kant is quoted in E. D. Hirsch, *Wordsworth and Schelling* (New Haven CN: Yale University Press, 1960), p. 19. These forms of separation and reflexivity reach one kind of culmination in the transcendental phenomenology of Edmund Husserl, with its phenomenological reduction or *epoche*. Husserl claims that the phenomenologist's attitude is destined to effect "a complete personal transformation, comparable in the beginning to a religious conversion, which then, however, over and above this, bears within itself the significance of the greatest existential transformation which is assigned as a task to mankind as a whole" (*The Crisis of European Sciences and Transcendental Phenomenology*, trans. D. Carr [Evanston IL: Northwestern University Press, 1970], p. 137).

[36] Elias, *The History of Manners*, pp. 129, 260, 253, 258. Similar tendencies toward increasing discipline, organization, and self-scrutiny are traced in Michel Foucault's *Discipline and Punish: The Birth of the Prison*, trans. A. Sheridan (New York: Vintage Books, 1979).

[37] Ong, *Presence of the word*, pp. 63, 136-37. The shift from an oral to a literate or alphabetical culture: can be seen as part of an even larger mutation with similar implications for consciousness and the self: the growing predominance of vision over other sensory modalities. See W. Ong, "World as View and World as Event," *American Anthropologist*, 71, 1969, 634-647.

[38] According to George Devereux, "the ethnic personality of modern man is basically schizoid" (*Basic Problems of Ethnopsychiatry*, trans, . M. Gulati and G. Devereux [Chicago: University of Chicago Press, 1980], p. 219).

[39] J. Lang, "The other side of the affective aspects of schizophrenia," *Psychiatry*, 2, 1939, 195-202, pp. 196, 197, 200. Interestingly, however, Lang also acknowledges that ideocentrism may not be an ultimate cause, but may be physiological operations of the organism (p. 201).

[40] See Nietzsche, *Human, All Too Human*, trans. H. Zimmern and P. V. Kohn, in *The Complete Works of Friedrich Nietzsche*, ed. 0. Levy, 18 vols. (New York: Macmillan, 1909-11; originally publ. 1878), sec. 16.

[41] Heidegger locates the source of his subjectivism in Descartes' attempt to found being itself on the self-certainty of a representing consciousness ("The age of the world picture," in *The Question concerning Technology and Other Essays*, trans. W. Lovitt [New York: Harper and Row, 1977}, pp. 127, 139-141). Quotations in this paragraph from this essay, pp. 128-30, 132, 147; and from Heidegger, "The Word of Nietzsche: 'God is Dead'", in *idem*, p. 68.

[42] It is in this sense that the human being, in Heidegger's words, "'gets into the picture' in precedence over whatever is ... set[ting] himself

up as the setting in which whatever is must henceforth set itself forth, must present itself [*sich prasentieren*], i.e, be picture" ("Age of the world picture," pp. 131-132).

43 Heidegger, "Age of world picture," p. 142.

44 Heidegger quoted in H. Richter, *Dada: Art and Anti-Art* (New York and Toronto: Oxford University Press, 1965), p. 91.

45 Laing, *Divided Self*, p. 146.

46 Quoted in C. Landis, ed., *Varieties of Psychopathological Experience* (New York: Holt, Rinehart and Winston, 1964), pp. 192-3.

47 Quoted in A. Hiedsieck, "Kafka's narrative ontology," *Philosophy and Literature*, 11, 1987, 242-57, p, 249.

48 Nietzsche, *The Will to Power*, trans. W. Kaufmann and R. J. Hollingdale (New York: Vintage Books, 1968; first publ. 1901), #22 and #23, pp. 17-18.

49 Nietzsche, Will to Power, p. 17.

50 For Rorschach examples, see S. J. Blatt and C. M. Wild, *Schizophrenia: A Developmental Analysis* (New York: Academic Press, 1976), pp. 144, 149; e.g., "two people in a stylized position, leaning over a pot... the quality of theatre about them as though somewhat acted."

51 C. Rycroft, "On the defensive function of schizophrenic thinking and delusion-formation", in *Imagination and Reality* (London: Hogarth Press, 1968), 84-101, pp. 86-7.

52 Laing's "inner self" should not be confused with Winnicott's "true self": the first is primarily mental, the second instinctual. Whereas the schizoid is identified with the first, he or she is alienated from the second.

53 See Arieti Interpretation of Schizophrenia, pp. 107-8.

54 Laing, *Divided Self*, p. 70.

55 Kretschmer, *Physique and Character*, p. 196.

56 See A. Macintyre, *After Virtue* (Notre Dame IN: University of Notre Dame Press, 1981), pp. 115-19.

57 Godfrey Lienhardt, *Divinity and Experience: The Religion of the Dinka* (Oxford: Clarendon Press, 1961), pp. 149-51. See also Tuan, *Segmented Worlds and Self*, p. 139-67.

58 Francis Yates quoted in L. Trilling, *Sincerity and Authenticity* (Cambridge MA: Harvard University Press, 1972), p. 19.

59 Georg Simmel and more recently, Peter Berger, are among those who have made this point; see, e.g., P. Berger. B. Berger and H. Kellner, *The Homeless Mind: Modernization and Consciousness* (New York: Vintage Books, 1974), pp. 63-82.

60 See S. Greenblatt, *Renaissance Self-Fashioning* (Chicago and London: University of Chicago Press, 1980), p. 2. Also see Trilling, *Sincerity and Authenticity*, pp. 12-16.

61 D. M. Lowe, *History of Bourgeois Perception* (Chicago: University of Chicago Press, 1982), p. 99.

[62] Berger, Berger and Kellner, *Homeless Mind*, pp. 83-96.

[63] This is part of what Richard Sennett means by the "fall of the public man"; Sennett, *The Fall of Public Man* (New York: Vintage, 1978).

[64] Quotations in this and the following paragraph are from N. Sarraute, *The Age of Suspicion*, trans. M. Jolas (New York: George Braziller, 1963), pp. 29, 61,67, 75, 82, 84, 95, 97.

[65] *The Story of Mary MacLane* (Chicago: Stone, 1902), pp. 134-36.

[66] Laing, *Divided Self*, pp. 140, 144, 47-8. The patient who withdraws from his public performance is also likely to feel clumsy and awkward, and to worry that others may see through his shamming and pretence; see case of Peter (p. 124).

[67] Laing, *Divided Self*, p. 49.

[68] E. Bleuler, *Dementia Praecox, or the Group of Schizophrenias*, trans. J. Zinkin (New York: International Universities Press, 1950), p.106.

[69] Nietzsche, *The Gay Science*, trans. W. Kaufmann (New York: vintage Books, 1974; first publ. 1887), #335, p. 266.

[70] Nietzsche, *The Will to Power*, #962, p. 505.

[71] Trilling, *Sincerity and Authenticity*, p. 27, see pp. 26-52. My discussion in the following pages follows Trilling's argument rather closely. The relevant pages from Hegel are: G. W. F. Hegel, *Phenomenology of Mind*, trans. J. B. Baillie (New York: Harper and Row, 1967), pp. 509-48. Relevant passages from Hegel not otherwise noted are quoted in Trilling, ibid., pp. 31, 35, 36, 38, 46.

[72] Hegel, Phenomenology of Mind, p. 548.

[73] Hegel, *Phenomenology of Mind*, p. 546, emphasis added.

[74] Wilde quoted in Trilling, *Sincerity and Authenticity*, p. 118.

[75] Baudelaire, "The dandy," in "The painter of modern life," in P. Quennell, ed., *The Essence of Laughter and Other Essays, Journals, and Letters*, (New York: Meridian Books, 1956), 46-50, p. 48.

[76] Laing, *Divided Self*, pp. 70-71, 102.

[77] H. C. Rumke, "The nuclear symptom of schizophrenia and the praecosfeeling," trans .J. Neeleman, *History of Psychiatry*, I, 1990 (originally publ. in 1941), p. 336.

[78] R. Rosser, "The psychopathology of thinking and feeling in a schizophrenic," *International Journal of Psychoanalysis*, 60, 1979, p.178. A polarity within dementia praecox that was described by Emil Kraepelin sounds virtually identical to Kretschmer's distinction between hyperaesthetic and anaesthetic forms of schizoid personality. See Kraepelin, *Dementia Praecox and Paraphrenia*, trans. R.M. Barclay [Huntington NY: Krieger, 1971; first English ed. 1919], 24, 34).

[79] Phrases from Erwin Stransky and Emil Kraepelin (M. Bleuler, *Schizophrenic Disorders*, pp. 491, 499).

[80] C. Schooler and W. Caudill, "Symptomatology in Japanese and American schizophrenics," *Ethnology*, 3, 1964, p. 177.

[81] E. Bleuler, *Dementia Praecox*, pp. 192-93.

[82] Manfred Bleuler's words, paraphrasing Kretschmer (*Schizophrenic Disorders*, p. 29).

[83] E. Bleuler, *Dementia Praecox*, p.93.

[84] E. Bleuler, *Dementia Praecox*, p. 215, emphasis added. Bleuler mentions that the "buffooneries" of "spiteful hebephrenics" have a rather different quality. John Cutting notes that negativistic actions in schizophrenia are often difficult to distinguish from "playfulness " or "bloody-mindedness" (*The Right Cerebral Hemisphere and Psychiatric Disorders* [Oxford UK: Oxford University Press, 1990], p.298).

[85] M. Bleuler, *Schizophrenic Disorders*, p. 488.

[86] Sullivan, *Clinical Studies in Psychiatry* (New York: Norton, 1973), p. 185.

[87] Schlegel, "On incomprehensibility," in K. M. Wheeler, ed., *German Aesthetic and Literary Criticism: The Romantic Ironists and Goethe* (Cambridge UK: Cambridge University Press, 1984), 32-40, pp. 36-7. Also see P. de Man, "The rhetoric of temporality," in *Blindness and Insight* (Minneapolis: University of Minnesota Press, 1983), 187-228, pp. 208-28.

[88] Thus Freud conceived of a rational inner observer who watched the progression of the illness from some recess in the psychotic's mind; see J. E. Gedo and A. Goldberg, *Models of the Mind; A Psychoanalytic Theory* (Chicago: University of Chicago Press, 1973), p. 130.

7: Laing and Philosophy

Douglas Kirsner

Laing and Philosophy

Douglas Kirsner

Most of Laing's concerns were philosophical. For him, issues of mental illness were an application of fundamental philosophical inquiry. In common with philosophical and religious traditions of inquiry, Laing regarded being human as a mystery.

It strikes me that many of Laing's concerns surrounded the four questions that the eighteenth century philosopher, Immanuel Kant raised about fundamental issues that philosophy needed to investigate. Kant wrote; 'All of the interests of my reason, speculative as well as otherwise, combine in the three following questions:

1. What can I know?
2. What ought I to do?
3. What may I hope?'

To these Kant later added a fourth question that combined the first three, 'What is man?'

Laing was always vitally concerned with such questions and found his patients also to be centrally concerned with such issues. Laing's legacy will, I think, lie in his stance, his approach, his sensibility more than any particular positions he adopted in relation to such questions. This includes, for example, the extent to which schizophrenia is psychological, familial, social or biological. As he said in an interview with me, 'Man is the being whose being is in question to himself. There is this problematic about ourselves to ourselves' (Kirsner 1997, p. 39). What is crucial is questioning, and the questions he asked.

Today I think that Laing's idea that schizophrenia could be context-dependent has been integrated into contemporary thinking on mental illness. Laing's view that psychosis could be at least partially psychodynamically intelligible in terms of agency, meaning and context has also been integrated into most approaches. Schizophrenia is an illness yes, but important psychosocial modifiers need to be taken into account as well. Also, the critique of normality as intrinsically related to society is now widely assumed to be a factor to take into account in understanding unusual individual behaviour. In general, the idea of taking individuals seriously as agents is more prevalent. Certainly, putting people directly into institutions for unusual behaviour has declined considerably, to the extent that nowadays it is often difficult for patients to be admitted to psychiatric institutions when they need to be. I think that the kind of critiques Laing made in the sixties have been so successful that many of his direct critiques of psychiatry now seem anachronistic. This happened, not just as a direct result of his own work, but partly because of the development of new psychotropic drugs, partly because of changes in government policies and funding and partly because he was riding a wave.

Laing responded to the fact that psychiatry viewed schizophrenia as 'ununderstandable' — as Karl Jaspers' classic psychiatric text, *General Psychopathology* has it — and therefore not possible to investigate in terms of meaning and significance. For Jaspers, psychotic phenomena manifested an 'abyss of difference' between sane and psychotic experience, a dichotomy Laing constantly challenged throughout his life (see Kirsner 1990). In 'The Obvious', his contribution to the Dialectics of Liberation Conference held at the London Roundhouse in 1967, Laing made the point that the 'obvious' was what stood in front of us but we didn't see. He claimed, 'What is obvious to me might not be obvious to anybody else. The obvious is literally that which stands in one's way, in front of, or over, or against oneself. One has to begin by recognizing that it exists for oneself' (Laing 1967). The conference was held during a momentous political period of change and protest. It was the height of the Vietnam War, and the period of Alexander Dubcek's 'socialism with a human face', the era of the civil rights movements in the US and the rise of the counter cultural and New Left movements, and the year before the student revolt in Paris. Laing's contribution to the symposium not only clearly related to the politics of the time, but also to the problem of treating psychiatric symptoms as illness rather than as communication, at least partly. His was a fundamental phenomenological approach to understanding what stood in front of us, with as few preconceptions as possible. However, it should be asked how many taken-for-granted preconceptions were left unchallenged at the time — and later. What was *obvious*, 'standing in front of us', at the time was the struggle against the 'evil' US imperialist government by the 'wretched of the earth', the 'authentic' New Left and the 'heroic'

South Vietnamese National Liberation Front. Yet, if we are to be honest, shouldn't we ask some uncomfortable but *obvious* questions such as — Was the New Left really that good and the US that bad? Was the defeat of the US such a good thing given that South Vietnam became part of a communist dictatorship with an abysmal human rights record, which remains very much in power today? Weren't the USSR really ultimately the bad guys during the Cold War? (I write this as a New Left activist at that time myself). It wasn't hard to attack the modern life or Western governments at that time, especially in a revolutionary atmosphere such as the London Roundhouse, where speakers vied with each other to be the most radical. Any approach that challenges preconceptions ought to let the chips fall where they may, not just bolster whatever strongly held beliefs happen to be held, whether anti- or pro- establishment.

Laing had both the strengths and weaknesses of a romantic who believes that things were so much better and real in the old days and also that the only thing preventing the institution of a utopia is a bad social system that produces ills from schizophrenia to poverty. I am referring to the idea that there are no intrinsic flaws in human nature and that evil arises simply from a corrupt society. Laing's approach is reminiscent of Jean-Jacques Rousseau's view of the natural goodness of noble savages, people who had not been corrupted by civilization: 'Man is born free but everywhere he is in chains'. This is opposed to Freud's anti-romantic Hobbesian view of the human condition which Sartre shared. Laing's view, at least as expressed in *The Politics of Experience*, is a romantic one: we are inherently and naturally good, if only the world would leave us alone; schizophrenics might be in a better state if only psychiatrists would not interfere with them. We find here the idea of a basic goodness in human nature that could supervene in a society that did away with the corruption that derived from poverty ownership, for example. This is reflected in the idea of a state of nature of the noble savage, or of bygone eras when human beings were not as pervasively conditioned by power elites, media and ideology.

I have become increasingly sceptical of the idea that things used to be better than they are now psychologically, that life was real then but that we are now mesmerized by 'McCulture'. I think, by and large, that the vast majority of us, especially in the West, are far better off than we used to be 1000, 2000 or

3000 years ago physically and spiritually. Clearly, we're far better off physically, but we have far, far better political systems, science, medicine, media, information, justice, political freedom, and so forth. Obviously, there have been truly terrible, relatively recent blots (the Holocaust stands out). Plainly too, with the advancement of science, there has been the development of weaponry that can be used by evil people for ' evil purposes. However, on the whole, things are incredibly better than a hundred or thousands of years ago. With all their faults, science and liberal democracy are clear pluses for the vast majority of people. Much discussion about the contemporary 'devastation of experience' is markedly exaggerated rhetoric that of course fits a romantic state of mind where people can have their cake and eat it too, enjoying all the concrete benefits of advanced democratic capitalism while abstractly railing against it.

Despite statements that are essentially confined to the late 1960s in 'The Obvious' and in *The Politics of Experience*, Laing was mostly smarter than that. I think seeing society as the cause of human problems was an experiment he tried and which failed. As I argued in *The Schizoid World of Jean-Paul Sartre and R.D. Laing*, Laing was interested in situating our problems in context, and when the social context did not provide the rationale, he moved on to the next context in which to situate the social context – the cosmic or mystical context. Later, after his visit to Ceylon, he abandoned that position and returned to the perspectives he held prior to the mid-sixties. Laing took liberalism very seriously and was I think principally concerned with limiting society's interference with the individual's wishes. Much of Laing's work is about protecting the individual from the incursion of other people on individual experience. I remember hearing one of Laing's lectures in 1975 in London in which he said that the main fear people had was 'the fear of other people'. He was far more John Stuart Mill than Karl Marx.

Laing's 'half-in, half-out' positions on issues ranging from the causes of schizophrenia to political, reflect his attempts to wrestle with real ambiguities. Laing argued for the greater social intelligibility of schizophrenia, not for the total explanation in social terms. Laing preferred the dentist to use his or her scientific 'look' in examining his teeth but emphasized the inappropriateness of exclusively using such a 'look' by a doctor at childbirth. The emphasis on the primacy of experience is as a redress to simply looking at outcomes of effects. As Laing argued in *The Divided Self*, science deals with what is appropriate to it. So the science-based art of dentistry, for example, studies teeth and their relation to the mouth. But the study of a mental illness deals with the mind attributes, however 'mind' is defined. This does not imply that there is a mind-body split that Descartes proposed when mind and body are totally separate and function on different principles. Laing was a psychiatrist who never assumed there was no role for biology. Laing was influenced by Maurice Merleau-Ponty's position that we are 'embodied subjects'. The starting point for Laing for such a science is that it is a 'science of persons', as first adumbrated in *The Divided Self*. This starting point is the apprehension of the personal, as a self-acting agent who always chooses, whether he or she likes it or not. Laing's commandment: Always treat a person as an agent, a choosing being, not a thing. Martin Buber's I-thou division as apposed to I-it is central in *The Divided Self* and continued to underpin Laing's future work.

Nonetheless, in this, as in so much else, Laing essentially follows Sartre too. I have read through Laing's very careful and copious notes on his minutely detailed reading of *Being and Nothingness*. Laing together with David Cooper summarized three major later works of Sartre as *Reason and Violence*. Like Sartre, Laing's approach was existential phenomenological, that consciousness is always consciousness of something, that it cannot be seen just as in itself but is always directed and in relation to something or someone. Laing's primary apprehension is that the person cannot be reduced to a thing as the person is always choosing and deciding, which a thing doesn't.

I have emphasised in *The Schizoid World of Jean-Paul Sartre and R.D. Laing* (Kirsner 2003) how very much Laing focused on context and the problems of acting meaningfully within it. As inherently social beings, we are always insignificant relationships with others. Social phenomenology is an application of phenomenology that provides better and more detailed understanding of social relationships.

Laing's approach to schizophrenia should be viewed in terms of his focus on the importance of looking at the invalidation of the person's inner world. For Laing, at least in *The Politics of Experience*, violence has been so successful in seeming to take this realm from the rest of us that schizophrenia can be seen as a last-ditch chance we have of encountering this lost world. Whether any transcendental experience is mad or mystical, it testifies to the importance of inner experience which has been devastated by the outer but which is so essential to a sane, whole way of living.

Freud thought that slips of the tongue and other marginalia of the psychopathology of everyday life could provide us with important discoveries about the nature of the human mind. I think that for Laing schizophrenia plays a similar role in providing a way into understanding the lost world of human experience. I think one of the reasons that Laing so often felt he had been misunderstood is that his project was larger than understanding schizophrenia. It is as though Freud were saddled with his major achievement as the discovery of Freudian slips – Freudian slips were a way-station and not any kind of end-point. I think Laing's end-point is the role of the loss of the world of valid experience as the problem of our age. This has consequences for our view of the world beyond mental 'normality', such as the place of science and how alienated medicine becomes when we think that it is an achievement for a woman to be able to read a newspaper while she has a baby. Issues about the central denial and violation of the realm of experience in the modern world persisted for Laing until the end of his life. These included his interest in Francis Mott's ideas about pre-birth experience, the importance of the voice of experience and its relation to the scientific 'look', the asylum communities in London, what we do to ourselves and others in order to not see what we experience, and lies and deceit in love. Scientific objective rationality systematically contributes to the destruction and invalidation of the primacy of experience as specifically human. In his social phenomenology Laing illuminates a specific type of *sensibility* to experience, a natural way of being alive to oneself and others which has been lost.

Laing was especially influenced by Sartre's later social theory about the constitution and impact of social groups upon the individual. *The Divided Self*, completed in 1956 before Sartre published *The Problem of Method* and *The Critique of Dialectical Reason* was, among other things, clearly an application of Sartre's early theory of self deception to the schizophrenic. *The Self and Others* concerned the self in relation to the other where

Laing moved from a focus on meaning expressed in the intrapsychic life of the individual to the context of the interpersonal space of two persons. It was also strongly influenced by Sartre's early work. *Sanity, Madness and the Family* and other works around the family were based on later Sartre works, especially his *Critique of the Dialectical Reason* with its emphasis on the impossible dialectic of individual and group where the individual freedom is an inevitable casualty. In these works Laing located mental illness within the group or family context. Laing was interested in how the family constellation provided the context in which the individual schizophrenic experienced could be understood as a rational strategy.

The Politics of Experience explores this problem further in the social context whereby Laing saw the individual as almost inevitably at the mercy of society. For Laing this group context existed within a society which was part of the context of the Total Social World System which is in turn part of the cosmos. In *The Politics of Experience* Laing understood the Total Social World System as providing the social context in which schizophrenia was an understandable reaction. In *Knots* and also in parts of *The Politics of Experience* Laing thought that mystical experience might explain seemingly irrational experience and behaviour in term of the biggest meta-context of all. Mysticism was the limit of contextualizing and while Laing went to Ceylon to meditate, Sartre was too much a rationalist to make Laing's next move that situated the social world within the mystical.

However, the methodology of investigating particular 'situations', as Sartre described them, illustrates Laing's basic approach and abiding project because, like Sartre, Laing appreciated individuals in their singularity at the same time as they represented something more general. Contexts for Sartre and Laing were the conditions of human action that affected the way we understand the field we act in. In so far as the context provided the parameters within which we could choose our action, we are all in Sartre's term, 'universal singulars', individuals who could be cross-referenced with their time.

Laing focused on many issues throughout his career: schizophrenia, birth and pre-birth experience, family dynamics, the impact of the modern world of science and technology, social institutions, politics, the impact of psychiatry, patients' rights, the vagaries of love, and many more. But one vital link permeated them all, one which originated with what is central to Sartre — *the distinction between two realms, the human and the nonhuman, and the consequences of treating human beings as though they were objects or things.* Like Sartre who began with the radical ontological division of the world into human and nonhuman, 'being for-itself' and 'being-in-itself'', existence and essence, free and unfree, Laing took as his starting-point that no matter how alienated they were, every human being was free and needed to be treated as a free agent. On this premise, it is inappropriate to talk about human beings in 'thing' language, and language about things or processes is never appropriate for ultimately understanding human beings. It is as though this was Laing's 'global project', as Sartre might have put it.

Different consequences accrue from whether we initially see someone as a person or as an object. As the observer is always part of the observational field, how we treat someone impacts on how they react and how they are then viewed. Since for Sartre consciousness was never an independent faculty but always consciousness of something — our stance determined what we saw. This phenomenology of ways of seeing is clear in Laing from the beginning. As Laing put it in *The Divided Self*, 'The initial way we see a thing gives rise to all our subsequent dealings with it' (Laing, 1965, p. 20).

Laing carried the implications of our invariably starting from a point of view much further in his later work, making the concept of 'the normal' itself a focus of investigation and critique. It would be interesting to discover how much his critique of normality effected the post-modern turn where taken-for-granted assumptions about the positions we occupy are challenged. The idea of the identity of the author or agent was under question as was authority and expertise as such during the sixties and seventies. The concept of normality goes right into the centre of social harmony and structure since a norms reflect how most people think and behave. The possibility that sanity is different from normality or even that the mad might be sane opened up fundamental questioning and brought a different yardstick to bear in questioning the intrinsic goodness and rightness of the society. Laing's challenge to normality might have been epistemological, but it was taken on politically by a generation and Laing did nothing to disabuse them of the difference.

When Laing visited the back wards during his medical training in Glasgow, he simply could hear and understand what the schizophrenics were saying. He just had an uncanny ability to be able to hear the communications. As a highly intelligent person, he was able to play with concepts and challenge the ones he used. But I think his therapeutic intelligence went beyond the ability to listen and empathise with others like him or quite different from him. He was comfortable with constantly challenging our mindsets and was able to live with not knowing. This is the attitude of scepticism that came with his fellow Scot, David Hume as well as the Greeks. Dichotomies, such as 'inside-outside', 'mind-body', 'self-other', 'society-individual', 'mad-normal', were, as he constantly put it, 'up for grabs'. Philosophy, especially existential philosophy and phenomenology, suffused his work with the clinical data gleaned from his work as a psychiatrist and psychoanalyst as concrete material to further explore the humanity or lack of it in the human world. However, even beyond psychological comfort and attitude is the capability to conceptualise. Laing's uncommon intelligence meant that he was able to think in a complex way. (Masud Khan told me in 1976 that Laing was the most brilliant in his generation of psychoanalysts). He did not use stereotyped, template thinking but thought counterfactually [if x, then y, if not x then z, etc.], using parallel process thinking as described by Elliot Jaques (Jaques and Cason 1994).

A good way of highlighting the philosophical perspectives that Laing adopted is to examine some of the philosophy behind his two most best known and quite different worlds, *The Divided Self* (1960) and *The Politics of Experience* (1967). Separated by a decade, these two books encapsulate important aspects of his approach and influence and show deep contrasts as well as continuations.

1.   *The Divided Self*

The Divided Self (Laing 1960) was a study of schizoid and schizophrenic people; its basic purpose, Laing claimed, was 'to make madness, and the process of going mad, comprehensible'. Laing was also trying to give an existential account of some forms of madness. But Laing was not attempting to present a comprehensive theory of schizophrenia nor to explore constitutional and organic aspects (p. 9).

The publication of *The Divided Self* in 1960 was an important moment in the history of psychiatry. Laing's book was a pioneer in systematically trying to be where the psychotic patient was 'at'. During the 1950s when Laing was working in back wards and later at the Tavistock Clinic, many psychiatrists accepted that the speech of neurosis and not psychosis was intelligible. Freud had insisted that neurosis was intelligible, that dreams, slips and symptoms were disguised expressions of human subjectivity which could be understood using free association. Laing did for the psychotic what Freud had done for the neurotic — Laing listened to psychotic patients and treated their speech and actions as potentially understandable and meaningful. Psychosis is, as Laing says in *The Divided Self*, the product of a disjunction: 'sanity of psychosis is tested by the degree of conjunction or disjunction between two persons where one is sane by common consent. The critical test of whether or not the patient is psychotic is a lack of congruity, an incongruity, a clash, between him and me' (p. 36). Psychosis always involves problems of communication; 'Schizophrenia', Laing told me in 1980, 'is the name a psychiatrist gives for somebody who can't understand' (Kirsner 1997), p. 50). Never having found difficulty in listening to schizophrenics Laing could not resonate with Bleuler's remark that when all was said and done schizophrenics were a stranger to him than the birds in his garden (p. 24). For Laing, such a lack of understanding of the world of the psychotic was not so much given as constructed. In *The Divided Self* the thoughts and actions of psychotics were understood to be expressions of human subjectivity, not simply emanations of psychobiological processes. Seen in context and from the point of view of the patient as agent, madness could be understood as resulting from choices within psychosocial and biological parameters.

We all make fundamental assumptions about the world that determine many of our beliefs and actions. One prevalent modern assumption is that despite our feelings to the contrary, we are in reality complex machines or even computers. Such an assumption has major consequences for our view of the nature of neurosis and madness and how they should be treated. The psychiatrist may collude with the schizophrenic in assuming that he or she is primarily a machine. For Laing, 'one's relationship to an organism is different from one's relationship to a person' (p. 21). But in Laing's view diagnosis is literally 'seeing through', both looking *at* the categories that we see through, and seeing *through* what appears so concrete — the standpoint we adopt conditions what we see, whether we attribute agency or mechanical processes to ourselves or patients. For Laing, attributions of autism, lack of affect and relationship applied at least as much to those doing the diagnosing as those diagnosed. In Laing's view the scientific objective 'look' stands opposed to empathic approach — one cannot move into an empathetic mode while retaining a view of the patient as an organism. 'To try to find understanding within that way of looking', Laing told me, 'is like trying to buy a camel in a donkey market'.

Laing emphasized the importance of the point of view of the observer who partly determined the observational field: 'the standard psychiatric patient is a function of the standard psychiatrist and the standard mental hospital' (p. 24). In his 1964 Preface to *The Divided Self*, he lamented that he had written 'too much about Them and not enough about Us' (p. 11). Much of his later work would rectify this flaw; he systematically concentrated on contexts and meta-contexts in his project to render mental illness more intelligible.

The Divided Self was a radical book when it appeared — it remains a remarkable one. It is still refreshing in its closeness to schizophrenic experience and in its attempts to find at least part of an explanation in terms of human agency. In a period in which the biological psychiatric standpoint has become dominant, *The Divided Self* remains a powerful reminder of the advantages of a sensibility which adopts an existential, psychodynamic, philosophical point of departure that takes the full significance of human agency into account instead of denying it.

The Divided Self was the first major work in existential psychoanalysis to make a mark on the English-speaking world. The existentialist collection, *Existence* (May et al 1958), with its complex Heideggerian focus, appeared just two years earlier but its influence did not extend beyond a limited umber of psychotherapists and academics. In contrast *The Divided Self* became popular, resonating with a far wider audience. Undoubtedly *The Divided Self* is indebted to the object relations theories especially of D. W. Winnicott. Laing's discussions of the 'true self' and 'false self systems' (not one but a number of false selves' owed much to object relations theory, particularly D.W. Winnicott with whom Laing worked. Laing sent his manuscript to Winnicott 'I've written a study (c. 80,000 words) on schizoid and schizophrenic states, in particular trying to describe the transition from a sane to a mad way of being in the world. It draws its inspiration very largely from your writings'. Winnicott was so enthusiastic that he read it in two hours (Rodman 2003, p. 243). According to Laing, the schizophrenic's vulnerable true self does not feel it is participating in the activities of the false self systems which mask it (p. 74). Although such an object relations view is, I believe, quite incompatible with Sartre's view which assumes there to be no human nature or essential self with any characteristics except the inevitability of agency and choice, Laing's false self systems or personas can be understood as cases of Sartrean self-deception. In fact, Laing highlighted the importance of understanding truth, deception and mystification in the world of the schizophrenic. Listening as a way of reaching the patient's truth was as important for Laing as it was for Freud.

As I have said, Laing's position owed much to the philosophy of Jean-Paul Sartre. Sartre had become well-known at the time in Anglophone countries largely through his plays and novels as well as though his role as a public intellectual. Sartre's basic tenet was the ineluctable freedom and agency of all human beings. The world, for Sartre, was divided into 'being-for-itself' (the non-human world). Human beings are characterized by freedom and agency no matter how much we attempt to escape this situation — our being is always in question and, while we are alive, we are never identical with what we have been or done. The non-human world is that of identity, it belongs to things and processes which do not have transcendent goals, Sartre coined the term '*mauvaise foi*' ('self-deception') for our efforts to escape our responsibility as free agents by treating ourselves or others as things. Given freedom as the point of departure, for Sartre, 'mental illness' can be seen as a way out — perhaps, as Laing was to put it, an attempt to live in an otherwise unliveable situation: No matter how alienated they may be, patients, like all other humans, always exercise some degree of choice. The task of existential psychoanalysis is to explore how patients' original and subsequent choices contribute to their present predicaments and self-deceptions (Sartre 1943).

The Divided Self was Sartre's existentialism blended with psychoanalytic object relations theory without the unconscious. Like Sartre, Laing rejects the Freudian concept of 'the unconscious; it is only mentioned in *The Divided Self* to disagree with the application of the concept to the patient's basic existential position of wanting to achieve 'ontological security'(pp. 56-7). Nevertheless, Laing like Sartre respected Freud's inspiration — Freud was 'the greatest psychopathologist', a 'hero' who 'descended to the "Underworld" and met there stark terrors. He carried with him his theory as a Medusa's head which turned these terrors to stone'. For Laing the confrontation with the 'terrors' had distorted and ossified the psychoanalytic vision (p. 25).

Laing was profoundly interested in investigating the patients' experiences of interpersonal relationships, familial, social and psychologist situations. In a real sense, his work tried to be a living phenomenology. The households or asylum communities he was responsible for setting up in London from the late 1960s onwards took primacy of experience of the often psychotic residents as their basic ground. By having their experience taken seriously instead of being invalidated, the patients felt heard. Often for the first time. These therapeutic communities were homes or dwellings in which the normal social stigmas and censures did not prevent patients exploring their own personal and interpersonal worlds (Kirsner 1976).

Laing's crucial philosophical concepts of 'ontological security' and 'ontological insecurity' are about our 'at-homeness` in the world we owe much to Martin Heidegger. For Laing, the ontologically secure person feels his or her life as 'real, alive, whole; as differentiated from the rest of the world in ordinary question' (p. 41). This is not the case for the ontologically insecure person who in ordinary circumstances 'may feel more unreal than real; in a literal sense, more dead than alive; precariously differentiated from the rest of the world, so that his identity and autonomy are always in question' (p. 42).

It is striking how much *The Divided Self* adopts and develops Sartre's existentialist positions, particularly Sartre's concept of self-deception. *The Divided Self* is structured around ideas such as anxiety, implosion, petrification, engulfment, ontological security, reality, dread, being at home, alienation, agency and responsibility. These existential concepts focus on the vagaries of the relationship of freedom and the self and form part of a phenomenology of mental illness in which interaction between self and others affect the very constitution and experience of the 'self' and 'reality'. More importantly, the psychotic is understood in terms of attempts to solve existential problems through the use of the person's ineluctable freedom and subjectivity. In this Laing is a firm follower of Sartre. The hysteric's disassociations are for Laing best described as Sartre's concept of 'self-deception'. Laing sees much of schizophrenia as simply nonsense, red-herring speech, prolonged filibustering to throw dangerous people off the scent, to create boredom and futility in others. The schizophrenic is often making a fool of himself and the doctor. He is playing at being mad to avoid at all costs the possibility of being held responsible for a single coherent idea, or intention (p. 164).

Even in this early work Laing takes note of the family's role in the occurrence of schizophrenia. The mother and the family may 'impede rather that facilitate the child's capacity to participate in a real shared world, as self with other'. For Laing 'schizophrenia is a possible outcome of a more than usual difficulty in being whole person with the other, and with not sharing the common-sense (i.e. the community sense) way of experiencing oneself in the world' (p. 189). The development of this approach involving the role of the social context in which schizophrenia takes place forms the axis of Laing's concerns throughout his career about schizophrenia.

Laing's explanations for the phenomenology may be questioned but his sensitive and rich descriptions of schizophrenics' experiences reveal how much of schizophrenic behaviour consists of strategies to live in what schizophrenics feel to be an unlivable world; these behaviours are ways out which take the less unattractive and threatening horn of a dilemma. Laing asserts that even the schizoid state 'can be an attempt to preserve a being that precariously structured' (p. 77). In other words, it is the result of an active choice within certain parameters.

The intelligibility of social events must be seen in the contexts of time and space, an explanation of what seems to present itself must not be taken for granted. One of Laing's most important gifts was the ability to suspend judgment and listen to what was in front of him. *The Divided Self* is a sceptical book which does not so much provide answers as stimulate more questions and challenges. Almost every page of this, still very stimulating and lively, book challenges us to rethink our conceptions in the direction of reaffirming that both doctors and patients are first and foremost human agents.

However, Laing almost certainly overrated the magnitude of the patient's choices in schizophrenia — by challenging the role of unconscious factors as well as organic ones, he was left with little alternative. But he had tried to redress the balance a little in favour of the schizophrenic not being merely the victim of an organic process. Laing's later ideas which developed the role of the family and society caused much further debate — many clinicians now see psychosis as the result of psychological factors together with biological ones.

2. *The Politics of Experience*

Although published in 1967 *The Politics of Experience* represents the development of Laing's views between 1962 and 1967. Here, Laing focuses on the centrality of the concept of experience, evidenced by the chapter titles: 'Persons and Experience', 'The Psychotherapeutic Experience', 'The Mystification of Experience', 'Schizophrenic Experience', Transcendental Experience,' as well as the end part which dealt with a ten day experimental voyage. For Laing our data are first of all experimental. As I noted above, Laing was influenced by David Hume. For Hume, the archetypal empiricist, all we can know is the experience which provides our starting point. Like Hume, Laing was a profound sceptic, fundamentally questioning established ways of thinking, moving from physical and interpersonal 'reality' to interpersonal space as the given ground of experience.

The Politics of Experience is a mixed bag. From a contemporary perspective, it stands out as part of the climate of sixties opinion and a dramatic clarion call to that generation. The introduction describes our setting in the very New Left terms of our time:

> There is little conjunction of the truth and social 'reality'. Around us are pseudo-events, to which we adjust with a false consciousness adapted to see these events as true and real, and even as beautiful. In the society of men the truth resides now less in what things are than in what they are not. Our social realities are so ugly if seen in the light of exiled truth, and beauty is almost no longer possible if it is not a lie. We are still half-alive, living in the often filibrating heartland of a senescent capitalism (p. 11).

In this setting it is 'the requirement of the present' to 'provide a thoroughly self-conscious and self-critical human account of man'. But while our starting point is always our 'alienation', for Laing, 'we are all murderers and prostitutes,' Humanity was estranged from its authentic possibilities. Fiery and relevant language 35 years ago when it became the hallmark of a generation, but we may ask now, if not then, what exactly does all this mean? Does it make much sense? Laing had constantly protested that he had been misinterpreted, which he probably often was, but the introduction to *The Politics of Experience* certainly gives credibility to some of the views of Laing as a counter cultural, new left political radical who added personal and transcendental experience to a location within social and political categories. Our alienation which, for Laing, goes to the roots, forms the foundation of any investigation of the sanity of common sense or the madmen. As 'crazed and bemused creatures' we can barely glimpse our true selves and are strangers to each other.

In *The Politics of Experience* Laing closely linked the idea of the false self or mask with the new left and Marxist 'false consciousness' of the social totality. Combining Marxism and existentialism Laing maintained that our alienation was the social product of the violence of human beings upon one another.

Although it struck a chord with so many at the time, such rhetoric gives Laing a lot to answer for. It was framed in the excessive language of the time, making generalizations about whole cultures by placing all-encompassing, collective abstract nouns as the subjects of very emotive sentences. *The Politics of Experience* is at bottom a work of rhetoric, enjoining us to question our categories — but exactly who are 'us' and who are 'them'? The world seems to be simplistically divided into good and bad. Especially on a rereading the rhetorical power of *The*

Politics of Experience is striking. In contradistinction to *The Divided Self* and *Self and Others*, much of *The Politics of Experience* is really quite extreme. The tone is oracular, prophetic, and full of hyperbole. These are strings of emotional assertion upon generalization upon assertion which struck the mood of the times among 'us', if not among 'them'.

Laing begins the section 'Persons and Experience' with the assumption that we experience only each other's behaviour and that the task of social phenomenology is to relate my experience of the other's behaviour with the other's experience of my behaviour as inter-experience (p. 15). Once the divide is made between experience and behaviour, it becomes clear that experience must be an intrinsically private event. This is very much an assumption — people can be very unempathic, empathy can certainly be abused, but is empathy intrinsically impossible? Are we so different from each other? We should remember that Laing follows Sartre in claiming that violence dictates so many interpersonal experiences and that attributions of sanity and madness are used in promoting this agenda. Although this is more akin to rave than argument, I think Laing's point is that we should not *presume* that we know what the other person is experiencing, certainly not without asking him or her, that we should not equate real categories of sanity and madness with the way people behave socially. Laing wants us to adopt an individual sensibility, it is an approach toward another person that brackets out assumed knowledge of them. Yet it should be borne in mind that the radical subjectivity assumed in the experience-behaviour dichotomy makes community impossible except by contract. Throughout *The Politics of Experience* the major thrust is existentialist rather than Marxist. In fact, Laing told me that by the time he was writing *The Politics of Experience*, he was in no way an ideological Marxist. 'For me, academically, I had never studied Marx enough to entitle myself in my own view to call myself a serious 'in' professional Marxist. I have read most of the major things of Marx, I didn't make a further special study of him because I didn't feel it was worth my while — I couldn't reconcile the tremendous building up of a picture with a serious study of the facts. I was never a Marxist' (Kirsner 1997, p. 44).

For Laing, 'experience is the *only* evidence'. While our experiences of each other are not 'inside' our physical bodies, nonetheless our experiences are invisible to each other. While I do not experience, I do experience you as experiencing, and infer from my experience of your experience of my experiences, etc. The science of social phenomenology is distinct from a natural scientific approach where a science is a form of knowledge adequate to its subject. Laing maintains that the distinction between 'inner' and 'outer' makes assumptions that stand in the way of our making sense of the data of inter-experience.

Laing defines a 'person': 'in terms of experience, as a centre of orientation of the objective universe; and in terms of behaviour, as the origin of actions. Personal experience transforms a given field into a field of intention and action' (p.20). Often fields of intention and action are treated as objectives by natural scientific approaches, the objective becomes subjective through our involvement. We often attempt to escape from personhood, once again, although Laing does not say so, we have Sartre's *mauvaise foi* where we treat ourselves and others as though we or they were things, as though we were not responsible for our actions.

Laing claims that Freud's major contribution was his '*demonstration* that the *ordinary* person is a shriveled, desiccated fragment of what a person can be' (p. 22). We have forgotten our dreams, our fantasies, deny the inner world — all of which represents a devastation of our experience, based on the divorce of experience from behaviour (p. 23). I cannot imagine that Freud would have agreed — Freud's view was tragic, not romantic. For Freud civilization was inherently flawed in its Mephistophelian pact that exchanged happiness for a degree of security and sublimation for love, all under the influence of the death drive. Even early on Freud thought that the aim of analysis was 'to transform hysterical misery into common unhappiness' and later argued with Einstein about whether human aggression was innate and was not socially produced. The Id was not the repository for what was truly good and the soft voice of reason was significant in keeping the irrational from total domination.

But for Laing, so-called 'normality', is the product of repression, denial ' etc. which are destructive to our experience, estranging us from the structure of being (pp. 23-24). 'The condition of alienation, of being asleep, of being unconscious, of being out of one's mind, is the condition of the normal man'

(p. 24). Now, since 'normal men have killed perhaps 100,000,000 of their fellow normal men in the past fifty years', the relation between normality and violence demands investigation and the relation between sanity, madness and normality. Since our behaviour is a function of our experience, if our experience is destroyed, our behaviour will be destructive (p. 24). But all is not lost. Disagreeing with Herbert Marcuse, Laing says, somewhat sentimentally, that every time a new baby is born, there is hope. Again, we find the Sartrean ineluctability of freedom thesis and an emphasis on seeing through deceptions.

According to Laing, the only way we can act is on our own or on the other's experience. In so doing I can confirm or encourage or deny or discourage my or his or her experience (p. 29). We can dissociate ourselves from our own actions by using defence mechanisms which can devastate the person's experience. Importantly, another can invalidate my experience by saying it is unimportant, can change its modality from memory to imagination and invalidate its content. This Laing does by borrowing Marx's concept of 'mystification' without attribution (p. 31).

But, explicitly following Sartre, Laing writes of the centrality of negation, of the injection of non-being into the world breaking the plenitude of being. And if we strip away the social 'things' and reveal who we 'really' are, Laing avers there is no-thing between us. Again, this is high rhetoric — there is a romantic vision of the real self or nothingness below, after the diagnosis of mystification has revealed how ordinary social life is so extraordinarily oppressive. In *The Politics of Experience* Laing himself invalidates and deprecates ordinary experience as was the norm in the 'Little Boxes' era. During the early 1970s after his return from Ceylon, he began to move away from such extremes. But for the Laing of *The Politics of Experience* the creative person was in touch with his or her nonbeing and to that extent estranged from the pseudo-wants, pseudo-values and pseudo-realities of the epidemic delusion of life or death and give us 'the acts of creation that we despise and crave' (p. 37). Our fundamental nonbeing is the creative source which must be recognized and tapped. According to Laing, I am disjoined from my behaviour, my behaviour and experience are disjoined from others' behaviour and experience. But this is the beginning point of the schizoid experience — I am never a whole person, my body and mind are quite separate even if somehow related.

'The Psychotherapeutic Experience' again contains a romantic vision of an unalienated situation. Psychotherapy involves 'the paring away of all that stands between us, the props, masks, roles, defences, anxieties, projections, introjections, in short, all the carry-overs from the past... that we use wittingly or unwittingly as our currency of relationships. It is this currency, these very media, that re-create and intensify the conditions of alienation that originally occasioned them', (p. 39).

The aim then of therapy is to eliminate that which stands in the way of fully meeting each other. What we need, according to Laing, are concepts that will enable us to understand the relationship between our experience and behaviour in the context of the relationship between therapist and patient. A critical theory must be able to place all theories and practices within the ontological context of being human. Laing emphasizes the central importance of persons in understanding the relation between experience and behaviour.

Laing believes that the mystification of experience is ubiquitous in the contemporary world, at least of *The Politics of Experience*. Normality is achieved when by the age of fifteen a human being is a 'half crazed creature, more or less adjusted to a mad world'. This 'mad world' is characterised by the reign of violence masquerading as love, where violence constrains freedom with a lack of concern. The devastation of experience takes place through violence by the world and by ourselves on ourselves (p. 50-1). In fact 'only by the most outrageous violation of ourselves have we achieved our capacity to live in relative adjustment to a civilization apparently driven to its own destruction' (p. 64).

In Laing's discussion of 'Us and Them' Sartre's later concepts in *The Critique of the Dialectical Reason* (1960) are importantly represented. It should be remembered that Laing and Cooper summarized Sartre's *Critique of Dialectical Reason* in *Reason and Violence* in 1964. There and here Laing discusses the inherently violent nature of groups, the relations between the individual and the group, and that of series and nexus in the family.

Given Laing's stance in terms of violence and groups, it is no great step to attempt to locate and understand the role of the major diagnosed mental illness, schizophrenia, as a function of social relationships. Laing uses labeling theory to understand diagnosis as an interpersonal event, to explore how roles develop in psychiatrist and patient, and particularly how the experience of the patient is invalidated. Gregory Bateson's 'double bind' theory (which explains the enjoining of contradictory behaviours on different levels) provides an alternative passway to understanding the confusional states in schizophrenia (pp. 88-98). Laing goes still further than this too. The schizophrenic may find himself or herself on a journey within the lost inner realm, a voyage which just might be part of a natural healing process. Perhaps, Laing suggests, we should accord the schizophrenic who has come back to us no less respect than returning explorers were in the Renaissance. Laing believes that future generations will view our present age as an age of darkness and that schizophrenia was a way that some ordinary people had of seeing the light break through (p. 107).

I think that Laing's approach to schizophrenia should be viewed in terms of his focus on the importance of looking at the invalidation and loss of a whole realm of experience of the inner world. For Laing, violence has been so successful in seeming to take this realm from the rest of us that schizophrenia can be seen as a last-ditch way we have of encountering this lost world. Whether any transcendental experience is mad or mystical, it is testament to the importance of inner experience which has been devastated by the outer but which is so essential to a sane, whole way of living.

The Politics of Experience was excessive, romantic, rhetorical, oracular, and very much a sixties book. However, its sensibility and preoccupations with the value and validation of experience in its social context put *The Politics of Experience* right at the heart of Laing's project, making it a fascinating continuation of *The Divided Self*, as well as a work that can help to make *The Divided Self* more intelligible in broader terms. Clearly, the tone of these works is quite different. The first was the product of the mid-fifties, the second of a radically different time a decade later. *The Politics of Experience* has many faults, but some serious and important ideas which develop earlier themes can be found among the rhetoric. Although *The Politics of Experience* was his most well-known work, that book was not typical of his approach either before or after the mid to late 1960s.

I believe that throughout his career Laing covered the range philosophical problems described by Kant. He applied them in particular to his chosen field of investigation, the exploration of the interconnections between human nature, experience, relationships, mental illness and society. The interrogatory nature of his endeavours, which asked us to question fundamental assumptions in our attitudes, is a significant contribution to our ways of seeing and knowing.

references

Jaques, E and Cason, K. (1994). *Human capability: A study of individual potential and its application*, Cason Hall, Falls Creek VA.

Kirsner, D. (1976). 'The Primacy of Experience', *Meaning Quarterly*, XXV, 3: 300-6.

Kirsner, D. (1990). 'Across an abyss: Laing, Jaspers and Sartre'. *Journal of the British Society for Phenomenology*, 21, 3, October, 1990: 209-216.

Kirsner, D. (1997). 'Douglas Kirsner'. Contribution to Bob Mullan (ed.), *R.D. Laing: Creative Destroyer*. Cassell, London, pp. 30-51.

Kirsner, D. (2004). *The Schizoid World of Jean-Paul Sartre and R.D. Laing*, Other Press, New York. Original publication 1977.

Laing, R.D. (1967). 'The Obvious'. In D. Cooper (ed.), *The Dialectics of Liberation*, Penguin, Harmondsworth, pp. 13-33.

Laing, R.D. (1960). *The Divided Self*. Tavistock, London. Pelican ed. 1965.

Laing, R.D. (1967). *The Politics of Experience and the Bird of Paradise*. Penguin, Harmondsworth.

May, R, Angel, E. and Ellenberger, H. (eds.) (1958). *Existence*. Basic Books, New York.

Rodman, F.R. (2003). *Winnicott: Life and work*. Perseus, Cambridge MA.

Sartre J-P. (1943). *Being and Nothingness*. tr. H. E. Barnes. New York: Washington Square Press, 1966.

8: Normality and the Numinous: The Gnostic Thread in R.D. Laing

Daniel Burston

Normality and the Numinous: The Gnostic Thread in R.D. Laing

Daniel Burston

Unlike the majority of mental health professionals, Laing did not equate statistical normality with mental health, or make a fetish of "adaptation". On the contrary, he thought that adjustment to prevailing social realities entailed a progressive attenuation of 1) "the holy" as a category of normal human experience, 2) our capacity to think critically about our social surround and 3) an increase in the scope and scale of (individual and collective) violence. In formulating his critique of normality, Laing drew extensively on Jung and Heidegger. (Resemblances to Lacan are also noted).

Using the Diagnostic and Statistical Manual of Mental Disorders, recent studies suggest that 30% of the general (adult) population will suffer from severe mental illness this year, while another 60% are expected to suffer symptoms of mild to moderate severity at some time in their lives. The difference is clear. Less than 15% of the adult population is expected to enjoy continuous, uninterrupted and vibrant mental health during their lifetime. In a field where normality is defined by the absence of the symptoms, this can only mean one thing: normality isn't normal anymore — if indeed, it ever was.

Despite the intriguing oddity of this situation, the fact remains that defining mental health as the absence of symptoms is quite convenient for a discipline that seeks to normalize behaviour without reflecting too deeply on the nature of its commitment. But what if normality and mental health are not synonymous, as prevailing usage implies? That is the view that Laing espoused. Laing's thoughts on the matter unfolded in several stages. In *The Divided Self* for example, he noted that the "normal" individual enjoys a stable sense of identity and of personal autonomy that emanate from a state of primary ontological security. And like the majority of his colleagues, at this point, he tended to equate normality with sanity or mental health.

However, in *Self and Others*, Laing abruptly changed his tune, and defined normality as a state of unconscious complicity in "social phantasy systems" — an argument related with considerable vehemence in *The Politics of Experience*. As Laing depicted it, the alienated pseudo-sanity of the normal person fosters a progressive attenuation of their critical faculties and their openness to transcendental experience. Instead of stressing the advantages of normality as he did in *The Divided Self*, Laing now reversed his initial emphasis completely. What is lost to normals, said Laing, are not merely instincts, or the memory of specific events or losses, but whole modalities and possibilities of experience that are proscribed by society at large as irrational, excessive, infantile and so on. The awareness of the tragic, the sublime, the absurd, of the prevalence and persistence of evil, of the peace that passeth understanding – these innately human sensibilities are severely stunted, if not entirely extinguished in the struggle to adapt.

True sanity, said Laing, involves the dissolution of the adjusted ego in a process which, following Jung, he termed "metanoia". The transcendence of the ego can be sought deliberately through mediation and spiritual practices, or it can occur spontaneously. The mad person, said Laing, has been catapulted into this process unawares, and without skillful guidance, will go astray. So the therapist becomes a spiritual midwife or a shaman of sorts, while his patient becomes a "hierophant of the sacred".

Re-reading *The Politics of Experience*, it is interesting to note how often and how earnestly Laing disparaged normality with religious tropes and metaphors. In chapter three, for example, he says (p. 68): "We are all fallen Sons of Prophecy, who have learned to die in the Spirit and be reborn in the Flesh". And again, in chapter six:

> "There is a prophecy in Amos that a time will come when there will be a famine in the land, 'not a famine for bread, nor a thirst for water, but of hearing the words of the Lord'. That time has now come to pass. It is the present age (p. 144)."

Without stating so in quite so many words passages like the preceding, atrophy of the numerous as a feature of normal experience is linked with the problem of violence. In chapter one, Laing noted that normal men had killed approximately 100 million of their own kind in the preceding fifty years — a figure that has doubled since then. Nevertheless, said Laing, the escalating scale and widening scope of violence is not the result of innate propensities to violence and indiscipline — a "death instinct", as Freud thought — but of our efforts to adapt to an irrational world bereft of transcendence. Laing therefore implied that there is a strong correlation between the progressive secularization of society and the efflorescence of evil in our time.

Many took offence at Laing's religious imagery, and said that his prophetic airs ill suited a man of science. But, in fairness to Laing, he did not actually claim that the increasing secularization causes violence. That would have put him in the same company as Joseph de Maistre, and in opposition to the whole Enlightenment tradition that welcomed secularization as a necessary prelude to general human emancipation. Though wary of Enlightenment rationalism, like all existentialists, that was just not his style.

No, Laing's approach to transcendental experience was more complicated. Laing argued, in effect, that the violence we do to ourselves in the process of normalization is reflected, *among other things*, in the decline of the numinous as a dimension of normal human experience. Much as he lamented the loss of the numinous, however, Laing was not advocating a return to a repressive, theocratic society, or advocating the revival of religious creeds based on particular forms of belief. In fact, like Jung, Laing contrasted religious experience with religious belief, and disparaged the latter as a poor substitute for the former. As he said in chapter six of *The Politics of Experience*: "Having lost our experience of the spirit, we are expected to have faith" (p. 144).

Though seldom mentioned, the parallels to Jung in *The Politics of Experience* are extensive. Jung also distinguished between a creed (or faith), or a system of belief which draws its authority from consensus and tradition, and the self-authorizing, self-validating transcendental experience that presumably gives rise to religious symbols. The main difference, between Jung and Laing is that Jung's Gnostic affinities were overtly and articulately expressed, while Laing's were merely hinted at. Nevertheless, the Gnostic thread in Laing is ubiquitous. It is apparent in a footnote of chapter four of *The Divided Self*, where Laing notes the resemblance between the schizoid patient's pursuit of disembodied selfhood and the Gnostic's disincarnate spirituality. It is apparent in *Self and Others*, when Laing invokes the old Gnostic imagery to describe the common run of humanity: that we are dead, but think we are alive; asleep, but think we are awake; mad, but have no insight, etc (Laing, 1961, p. 38). *The Bird of Paradise* opens with a quote from the Gnostic *Gospel of Thomas*, and Laing's intense preoccupation with the Gnostic ideas of *Pleroma* and *Creastura* (circa 1968) figured strongly in Jung's life as early as 1916.

Laing's critique of normality also leaned on another modern Gnostic, namely Martin Heidegger. Heidegger was not preoccupied with the psychology of religion, but like Hegel and Marx, was preoccupied with the problem of alienation. Alienation, in the first instance, connotes a state of a process whereby one becomes estranged from one's original condition, hopefully as a prelude to a subsequent return of recovery of it. For example, in Heraclitus, the Stoics and in neo-Platonism, one is alienated from the Absolute until death, when the divine spark entrapped in our mundane body returns to the One, the World Soul of Primal Fire. And in Christian theology, alienation from God through the Fall (original sin), is remedied by repentance, faith and — for some believers — good works; works which promote reconciliation with the Deity.

Ancient concepts of alienation were invariably cast in religious or cosmological terms, and seeped onto our collective consciousness through neo-Platonism and negative theology. Hegel was deeply versed in these traditions, but gave alienation a new and more specific meaning. Hegel construed history as a process wherein God — or Absolute Spirit — loses and recovers itself, using successive phases of human civilization as way-stations on the path to self-knowledge. And if history is the process, humanity is the vehicle, whose various faiths and philosophies represent successive stages in the evolving self-consciousness of the Deity.

By the contrast with Hegel, who retained a religious dimension in his concept of alienation, Marx secularized it completely. But despite his critique of Hegel's religiosity, Marx also saw history as a (more of less) cumulative, unilinear progression in which alienation would ultimately be transcended – not merely in the consciousness, but practically, in a society free of exploitation and oppression.

In dramatic contrast with Hegel and Marx, Heidegger did not conceive of human history as a cumulative, unified and linear process resulting in Absolute Knowledge or in general human emancipation. Heidegger's concept of alienation was articulated in terms of Dasein or the "public world". When Dasein, or the distinctively human way of "being-in-the-world" shuts out the "noise" of the world, it experiences a state of *unheimlichkeit* or the uncanny, in which it is finally free to experience its own inner nature. As Heidegger says: "In uncanniness, Dasein stands together with itself primordially".

Heidegger's notion of alienation is profoundly counter-intuitive to most people. When you or I talk of feeling "alienated" from someone of something, we usually mean that we feel distinctly ill at ease in their presence, or deeply at variance with their way of being. But when estrangement from others crops up in *Being and Time*, Heidegger puts a positive spin on it, because he regarded alienation from the public world as a prelude to authentic self-recovery. By his reckoning, being "at home" or comfortable in the public world is a symptom of the numbing of our authentic inner voice, as he insisted in his reflection of conscience. Thus, he said,

"In conscience, *Dasein* calls itself" (p.320)...

And again

"The caller is unfamiliar to the everyday *they* self; it is something like an alien voice. What could be more alien to the 'they', lost in the manifold world of its concern, than the Self which has been individualized down to itself in uncanniness" (pp.321- 322).

Or again:

"The call of conscience...makes known...what we have hitherto merely contended: that uncanniness pursues Dasein and is a threat to the lostness in which it has forgotten itself" (p.322).

To restate this idea in ordinary English, the fact that conscience emerges as an "alien voice" is a symptom of our self-alienation. Moreover, alienation from the public world heralds growing self-awareness, and in the absence of the requisite estrangement from others, genuine self-knowledge cannot be achieved. That being so, the recovery and/or preservation of authenticity is never a fait accompli, but an ongoing project for the resolute individual. No radical reform or social transformation can alter the self and its dispersal in (and recovery from) "the they". This is the critical divergence from Marx.

In 1954, Hans Jonas called attention to the Gnostic tropes in *Being and Time*. The theme of an alien voice recalling the individual from his lostness or dispersal in the collective false-consciousness is one. And so indeed are the suggestions that the sense of dread, of the uncanny, are a prelude to, or corollary of, the soul's discovery of its basic situation, and that the general run of humanity tries to avoid or evade an authentic self-awareness by immersion in the *lethe* or oblivion of the crowd. Finally, there is the antinomian thread in Heidegger's discussion of conscience, where he opposes the authentic conscience of the individual with his inauthentic (public) conscience (Jonas, 1963).

The first indication of Heidegger's influence on Laing is the discussion of existential guilt in *The Divided Self*, which follows Heidegger closely. Another indication is in *Self and Others*, where Laing cited Heidegger's concept of the truth as *aletheia*, or uncovering (Laing, 1961,p.129) from the book on *Parmenidies* (Heidegger,1982). Another indication of Heidegger's influence is in *The Politics of Experience*, chapter five, where Laing asked us to imagine a group of airplanes in flight where one pilot strays deliberately from the rest of the formation. In the eyes of the other pilots, this one is "abnormal" or "deviant" even if the formation as a whole is unwittingly off course. And he warned us not to assume that because a group are "in formation" that they are necessarily "on course". From the ontological standpoint, said Laing, the abnormal one's orientation may actually be more congruent with reality — or not, as the case may be. Using this Heideggerian metaphor, Laing was saying, in effect, that statistical normality and genuine sanity may or may not coincide, and that there is no compelling reason to assume a priori that they do.

Finally, no discussion of Laing and Gnosticism would be complete without some mention of Jacques Lacan (Lacan, 1973; Schneiderman, 1984). I am not suggesting that Lacan *influenced*

Laing. But the resemblances are striking. The Gnostic thread in Lacan is evident in his characterization of the ego as a creature of "spectacular identification", an illusory and artificial construct embedded in "the discourse of the other", which is really a restatement of Heidegger, mediated through Kojeve. Rather than supporting and strengthening the ego, Lacan said the goal of analysis was to *deconstruct* it. This therapeutic objective echoes the Gnostic view that all but a handful *of cogniscenti* fundamentally misrecognize themselves and their condition. They imagine that they are free, that they know who they are, but their sense of identity is a chimera born of unconscious subjection.

Laing's hostility to ego-psychology bears resemblance to Lacan's. But, to his credit I think, Laing did not misattribute his antinomian spirit to Freud, then stake his identity and reputation on a muddled and exaggerated notion of fidelity to "the master". Like Sartre, Laing saw the ego as a largely illusory entity, but did not dismiss the existence of the self (Sartre, 1936). How could he? If you eliminate the self, you cannot explain human consciousness or human agency effectively, except as an artifact of non-personal processes or entries-in-relation, which is what structuralism and post-structuralist thought would attempt to do.

By curious coincidence, Sartre's distinction between the ego and the self converges with the ideas of Jung and Winnicott. Like Sartre, though for different reasons, they both distinguished between the ego and the self, and Laing found their formulations quite useful clinically. By their reckoning, the fact that the conscious ego is largely an illusory entity born of unconscious fear and vanity, and fashioned in the struggle for survival, does not nullify the existence of the self, though it does obstruct access to it much of the time.

Another factor influencing Laing's divergence from Lacan was his indebtedness to Martin Buber and John MacMurray. Laing was aware that the claim that consciousness and agency are not primary data, but artificial and illusory, is quite defensible on logical grounds. But, to paraphrase Laing, our experience is our psyche. The experience of consciousness and of personal agency is a self-validating, self-authenticating certainty that requires no support or sanction from the natural sciences. To invalidate our experience by trying to reduce or annul these elementary facts of life in deference to some higher authority is not science, but scientism. Laing's rejoinders to natural scientism apply with equal force to recent trends in the human sciences which invalidate the experience of consciousness, agency, selfhood and so on by treating them as the epiphenomenon of social structures and systems, rather than purely natural systems. So while Laing felt a much greater kinship with these theorists, as he frequently acknowledged, he refrained from joining them wholeheartedly.

Finally, despite his varied reputation as a militant atheist and electric mystic, the sad and simple truth is that Laing spent most of his adult life as a reluctant and often anguished agnostic who longed for the consolations of faith and a personal relationship with God.

In Laing's scheme of things, the ego is perfectly expendable, perhaps. But the terms self and salvation are correlative, so to reject selfhood would entail a symbolic foreclosure on this avenue of transcendence, and this Laing could (or would) not do.

To conclude, Laing's deep though unconventional religiosity attracted him to Jung and Heidegger, and rendered him unable to treat mental health and normality as synonyms, and to invert common-sense assumptions about normality to see where these transgressive thoughts would lead. Or as he remarked to Douglas Kirsner:

> "If we take the world's... spiritual teachers from the Buddha to the Judaeo-Christian tradition, to the Greek tradition and the Islamic tradition, it is said all over the place that most people by any rigorous standard are pretty daft... so I don't think I am saying anything unusual here".
> (Laing in Mullan, 1997, p.43)

9: Shamanism, Healing and R. D. Laing

Francis Huxley

Shamanism, Healing and R.D. Laing

Francis Huxley

Times do change. Fancy being asked to speak on the subject of shamanism, healing and R.D. Laing - of Laing, who was not a shaman but a psychiatrist, and here, under the auspices of what he took to be the House of Rimmon, the temple of anti-psychiatry, where he figured as the antipsychiatrist in person. I might not have so readily agreed had not Laing once told me that, when invited to meet the Pope, he refused because, he said, he'd never live it down if he did — but now that he'd missed the chance, he hardly knew how to live that down either.

I am a social anthropologist, and before I met Laing I had the chance to live with a Brazilian tribe and learn about shamans and cannibalism, amongst other things; to have worked in an overcrowded Canadian mental hospital; to have taken an ethnopsychiatric look at vaudoun in Haiti; to have been intimate with a Brazilian practitioner who, though he came out of a possession cult, was shamanising as a solo act, etcetera etcetera etcetera, as Laing was wont to say.

Such are my credentials for speaking as I do, as they were for Laing when he invited me to join the Philadelphia Association. They also give me reason to ask why shamanism should be relevant when speaking of Laing, sexy word though it is these days. For Laing was not a shaman. It wasn't his style — he didn't beat drums, shake rattles, brandish crystals, blow tobacco smoke on his clients and make a show of sucking out the nasties. He didn't invoke his guiding spirit with songs and then fall into epileptoid fits; nor did he eat burning coals, slit his belly open, ventriloquise, get into sorcery or divination. He prescribed no remedies, did no conjuring tricks, did not hurl magic darts on the sly.

Nor was he a possession priest of a cult such as vaudoun, candomblé, makumba, umbanda, or spiritismo These are Haitian and Brazilian forms of African possession cults, and their initiates go all the way from being conventionally normal to unconventionally abnormal, sometimes with a vengeance. I found much of interest in these cults, such as their method of diagnosing an illness in terms of their client's daimon, his native character, rather than in those typifying the disorder per se. They do this by discerning which, of a pantheon of loa, of gods and spirits, is the ruling spirit of their clients, and by initiating them into the mysteries of possession by that particular loa, manage to expel those others that have arbitrarily installed themselves in their clients' psychic economy and so take over the direction of their lives.

The effectiveness of this highly ritualised approach may be gauged by what happened when a Haitian troupe put on vaudoun ceremonies in France some forty years ago. Quite a few spectators were then possessed by the relevant loa of the ritual moment even though the audience was entirely unfamiliar with such goings-on. (Maya Deren, in *The Divine Horsemen*, reported a more complex experience of this kind that happened to herself.) A sociologist who had witnessed the affair discovered that those possessed had all been under some form of therapeutic treatment, and that after their possession they felt so much saner that, for a year, none of them had found cause to return to medical forms of relief.

But Laing was not a possession priest any more than he was a shaman. Could you call him a nabi? Nabi is the Hebrew word the Bible translates as prophet (which Laing certainly was, in his own way) — those who speak vehemently in God's name, calling for repentance, admonishing the ungodly, and being consulted by kings about politics. They also heal: Elisha, for example, cured Naaman the Syrian of leprosy, who then declared he now believed there was no God except that of Israel, and asked forgiveness if he had to accompany his king into the House of Rimmon and bow there. (Go in peace, Elisha told him). Nabis of this kind are now defunct in Israel, though according to Margaret Field, in *Search for Security*, they flourish in Ghana as possession priests, diviners, magicians, healers and exorcists.

But are such latter-day nabis nabis proper? For that matter, what distinguishes them from shamans? Mircea Eliade, when discussing shamanism, defined that vocation as the ability to keep self-witness when taken by a fit of inspiration, and set it apart from possession cults in which self-witness is lost. There are so many exceptions to this rule in both camps, however, as to make it nugatory. Even in the heartland of shamanism proper, most shamans are possessed by their spirits — mounted by them, Haitians would say — before being able to ride them; while in vaudoun, the final stage of initiation, which authorises a servitor to set up a temple and control its activities, is known as *la prise* *des yeux*, the taking hold of the eyes. This is a state in which, for all the nearly intolerable turmoil occasioned by a full inspirational upsurge,* the privileged victims are able to retain self-witness. Such being the case, it is best to recast the question in terms of the inspirational fit and the different theatres of action in which it displays itself, the difficulty of retaining self-witness being the same whatever the style adopted.

There is yet one mark by which a nabi proper may be distinguished from one half-made or merely pretending, as there is with a shaman or a possession priest, this being what, in the Bible, is called the discernment of spirits — an instant recognition of what afflicts a client, together with the ability to get to the heart of the matter on the spur of the moment. True, the gift is not restricted to them, as I hardly need remind you: I have known a doctor who could diagnose at twenty paces, as well as a philosopher, a painter, a novelist, a psychotherapist or two of various persuasions, a garage mechanic, a priest and of course Laing himself, who could do as much. All the same, it is an arduous task to perfect this gift, for though it is native to us all it is commonly repressed — with some reason, for it goes to that place where the sense of one's self is permeated by the sense of others, often to one's confusion.

What then is the nature of self-witness? I take it that Coleridge was speaking to this point when he said that the organs of spiritual sense were consubstantial with their objects — a profound remark from a man who evidently knew as much by direct experience. And so was it with Coventry Patmore when he declared love to be

> "that marvelous state in which each of two persons in distinct bodies perceives sensibly all that the other feels in regard to him or herself, although their feelings are of the most opposite characteristics."

One cannot say as much, unfortunately, for Lévy-Bruhl, whose writings on mystical participation suffer accordingly or, for that

---

* This upsurge affects the inner ear and hence the postural reflexes it coordinates. The sense of balance being the first to go, it is soon followed by failure to control the movements of the limbs, also those of the eyes, which then roll upwards; meanwhile, notable changes occur in breathing and heartbeat. Following this large-scale dissociation, the loa responsible for the upsurge can then invest the locus of self-witness with their own characteristics.

matter, for modern physicists who hold, without even appealing to Heisenberg, that if two particles are identical in their behaviour, they may safely be counted as one.

As much to the point is the sense of being what one perceives during nightmares. I mention the nightmare for its close association with possession states, as the literature on the subject makes clear, while folklore records the saving grace of such an experience by advising the sufferer to take a nightmare by its toe, when it will transform into a voluptuous moment. This, along with what Coleridge and Patmore have declared, tells us that the two-fold sense of consubtantial mutuality is also the breeding ground of personifications, and raises the problem of how to deal with them when they get out of hand.

Here then is what I take to be the actual subject I have been asked to speak upon today, a subject whose natural focus is an I-Thou moment — this being when two-fold sense meets two-fold sense — whose energetics are well characterised in Jacob Boehme's words "the being of beings is a wrestling power".

Every shaman I have met, and every member of a possession cult, would agree that such is the case: as of course Laing would have, along with many another whatever their vocation. For shamanism is a vocation — the utmost of vocations — in that its practitioners are called to it, much as they might wish to avoid that laborious, painful and often alienating destiny. How should it not be so when they first hear its voice in a nightmare, into which they again fall should they cease to shamanise, as happened to Jonah — Jonah the scape-goat, the wounded healer?

I take it meanwhile that the awakening of the two-fold sense to its own existence is part and parcel of initiation in general, an event that is usually staged at puberty as a horror story accompanied by painful moments of every kind, with a view to awaken the young to their place in the scheme of things. However, quite a number of people wake up to this, their self-witness, at a much earlier age — Eileen Garret, who had once been Conan Doyle's trance-medium, told me that she woke up in this fashion when, at the age of four, she was harshly reprimanded by her parents for telling them of an event she thought natural but which they regarded as supernaturally disrespectful even to mention. Mid-life crises may also provide the occasion for such awakenings.

What has been called the shamanic illness usually strikes around puberty, but by no means always, and takes much the same form whatever the diagnosis according to Western custom. Epilepsy was, for a time, a favourite diagnosis, soon to be followed by arctic hysteria, which under other names was recognised by tribal peoples whose women-folk were especially prone to it — brought on by those long sunless winters, and blizzards in which, the Inuit say, one can hear the spirits of the dead howling their recriminations. Knut Rasmussen, that best of past ethnographers, tells of how they countered this dismal affect when he and a party of Inuit were caught in just such a blizzard. After slogging through it for terrible hours, they found shelter in the ruins of a summer dwelling. Rasmussen collapsed behind a wall, but not so his companions — to his amazed vexation, they set about making themselves snug, they talked, they laughed, they sang — "How can you be singing after all we've gone through?" he at last inquired. "Ah," said one of them, "if we weren't happy, we would die." This was also Laing's view: he not only extolled the virtues of conviviality, but made a point of setting it in motion by getting people to sing Noel Coward songs, or Victorian ones such as "O for the wings of a dove" or 'The Lost Chord', while accompanying them on the piano — though I admit there were other times when he was in such an unconvivial mood, his companions were afflicted with hesitation and gloom. He rather enjoyed such moments, I suspect, for the insights they gave him into what happens to a group when deprived of an agenda — a practice in which W.R. Bion excelled by remaining steadfastly unconvivial whatever the mood of his group.

Then there's tropical hysteria — that is, latah — for which quite another explanation must be found; there's the effects of traumatic shock, as when an Inuit had his kayak overturned by an enraged walrus, that tusked him through the lungs — his companions saw him to the shore of ice, built him an igloo and left him there for days without dressing his wounds, lighting an oil-lamp or providing him with food, and that's how he became an angekok, a shaman. And then there are shamans that have been diagnosed as schizothymic, schizophrenic, idiopathic-paranoiac, etcetera etcetera, who have recovered some if not all of their senses by undergoing the classical shamanic experience of being dismembered, tormented, and remade with iron bones or rock-crystals stolen from the sky, with one, two, even seven bones left over which represent new and special powers: powers which, alas, have to be paid for indirectly with the life of one of the shaman's immediate family. (Such things happen closer to home: see Laing's writings on the family.)

Having now sketched this outline of what it is to be a shaman I may now bring in R.D. Laing on his own count. For though he was a psychiatrist and not a shaman, I must now so far contradict myself as to hold that he yet had a shamanic temperament. I don't suppose this to be all that different from the creative temperament whether it be artistic or scientific — a notable instance of this last being Tesla, the ipsissimus of electricity — or psychologic, as exemplified by C.G. Jung in self, both of whom have left accounts of their awakening to its existence. I don't know when Laing woke up in like vein — fairly early I suppose, I never asked, though I do know under whose patronage he may be said to have done so, for he told me. He had just come back from Iona, and paid me an unexpected visit. I gave him a drink: he stood with an elbow on the mantel-piece and after a companionable silence told me he was, as it were, a reincarnation of St Odran, whose legend he started to tell me. He did so with such stumbles and rollings-up of the eyes, I thought to save him the trouble of switching on his memory by looking into the top of his head. "But I've just come across the story myself," I broke in. I found the book — *Ten Thousand Saints*, a study of Irish and European origins by Hubert Butler — turned to the page, and read the précis of the legend aloud:

> St Odran was a famous saint of Iona. It is said that St Columba, finding that demons were infesting a site [where he wished to build a chapel — St Odran's chapel, it is now called], discovered that only by burying a holy man alive could they be exorcised. St Odran volunteered but after three days Columba decided to dig him up again for news of Heaven. St Odran, on being uncovered, instead of giving suitable information said, "There is no wonder in Death, and Hell is not as it is reported." Thereupon Columba cried out furiously: "Earth, earth upon the mouth of Odran that he may blab no more!" And he was covered up again.

Laing heard me out with an approving smile, which I thought friendly of him, and then said that Odran must have been a priest of the Irish goddess before his conversion to Christianity, through which he had hoped to escape her attentions. (She is the Morrigan — mother of all, demons included, and vengeant queen of love in death). There was no need for me to do more than smile in my turn, though not without a sigh.

Earth, earth, upon the mouth of Laing that he should blab no more about there being no wonder in psychiatry, and that schizophrenia is not as it is reported. But I only learnt the context of this revelation at his funeral, when the Reverend Donald Macdonald mounted the pulpit to give the oration. He told of Laing's visit to Iona, their meeting, their hot-tempered quarrelling over religious matters, and the fight they got into before Laing submitted himself to the authority of the Church of Scotland — in proof of which he took a blood-stained prayer-book from his pocket, and held it above his head. The gesture was as eloquent as the words the Duke of dark corners spoke to the miserable Claudio in *Measure for Measure*

> Be absolute for death — death or life
> Shall thereby be the sweeter

Words I am sure Laing would have approved of when he came to require this unconditionality of himself. He was then trusting his inspiration without second thought, as he had not quite been doing when it had been his wont to say, "I don't even trust my own judgment unless I have to".

The being of beings is indeed a wrestling power, and in meeting it Laing had the advantage of being something of a Glaswegian brawler. How he liked fighting and putting himself to physical test, if it was only playing rugby when he was young — this in spite of all his piano teacher said against it, for sure enough someone stepped on his hand and broke some bones — not ruinously (for he was as deft in playing night-club music as that of Bach, where I most admired his talent) but enough to scotch any idea that he could make a career of it.

Instead he took to psychiatry as a profession, and as his shamanic temperament no doubt played a part in this choice, a brief word about its nature is due. He had no quarrel with his father (a professional singer) even though he had once been given such a beating by him that he had to enclose himself in a solitude so intense that he felt nothing but with his mother, he once told me. Was she perhaps, he wondered, Jewish — that would explain why, when he was a child, she kept his cup, saucer, plate and cutlery apart, with repeated injunctions to his father not to touch. (But touch he would on occasion, with a mocking smile.) She also insisted on giving him his bath till he was of an age to lock the door against her, and for all her hammerings, kicks and screams of rage, she had to own defeat. Much later he heard from someone in the family that she had made a doll in his name and was sticking pins in it. On his next visit he asked her about that. A short silence, and then "We don't talk about such things", she replied.

And there was that further time, quite early on, when his father gave her a present on her birthday. Never before had he known his father to give her anything on any occasion, but there it was — a small box neatly wrapped, tied with a ribbon. She looked at it for a while, then slowly unknotted the ribbon, unwrapped the paper, took the lid off, removed a layer of cotton wool, and what should she see but the clippings of ten fingernails and ten toenails in orderly array. Not a word said she, not a glance she gave to her husband, but rose from her chair and left the room, leaving a funereal silence behind her.

I heard this story years after I had ventured to give him a Christmas present. He showed me into his study, which I hadn't seen before, and was much impressed by the dark green of its walls in whose shade the most lonely could feel at home with the Alone, even in company. Laing unwrapped the small bronze Buddha hand that I had brought — he was then practising meditation — and when it lay open to his gaze I became acutely aware of the pugnacious wings of his nose and the scorn-lines that ran down from them. Then, after a moment's thought, he got up from his chair, opened a cupboard, reached in and came out with a sword stick, which he negligently handed to me.

It was a dreadful object, ugly, heavy, and unwieldy both as a stick and a sword; the handle was perfunctory, and the wood of the scabbard-stick worm-holed to breaking point. A real old-time blackguard's weapon it was, and I could just see him as a young man buying it in a Glasgow junk shop and keeping it until the telling moment arrived to rid himself of it at another's expense. As I accepted this dubious comment on myself, delivered as it was in the confines of his dark green room, I began to wonder what he thought I had thought I was doing in giving him a present.

He told me as much twenty years later, when I came with another gift for his last child, then just born. Again he bridled with distaste, remembering how our mutual friend Joan Westcott, an anthropologist who for a time had been his secretary, had once given him a crucifix made of rifle bullets with a tin Jesus soldered to it, First World War vintage. It wasn't that he didn't appreciate the object, for it was on his mantelpiece for years, but that Joan, noticing his discomfort, lectured him on the anthropology of the gift, of how it created a web of social relationships by putting the recipient under the obligation to give something back. "Obligation!" he repeated with horror.

To give is indeed a two-faced operation, for the same word does duty, in its various cognates, for giving, having, receiving and taking; while in German, *das Gift* means poison. It may rightly stand, therefore, as epitomising the double bind, such as makes a divided self of its victim. Laing got the term from Gregory Bateson, who had arrived at it after lengthily wrestling with a ceremony of role reversal, Naven by name, practised by a tribe in New Guinea: a knotty problem involving several forms of two-fold sense. Meanwhile Laing took the idea of a knot from a Sufi poem, and his book of *Knots* shows him at his minimalist best, though it does not include the most heart-rending of these sickest of jokes. This, which in his later years I would hear him repeat with heroic despair, represents — so Jutta Laing has told me — an interchange he had with his mother at an early age. It goes like this:

> Do you love me?
> Yes.
> Do you believe me?
> Yes.
> How can you love me if you believe me?

I am sorry to say that *The Lies of Love*, his last book, is still unpublished, for those who have read it tell me they were much engaged by its disturbing reports of similar interchanges. Laing indeed detested lies above all things, and would go out of his way to demolish liars. Nor did he ever forget his bafflement when a couple came to see him with such contradictory and yet persuasive stories that he was unable to determine which of the two was lying about what, such a mare's nest had they made for themselves to lie in together.

There were also times when Laing found himself in yet deeper and darker waters, which involved not just double binds — spells, an anthropologist might well call them — but curses. One instance, of which he published a brief account, had to do with a woman who cursed her son to the seventh generation so successfully that four generations later his sole descendant realised he would also be the last. He had made every effort to free himself from his fate but, he said, it was like one of those Russian dolls that had smaller ones inside, all of which he could deal with, but the innermost — entirely beyond appeal — was the mother still mouthing her implacable curse.

I have known of curses being removed by vaudouists, as long as the curser was still alive, but not when the curse had renewed itself over successive generations. A Tibetan exorcist might, from the little I know of such practitioners, have done better, though the wrestling power involved is beyond my comprehension, and by all accounts takes so much out of an exorcist that such men usually die in their thirties. Laing's nearest approach to such a feat that I know of concerned one of the first, most chronic inhabitants of a P.A. household, David by name, who had just returned from hospital in a high state of mania. Laing gave him what I once heard him call his undivided attention ("No thanks", was Andrew Feidmar's response when offered it, ha ha, as a birthday present). He did this silently and without looking at him, so well that David soon fell silent. Laing then told the others present what he had done, whereupon David took flight again. Laing once more set himself to attend, again David fell silent. What he had done, he later told me, was to take David's frenzy and contain it in himself. But the effect on him was so great that, when he left soon after to drive himself home, he collapsed in the car from the strain. David, meanwhile, was back in high-speed mania.

This same David spoke a rapid and advanced form of schizophrenese which, exhausting though it was to attend to, Laing said he sometimes could understand, much as shamans know the language of the birds. Less sophisticated cases gave him no trouble, nor did the wooden dumbness so often met with in divided selves under interrogation. In Haiti, as I have recounted in *The Invisibles*, this affliction is held to be the work of a loa called Great Tree, and is dealt with by the usual method of ritual incubation. Laing needed much less time, as witness a video made during his appearance at a Milton Erickson conference, he having offered to have a normal conversation, in public, with anyone diagnosed as schizophrenic, deemed intractable, and not under medication. Introduced to a homeless woman who fitted this bill, he so engaged her attention that after an hour she agreed to continue the conversation before a large audience, which she did with aplomb. Laing said that he had no technique in achieving this result: it was, he insisted, the result of empathy in the service of copresence — the state of mind I alluded to when quoting Coleridge and Patmore.

But the ability to empathise can be perilous. I met him one morning looking ghastly — ghastly was a word frequently on his lips at the time and yes, he said, that's how it was with him, he'd woken up from a dream in which he'd been a rat in a Hong Kong sewer. He was in much the same state at one of the weekly P.A. meetings, which I will give a brief account of, if only in order to give an idea of what I mean by a shamanic temperament. Instead of getting on with the agenda, Laing asked if we would help him, for he was in a peculiar state: he felt like exploding and breaking the furniture. As it was, he was filled with this dire impulse down to his feet, which he wiggled for the next hour to free them from cramp.

Knowing something of that state, I offered to give his feet a massage by way of emergency treatment, which he indignantly refused: just as well, he might have kicked my teeth in had I tried. Hugh Crawford then offered to put him through a formal inquisition, which Laing accepted by sliding off his chair onto the floor. First question: What brought it on? Laing replied that he'd just returned from Rome (this was the time when he'd refused to meet the Pope) and he and an Israeli doctor who like himself had a consuming interest in (here his voice faltered) fetuses, were sharing a bottle in a hotel bar. The doctor remarked: "Look at that woman, she's a coca-cola woman". Laing looked up, took her in at a glance and went off to vomit.

"Why", he asked of no one in particular, "do I take all this in? It lodges in my throat like a vampire." He was, he said, exsanguinated by it all, it must be because his umbilical cord had been cut as soon as he was born, much too early, his mother having already dissociated herself from his existence.

"That's a condensation," Crawford said. Laing ignored him, and with tears streaming down his cheeks told of the conflict raging between his two hemispheres. "I feel both of them," he said, "they alternate, I've seen them in detail in myself." A heterodyne effect, Crawford remarked. Yes, but what was it about? Laing gave the answer: it had to do with an incorrigible evil in himself that waited on the incorrigible necessities of life in general.

"Regard the condensation" Crawford continued; Laing obliged, adding that he could go on like this for months, he knew it all. Crawford persisted until, grateful though I was to have heard what Laing confided to us while under this interrogation, I lost patience and attacked Crawford ad rem. Leaving the fetal issue to look after itself, I asked if he didn't recognise a mild case of shamanic disorder when he saw it — the moment when the gear-box is seized up, and one can't shift either up or down — or know how to restimulate the works without further recourse to analytic procedure?

Crawford feigned not to understand -"You speak air," he told me. Laing broke in: "I breathe with my brain," he said, "I learnt to do that in order not to die during an asthma attack." * Crawford: "That's a metaphor. You breathe with your lungs." This scientistic remark infuriated me: I got on his case once more, and so we slanged each other for a time. Energised by this brawl, Laing soon joined in to slang Crawford on his own terms. He was now back in his chair with his gear-box unjammed, his hemispheres having found a common axis with his witness and spinning like a top. But what was his incorrigible evil, then asked Leon Redler. "Callousness", he replied, after a brief pause, and enlarged on that topic for a while. He was himself again.

Yes, Laing could be callous, and often was. It was, at best, part of his armamentarium against coca-cola women and the like; at worst, brutal — but then, we all have our little problems, do we not, complete with their own thick skins. Better to return to this account of a mild shamanic disorder by saying how much my contribution owed to that Brazilian I spoke of earlier, whose ability to shift gear caught my attention when I first met him. This was just before one of his shamanic performances, when he

---

* One of Laing's party pieces was a choke-by-choke rendition of this nightmarish malady, from which St Odran preserve us. Since Laing was sometimes accused of being schizophrenic, it is of interest that Dr Humphry Osmond, coiner of the word psychedelic, long ago observed that asthmatics find their breathing restored should they develop symptoms of schizophrenia, though when relieved of those symptoms they revert to the asthmatic mode. What is known of the physiology here involved suggests that those who wrestle with these and other double binds can indeed save their day by learning to breathe with their brains, a meditative practice of long standing.

was so self-absorbed I thought him autistic — an opinion that what he later told me of his childhood did something to confirm, as did his successful treatment of autistic children. (Here then may be another diagnostic category by which to understand the shamanic crisis). But he had discovered how to move in and out of this self-preoccupation: he went into first gear, if somewhat reluctantly, when I introduced myself to him, then into second when an attractive woman joined in, and into third when it was time for him to start his act. Then the spirit of the late emperor Nero (one of many that attended him) came into him and up he rose, like a spring, his face transformed, to work the audience until they hung upon his actions, and attend to his victim-patient — and he had a fourth gear ready for those moments when, having gone as far as he knew by himself, Messalina would animate his place of self-witness to do the necessary without him knowing. But the great difference between him and Laing was that I never saw Laing lose self-witness let alone indulge in such histrionics, even though he did acknowledge that some of his best moments were inspired by a clear-headed Kaliesque furor. But that was later, when he had abandoned the Philadelphia Association.

I have so far spoken but indirectly of shamanic healing. This is a subject difficult to do justice to in a few words, since it deals with spells, curses, breaches of tabu, underhand intentions, social dysfunction, soul-loss and other anthropological commonplaces, many of which have escaped psychiatric attention. The methods used to free the victim of such complaints are much the same the world over: shamans must establish a reflexive world animated by personifications of the forces active in this one, and employ their empathic sense to discern which personifications of spirit are involved in a particular disorder. This done, various arts of conjuration are employed to so fascinate the attention that the patient is freed from self-preoccupation and can re-establish normal relations with the world at large. The methods are not always gentle, and some shamans are notable for their intimate knowledge of sado-masochistic necessities.

Practices of this kind, along with religions, can be distinguished according to whether they follow the affirmative or the negative way, and traditional shamanism largely favours the affirmative one. Laing's method, as practised in the households of the Philadelphia Association, favoured the negative way, as befitted his minimalist and existential bent. His guiding line was the Hippocratic oath with its major injunction, to do no harm to those who consult you, to which he added his own gloss, that a human being should be treated as a human being and not suffer the consequences of being pathologised whatever the problem. Hence his refusal to set up a conventional regimen by which sufferers can be restrained and manipulated, and his horror of the unconvivial nature of psychiatric wards — a horror so large that, as I have mentioned, he constantly extolled conviviality as the eminent need for those in mental shipwreck.

His view of the households set up by the Philadelphia Association was that they provided asylum, and *asylums* was often his name for them. They had no resident therapists, the task of running a household being taken up by the residents themselves, who sometimes included apprentices; there was no prescription of drugs, and if someone should freak out, the residents were expected to form a safety-net on their own, and call on other households to help if necessary, with those who had oversight of these concerns also lending a hand.

There were no rules, in the formal sense of the word: the asylum was also a crucible in which, Laing used to say, rough edges were smoothed out little by little. An odd kind of crucible, I once remarked, with no cross marked on its bottom — at which pedantry he pshawed in reproof. No cross and no apparent limits either. Instead he appealed to the Golden Rule, to do nothing to others you would not like done to yourself, along with two others I once heard him appeal to, to make up for the lack of formal limits. One went:

> What is not forbidden is allowed
> What is not allowed is forbidden

whose rigour was mercifully put into question by the second rule:

> It's all up for grabs.

These rules generally kept things in order, and it was in this inchoate theatre, with no director, no script, no prompter, no stage props or effects, no drums or rattles, no invocations, prayers, chants, no mind-altering brews, that the Laingian mode

R. D. Laing

of spontaneous self-becoming could achieve the same general effects that are produced by shamanic initiation — of regression into nightmare, of its incubation, with a frenzy or two before the novice comes back into his senses — or hers, of course — with reintegrated faculties. The particular effects, however, were different, for no shamans were produced by this set-up. That was not the aim of the venture, which was to allow a mental disorder to be fully experienced as it ran its course, this being enough to ensure its happy outcome — no policing required. He was not interested in curing a disorder, I once heard him say, but in healing those distressed by disorder: in other words, he gave them their natural due, the chance to wise up to themselves by themselves.

I have but some further stories to tell you, to show him in action. The first concerns myself when I had a painful choice to make and could not see my way. I telephoned him one evening, asking for his help. All right, he said wearily, come over, and soon I was in that dark green room of his, telling him all about it. He bore with me patiently for quite a while, then got up and began walking to and fro in front of the curtains, back stooped, gesturing with his hands, eyes staring at nothing, silently jawing away non-stop. Alarmed by this parody of myself, my mind then cleared and I burst out laughing; whereupon he sat at his piano, opened a book of Noel Coward's songs, and so we passed the rest of a now convivial evening. I reminded him of the occasion years later, and he said — it was something of a reproach — there'd been times he wished someone had done as much for him.

Next, that unusual occasion in which I first saw him publicly engage in his speciality, which he later called psychic aikido. In contrast to usual shamanic and vaudouistic practice, in which the practioner uses his left hand alternately with his right — the right for white magic, in aid of a client, the left for black, to deal with the client's enemies — psychic aikido takes the client as his own worst enemy and launches the telling blow — by which hand makes no odds — at the solar plexus of the situation. In this case, however, Laing was dealing, not with a client, but with an established member of his own profession. This was Carl Rogers, who had invited Laing to put on a double act in London. Laing had accepted and in return had offered Rogers his hospitality for the duration. He had meanwhile summoned the

200

members and associates of the P.A. on the evening of his guest's arrival — who had come, I was surprised to find, with his own band. As surprising, was the silence that reigned over the room when I entered it, which continued until Rogers took it as his duty — Laing showing no such willingness — to introduce himself and his doings, after which his followers did likewise. There was another silence which, thinking that Laing needed a Mutt to his Jeff, I broke by following suit, to be followed in turn by the others of Laing's équipe. Silence once more, long but not too long. And then Laing launched his opening gambit: 'I see that we can work together, but I don't think we can ever be friends.'

Gasps. Rogers paled beneath his tan, and sat speechless. Not so his band, who were loud in outrage. When the clamour uneasily subsided, Laing proposed that, the meeting being over, we should all adjourn to the Chinese restaurant around the corner. He was there first, and seeing him installed with two others at a corner table already supplied with bottles, I took a seat elsewhere. Rogers came in next, and took the chair next to me. ("Serve you right for acting the gentleman," Laing sneered afterwards). We engaged in small talk and he was recovering his spirits when, as we were eating our noodles, two drunken Scotsmen lurched through the door. Laing shouted a welcome to them in broad Glaswegian, adding: "If you want to see a pairrson, he's sitting over there" — stabbing a finger in Rogers' direction.

Another hubbub arose, and the restaurant soon emptied. On my more leisurely return to Laing's house, I saw Rogers and his folk in anxious discussion on the other side of the street. Leaving them to it, I found Laing and some others at the window, looking down upon the scene with the relish St Augustine described as one of the chief pleasures of the blessed, namely, to observe the torments of the damned — a passage Laing had by heart. However, when he judged that enough was enough, he supposed he should go over and rescue Rogers from himself, which he did.

Next morning, the double act did very well. Laing was impeccable when introducing Rogers as the founder of non-directive, client-centered therapy, and in asking many an interesting question — for instance, 'How was it, do you think, that your psychology caught on so quickly in the United States?' to which Rogers replied, I thought without guile: 'I suppose I came along at the right time as a kind of a person or something.'

You may wonder what all this was about. If so, you should read the account of Martin Buber's public I-Thou encounter with Rogers, in Buber's *The Knowledge of Man*. Buber talked of such things as 'imagining the real', which Rogers failed to appreciate, and of a therapeutic dialogue being bounded by tragedy because of which, "Humanity, human will, human understanding, are not everything. There is some reality confronting us. We cannot forget it for a moment". Rogers agreed that, "there is an objective situation there, one that could be measured", which will give you some idea of the difference between the two men. Buber's final comment (with which Laing would have concurred) was that Rogers' concept of persons was little better than one of individuals, and that he was against individuals and for persons On the other hand he later said that he had never before attempted an I-Thou encounter in public, and found it to be not as impossible as he had supposed.

If only it had been Laing talking with Buber — Laing, for whom such public encounters came to be meat and drink! He would have known just how it was with Buber when he smashed a bible on the table, crying "What is the use of a book like that to us now?" — the time being the Nazi era, the event a rabbinical convention. And Buber would have appreciated Laing's remark that there were many people who, though worthy, he could not educate even if he wished to, because they did not entertain him.

I would be going beyond my assignment were I to speak of Laing's activities as a master of psychic aikido at the time he was preaching unconditional love, and being so unconditional in his treatment of others that, though they were at first appalled, they were soon effusive in their gratitude. Long before, I had occasion to bring up this unconditionality of his with Peter Mezan, and found myself saying that Laing was impossible; to which he replied "Obstinately impossible" and then retailed me this anecdote, whose tragic condensation brings me to a close. That morning he had paid Laing a visit, and found him entertaining a tall, thin Spaniard who, dressed in black — complete with cape and a slouch hat — was armed with an invitation to visit Madrid. There Laing would be given the keys of the city and meet the King. "You are as god to us," said he. "No-one has read your books, but we all want to meet you. We think of you as Jesus Christ, because you attempted the impossible and failed."

I don't know how Laing dealt with this challenge to his honour. What would you say, were you Odran *redivivus* and your works available, to an admirer who excused his failure to do the possible by making you that gift of gifts, a crown of thorns?

10: Psychiatry and Phenomenology Today

Thomas Fuchs

Psychiatry and Phenomenology Today

Thomas Fuchs

Summary

In today's psychiatry, phenomenology is still misunderstood as providing "first person data", based on introspective reports, as a raw material for aetiological research. Instead, phenomenology should be conceived as the methodical effort to describe the universal meaning of structures of conscious experience. By way of phenomenological reduction, it follows them down to the hidden structures of embodiment, spatiality, temporality, intentionality, intersubjectivity, etc. Moreover, genetic phenomenology analyses the way a person pre-reflectively constitutes her reality in a meaningful way, namely by what Husserl has called "passive syntheses". Thus it is capable of detecting the critical points where this constitution is vulnerable and open to distortions or deviations, apparent as psychiatric symptoms. By analyzing the structures of conscious experience in general, phenomenology provides the basic research for the understanding and the aetiological explanation of disturbances of consciousness in mental health disorders.

This paper illustrates the present role of phenomenological psychopathology by focusing on some of its major issues: embodiment of body, scheme, space, intentionality, time-consciousness and intersubjectivity. Special emphasis is given to the relation between phenomenology and cognitive neuroscience, a relation that has been viewed as "mutual constraint" or else as "mutual enlightenment". Here a new cooperation linking phenomenology, psychopathology and cognitive science begins to emerge. Phenomenology offers a methodically developed theory of human subjectivity which is indispensable to any attempt to understand, explore and treat psychiatric disorders.

Introduction

Ronald D. Laing is known as one of psychiatry's great dissenters, as a passionate advocate of patients' rights and a pugnacious fighter for a humane social psychiatry. However, Laing was not only a vehement critic but a profound philosopher of psychiatry as well. His subtle analyses of the phenomenology of experience and of interpersonality are still valuable for any existential or phenomenological approach to psychiatry. Therefore, the Royal College of Psychiatrists deserves special praise for recalling to mind this aspect of Laing's work. Considering the role of phenomenology in today's psychiatry may be one way to contribute to his memory and to carry on his work. Since space is limited, I will restrict my paper to the following questions:

(1) Why do we need phenomenology at all in present day psychiatry?
(2) What is the method phenomenology has to offer to the psychiatrist?
(3) Which areas of psychiatry might especially benefit from a cooperation of phenomenology and empirical science?

1) Why do we need phenomenology at all in today's psychiatry?

Not long ago, an editorial in *Biological Psychiatry* boldly proclaimed an end of the mind/brain controversy: "Neuroscience has now made it clear that the 'mind' is rooted in the brain"; and "...we can now safely predict that we shall succeed in understanding how the brain functions and how it dysfunctions" (Marazziti & Cassano 1997). The biological programme, with its twin pillars of molecular genetics and neuro-imaging, promises to explain the mind either by gene or by brain functions. Biological psychiatrists, neuroscientists, philosophers of mind and eliminative materialists of any provenance smile at seemingly outdated approaches to mental life *via* understanding subjective experience. For present day philosophers of mind such as D. Dennett there is only a unidirectional relationship between subpersonal brain mechanisms and personal experience – namely, the latter is entirely produced by the former. Consciousness is a byproduct of the brain's activity as a symbol-manipulating machine or an information processor. In this view, the riddles of mental illness will soon be explained by identification of localisable brain dysfunctions and transmitter imbalances. There is no need to rack one's brains about subjectivity and to indulge in the hair-splittings of psychopathology anymore.

However, this brave new science suffers from flaws. Firstly, subjectivity is not easily excluded and ends up returning by the back door. In usual neurocognitivist accounts of mental functions the brain is personalised: It "perceives", "sees", "learns", "computes" and "commands" as if it were a living being of its own. Neuronal circuits are attributed intentional and meaningful behaviour, as if they were some kind of homunculus. To a large extent, neuroscience uses an unreflective "as-if" language. This is only the counterpart of its reductionism: reducing personal consciousness to subpersonal mechanisms results in personalising these mechanisms. Nearly a hundred years ago Jaspers called this kind of science "brain mythology", and the German psychiatrist Erwin Straus coined a simple sentence which is still true today: "It is man who thinks, not the brain" (Straus 1956). The person is the proper subject of experience; meaning is not somewhere in the brain, but only in the interaction between the living human being and its natural and social environment.

This leads me to a second, more serious objection. Cognitive neuroscience stills rests on a passive concept of consciousness: There is an objective world "out there", and it is represented by images produced inside the brain that become conscious to us. But consciousness has the peculiar characteristic of being inseparably linked to what goes on beyond itself. It is not a passive container or a kind of screen on which the world is projected, but an active, self-organizing process of *relating and directing itself to the world*. This dynamic and intentional character of consciouness, however, is not covered by the concept of single mental events that could be translated into corresponding brain states. Therefore, the neurocognitive system cannot be grasped separately either: it exists only enmeshed in the world in which we move and live with others through our bodily existence. Growing research on neuronal plasticity has made it clear that the brain is not a prefabricated apparatus inserted into the world, but is structured epigenetically by the continuous interaction of organism and environment. Instead of representationalism with its fixed inside-outside distinction, we need what Varela (1996a) termed an "embodied" or "enactive cognitive science" that treats mind and world as mutually overlapping.

This "systemic" and "process" view of mental life has consequences for psychiatry as well. If consciousness is not conceivable separately, then mental illness cannot be understood in terms of single, circumscribed dysfunctions, but only as a disturbance of the patient's *relation to the world and to others*. And this view necessarily extends to the neurophysiological level as well: unlike neurologic diseases, psychiatric disorders cannot be related to discrete, localised brain dysfunctions, but rather to malfunctioning interconnections between neuronal modules and their interaction with environment. They have to be explored on the basis of the continuous self-organisation of the CNS as a living system (Parnas & Bovet 1995).

Now if the "systemic" view of mental illness is indispensable, then we cannot do without thorough analyses of its first-person experience. For subjective experience is not just an epiphenomenal picturing of underlying "real" processes, but *it is itself an essential part of the systemic interaction of organism and environment*. It is only by conscious experience that the organism is able to enter into a relationship with the world on a higher level of *meaning*, of integrated perceptive and cognitive units or "Gestalten", and these meaningful units in turn influence the plasticity, the structuring and functioning of the CNS. So when exploring a breakdown in the meaningful relations of a human being with his environment, where could we better start than with his subjective experience itself? Should we not initially set out to thoroughly describe the idiosyncratic way the patient experiences and structures his world? What could better guide us in searching for corresponding neurophysiological dysfunctions than the very sphere in which a meaningful world is originally constituted?

For these reasons, an adequate science of experience is foundational for psychiatry as well as for cognitive neuroscience. Without exploring the phenomenology of subjectivity we will not be able to identify the corresponding subpersonal mechanisms. Cognitive neuroscience will remain blind to its proper object as long as it operates without an appropriate methodological description of what it attempts to explain. Unless we overcome the present objectivistic, reductionist epistemology in psychiatry, empirical research will be seriously impeded. This leads me to my second question:

2) What is the method phenomenology has to offer to the psychiatrist?

In today's psychiatry, phenomenology is still misunderstood as the gathering of "first person data", based on introspective reports, as a raw material for aetiological research. However, this "descriptive phenomenology" *sensu* Jaspers stops half-way: it depicts only a catalogue of experiences in psychiatric illness. Instead, phenomenology should be conceived as the methodical effort to describe the basic structures inherent in conscious experience, such as, embodiment, spatiality, temporality, intentionality, intersubjectivity, etc. It starts with first-person accounts, but it arrives at substructures of consciousness, such as, the formation of perceptual meaning, action planning, temporal continuity or implicit memory. It focuses on the *form* and *building-up* rather than the *contents* of experience. By analysing the modes in which our world experience is constituted, phenomenology is also capable of detecting the critical points where this constitution is vulnerable and open to deviations which appear as psychiatric symptoms. By gaining access to the prethematic dimension of experience, the psychiatrist extends his scope of understanding to include phenomena which would otherwise only be taken as bizarre "secretions of the brain".

Of course, a thorough description of the phenomenological method would be beyond the scope of my presentation. Let me just give a short sketch of some of its basic features:

The starting-point of phenomenology as exposed by Husserl is the discovery that our primordial experience is always already covered under habitual beliefs and assumptions. The essence of experience, therefore, has to be uncovered by rigorous abstinence from all taken-for-granted convictions, by a suspension of the so called "natural attitude" to reality. We are requested to put in abeyance what we believe we "should" think or find, and especially any explanation that derives the phenomena from underlying causes not to be found in themselves. By this systematic disengagement, or *epoché*, as Husserl called it, the phenomenologist arrives at a "bracketing" even of the primordial belief in the existence of the world. As a result, he is able to turn his thoughts and acts into objects of his awareness, instead of being absorbed by their contents as we usually are. The direction of thinking is turned backwards towards the arising of thoughts themselves, towards their transcendental source (Varela 1996a).

This peculiar turn of his attention leads the phenomenologist to the fundamental or *"transcendental consciousness"*, which constitutes the world and always refers back to it. The world and all its phenomena become a correlate of this intentional consciousness. After this move, phenomenology aims at the *intuition of the essence* of the phenomena by imaginative variations which allow their invariants or essential features to appear. These essences have then to be described and translated into common language by an intersubjective process of mutual understanding in a scientific phenomenologic community. In the last step, the phenomenologist returns to experience itself — in our case clinical experience — in order to check for the appropriateness of his findings to the phenomena he encounters. By suspending our commonplace assumptions about reality, this whole process of the so-called "transcendental reduction" leads to a disclosure of the originary underpinnings of our experience. It follows the constitution of self and reality down to the basic structures of corporeality, temporality and intersubjectivity.

Now if the psychiatrist undertakes this process of epoché and reduction, he arrives at the prethematic dimension of experience, which is affected especially in psychotic disorders. For here consciousness loses its ground in the lived body as the seat of taken-for-granted habitualties; it loses its anchoring in temporal continuity and rootedness in the intersubjective common-sense. As Blankenburg (1979) has pointed out, one could say: what is performed actively by the phenomenologist is suffered passively by the schizophrenic patient, namely a shaking of the natural attitude, an estrangement from the common and taken-for-granted reality. The framework underlying our everyday experience is itself deranged and laid bare. The schizophrenic person suffers what Laing (1960) called an "ontological insecurity".

Therefore the way of phenomenological reduction is at the same time the way to come as near as possible to the disturbed processes of constitution in psychosis. Moreover, even in the erosion of the constitutional processes, the patient still strives for a coherent world view, even though this may only be possible in the form of delusion.

Phenomenology also explores the modes through which the patient tries to make sense of the basic disturbances and to re-establish some form of coherence.

This brief outline of the phenomenological method has highlighted its special affinity to the core of psychiatric disorders. This leads to my third question:

3) Which areas of psychiatry might especially benefit from a cooperation between phenomenology and the empirical science?

In what follows I will try to illustrate this fruitfulness in three areas: (a) embodiment, (b) time-consciousness, and (c) interpersonality.

a)   *Embodiment*

Phenomenologists such as Merleau-Ponty (1945), Straus (1956) and Schmitz (1965) have shown how our embodiment tacitly permeates all our experiences and bestows on them a sense of "mineness". Conscious experiences are thus essentially characterized by having a subjective "feel" to them, a quality of "what it is like" to have them (Nagel 1974). This holds true not only for bodily experience itself, but for emotions, mood or even perceptions: there is "something it is like" to taste an apple, to feel the sand of a beach, to hear the rhythmic sound of an African drum. Infant research has shown that the child's perception is permeated with bodily feelings and dominated by felt similarities of rhythm, intensity or tone. There is a primordial layer of a "bodily felt sense", a *"sensus communis"* that precedes the separation of proprioception, perception and emotion.

This sense is also the phenomenal basis of interpersonal perception: we experience a similitude or resonance between the outward expressivity of others and our own bodily expressivity which in turn is in resonance with our emotional states. The body works as a "felt mirror" of others. It elicits a non-inferential process of empathic perception which Merleau-Ponty called "transfer of the corporeal schema" and which he attributed to a primordial sphere of "intercorporeality". Infant research has confirmed this view by showing that even new-born babies are able to imitate expressions of others (Meltzoff & Moore 1977,

1989). By the mimetic capacity of their body, they also transpose the seen gestures and mimics of others into their own feelings. There is a sphere of embodied sensibility and mutual resonance that we all share from the beginning with others as embodied subjects.

Support now comes from neurophysiology and its discovery of so called "mirror neurons" in the monkey premotor cortex, which probably exists in humans as well. These neurons discharge both when the animal performs an action and when it observes a similar action by another individual (Gallese et al. 1996, Rizzolatti et al. 1996). They seem to represent a system that matches observed events to similar, internally generated actions, thus forming a link between the observer and the actor. This points to a neurobiological basis of mutual understanding, namely by mimetic or resonance behaviour, be it actual or only virtual.

These converging results from different research approaches are also highly important for psychiatric disorders, especially for schizophrenia. Growing evidence from phenomenological as well as empirical research points out that the schizophrenic person suffers from what could be called a *disembodiment* of experience. She does not "inhabit" her body anymore, in the sense of taking-for-granted its habits or automatic performances in order to participate in the world. The tacit "mineness" of experience is undermined, and an alienation of fundamental constitutional processes results. Laing described what he called the "unembodied self" in schizophrenia as follows:

> 'Such a divorce of self from body deprives the unembodied self from direct participation in any aspect of the life or the world, which is mediated exclusively through the body's perceptions, feelings, and movements (expressions, gestures, words, actions, etc.). The unembodied self, as onlooker at all the body does, engages in nothing directly. Its functions come to be observation, control, criticism *vis-à-vis* what the body is experiencing and doing, and those operations which are usually spoken of as purely "mental". The unembodied self becomes hyper-conscious' (Laing 1960, 71).

In order to compensate for the loss of automatic bodily performance, the patients have to prepare and release each single action consciously and deliberately, in a way that could be called a "Cartesian" action of the soul on the body. It is no wonder that they often speak of a split between their mind and their body, of feeling hollowed out, like a marionette or a robot; for the sense of being alive depends on being an incarnated subject, with integrated bodily performances at one's disposal. In the same way, we find a disembodiment of perception in schizophrenia: instead of simply perceiving the world, the subject, as it were, becomes witness to his own perceiving; hence the artificial or stage-like character of the environment in early schizophrenia.

This has consequences for interpersonal perception as well: There is a correlation between the disturbance of bodily self-perception and perception of expressive signals from others. Schizophrenic patients have marked difficulties in recognizing faces, in understanding mimetic expressions and gestures, as can be shown in interaction analyses (Berndl et al. 1986, Steimer-Krause et al. 1990). At the same time, they often show a strong impairment of self-actualisation in bodily expression. The alienation of the intercorporeal sphere that precedes any thematic verbal exchange led Kimura to view schizophrenia in the last analysis as a disturbance of the "between" or the interpersonal atmosphere. It may also be tempting to speculate on, and search for, a neurobiological basis for this disturbance, concerning neuronal mirroring or resonance behaviour, and its link to the bodily felt sense of self.

As we can see, phenomenology opens the access to a deeper layer of experience — here, embodiment — that is disturbed in mental illness. My next example is:

b) *Time Consciousness*

The basic temporal structure of consciousness was described by Husserl as an interweaving of *retentions* (an intending of what has just taken place and which still remains at the margin of the present experience), of *presentations* (an intending of what is immediately present) and of *protentions* (an intending of what is expected to be presented). Varela (1996b) has recently searched for neurological underpinnings of this subjective time-experience in nonlinear, dynamic systems theory: he used it as an example of the necessary cooperation of phenomenology and cognitive neuroscience, or of what he termed "neurophenomenology". I would like to point to a possible application of Husserl's model to psychotic experiences, though time will only allow me to give some hints on the issue (cf. Fuchs 2001).

The retentional-protentional structure of consciousness is essential for the temporal integration of the sequence of moments into "intentional arcs": e.g. to speak a meaningful sentence as well as to understand it depends on the continuous awareness of the words just spoken and on the anticipation of the words to come. The span of the intentional arc also helps me to keep my speech on track, and to inhibit inappropriate ideas or words from intruding. At the same time, this temporal integration of single moments is the presupposition for the sense of one's own continuity or identity over time. I am not only aware of the sentence I speak but also of myself speaking it and intending it. There is *a sense of mineness and of agency* built into the retentional-protentional structure of consciousness. It is the carrier of the unity of the self over time.

Now let us assume a weakening or intermittent failure of this retentional-protentional function in schizophrenia, i.e. *a sudden discontinuity of consciousness.* Then the constant intertwining of succeeding moments gets lost. All of a sudden, the anticipated goal of thoughts has vanished; for a moment, even the possibility of any future is abolished. This would be experienced as a kind of "blackout" or, in the patient's language, as a thought withdrawal. However, as a result of this discontinuity the inhibition of the unintended thoughts fails as well. Associations and ideas appear "out of the blue" and interrupt the intentional arc that the patient tried to draw. A thought occurring at this moment of discontinuity lacks the sense of mineness and agency. The intentional arc normally bestowing this sense on thoughts is broken. Such unbidden thoughts intruding into one's mental activity are experienced as alien and inserted, or even as "voices". The same may apply to motor impulses: a movement of my body that I did not anticipate appears as caused by someone else. Schizophrenic experiences of reference, persecution and control may thus be conceived as an *"inversion of intentionality"*: with the weakening and intermittent paralysis of the patient's own intentional activity, the direction of mental acts now emerging is reversed and turned against him, as if coming from the outside. Instead of actively perceiving, thinking and acting, he is being perceived, "being thought", and acted upon by others.

Thus from a phenomenological point of view, so-called "first rank symptoms" of schizophrenia maybe derived from a fundamental disturbance of the temporal integration of consciousness – from a discontinuity of the self. Of course this is just a very short outline of a theory that would have to be explained extensively and underpinned by evidence. A number of results from experimental psychopathology could be integrated into such a model. Thus Spitzer et al. (1994), working with the semantic priming-paradigm in schizophrenic patients, found a dopaminergic disinhibition of semantic networks with an extended scope of associations; this corresponds to a weakening of the intentional arc. Impairment of the attentional span, disturbances of working memory or executive control functions etc., may also be interpreted as due to the disintegration of the temporal unity of consciousness. Phenomenology may thus provide a framework for the integration of cognitive research results into higher order concepts. On the other hand, it also puts a constraint against attempts to explain the psychotic experience "bottom-up", i.e. by a simple increase of so-called basic disturbances that finally overburden the brain's capacity for information processing. Phenomenology, for its part, emphasises the "transcendental" source of the psychotic alienation, namely in the highest and most complex functions of human consciousness.

c) *The Interpersonal Sphere*

My final example concerns phenomena associated with perspective-taking in the interpersonal sphere. It was Laing (1966) who explored this sphere thoroughly and coined the term "self-other-metaperspective" i.e. the ability to imagine the other persons' mental states, thoughts or feelings. Laing also showed how his perspective-taking may spiral up on increasingly higher levels of complexity, according to the following pattern:

I am aware of you.
I am aware of your being aware of me.
I am aware of your being aware of me looking at you, etc.

Now this level of complexity apparently overburdens many psychotic patients. They may say for example:

> "The consciousness of others intrudes upon me and lets myself vanish" (Kant 1927). "When I look at somebody my own personality is in danger. I am undergoing a transformation and myself is beginning to disappear" (Chapman 1966).

So, instead of establishing a mutual understanding, the reciprocity of perspectives threatens the schizophrenic person with a loss of herself. How can we explain this? First we have to take into account the fact that this metaperspective is only a virtual one. Of course, when I am aware of your being aware of me, I do not become you. I do not lose my embodied being. Interpersonal perception implies a continuous oscillation between the central, embodied perspective on the one hand, and the decentred or virtual perspective on the other. The German philosopher Plessner (1975) coined the apposite term of man's "eccentric position", meaning the dialectical integration of both perspectives.

This integration requires the fundamental ability of *pretending*, or in other words, a *symbolizing* or *"as-if"-function* that appears to be a central characteristic of the human mind. This function allows us to suspend the validity of the immediate experience, and to take it to be something other that itself: e.g. a mirror image, a map of the town, a traffic sign, etc. The "as-if-function" is also necessary for perspective-taking and mutual understanding: I have to put my body-centred existence into brackets and for a moment pretend to be in the other's place. However, in order not to lose myself in this oscillation, it is also necessary to keep up the tension and the difference between the embodied and the virtual perspective. Though this happens in every conversation, it is nevertheless a complex task that requires a high intentional effort. A failure of the symbolizing function can be found in the autistic: they are usually impaired in representing mental states of others and in understanding pretend play (e.g. her mother using a banana as a telephone); they also confuse the personal pronouns which require a change of perspective (they may say: "you want biscuit" when they actually mean "I want a biscuit"; Frith et al. 1991, Leslie and German 1995). These phenomena illustrate the narrow connection between "as-if"-thinking or symbolising, and interpersonality.

In schizophrenia, a failure to symbolise becomes apparent mainly in concretism (the inability to interpret proverbs) or in the concretistic language of delusion. The tension between the symbolic and the concrete level of meaning cannot be kept up, and they are equated. For the same reason, perspective-taking in social situations threatens (with loss of) the self: the schizophrenic patient is caught in the decentred perspective and cannot maintain his own embodied centre. The perspectives of self and other are confused instead of being integrated. This short-circuiting of perspectives may lead to the experience of thought-broadcasting: all his thoughts are known to others; there is no difference between his mental life and that of others any more.

It is for this reason that schizophrenia manifests itself often in situations of social exposure and emotional disclosure, when the affirmation of one's own intentionality against the perspective of the others is at stake: e.g. when leaving one's parents' home, starting an intimate relationship or entering into working life. In such situations, the patient may lose his embodied perspective and get entangled in an imaginary view of himself from the outside: everyone seems to look or spy at him, everything is meant for him — he becomes the defenceless object of anonymous intentions. His intentionality is not strong enough to keep up the tension between embodied and virtual perspectives. Thus we find again what may be called a *disembodiment*, caused not by the loss of natural habits, but by a loss of self in the dialectical process of interpersonal perception.

Of course, this symbolising function is the highest of the human mind, and there is no easy way to explore its neurobiological underpinnings. We may at least assume that different brain regions have to work in interconnection to allow this metarepresentional function to emerge. And one may speculate that it could ultimately be based on the mirroring function of the felt body in intercorporeality that I mentioned earlier, which begins when the baby sees his mother for the first time.

Conclusion

I hope to have shown by these examples how the phenomenological approach may contribute to psychiatric understanding and research. Finally, I want to quote Laing once more:

> ...the theory of man as person loses its way if it falls into an account of man as a machine or man as an organismic system of it-processes. ...It seems extraordinary that ...an authentic science of persons has hardly got started by reason of the inveterate tendency to depersonalise or reify persons (Laing 1960, 21).

Laing reminds us that psychiatry as a science is always in danger of depersonalising the patient by viewing his behaviour and utterances only in terms of disturbed neuronal connections, transmitter imbalances, etc. This depersonalising tendency is partly due to the alienating effect of psychotic illness itself. Phenomenology may be a possible remedy against this danger: a scientific attitude that takes subjectivity seriously and by the epoché seeks to find the common roots of experience that connect the psychiatrist and the patient, even when there is a limit to mutual understanding on a symbolic level.

references

Burndl K, Cranach M, Grüsser OJ (1986) Impairment of perception and recognition of faces, mimic expression and gestures in schizophrenic patients. Eur. Arch. Psychiat. Neurol. Sci. 5: 282-291.

Blankenburg W (1979) Phaenomenologische Epoché und Psychopathologie. In: Sprondel WM, Grathoff R (eds) Alfred Schuetz und die Idee des Alltags in den Sozialwissenschaften, pp 125-139. Enke, Stuttgart.

Chapman J (1966) The early symptoms of schizophrenia. Brit. J. Psychiat. 112, 225-251.

Gallese V, Fadiga L, Fogassi L, Rizzolatti G (1996) Action recognition in the premotor cortex. Brain 119, 593-609.

Frith U, Morton J, Leslie AM (1991) The cognitive basis of a biological disorder: autism. Trends in the Neurosciences 14, 433-438.

Fuchs T (2001) The disturbance of inner time consciousness in schizophrenia. Psychopathology.

Kant O (1927) Zum Verständnis des schizophrenen Beeinflussungsgefühls. Z. ges. Neurol. Psychiat. 111,433-441.

Laing RD, (1960) The divided self. Tavistock, London.

Laing RD, Phillipson H, Lee AR (1966) Interpersonal perception. Tavistock, London.

Leslie A, German TP (1995) Knowledge and ability in theory of mind: one-eyed overview of a debate. In Davies M, Stone T (eds) Mental simulation. Evaluations and applications. Blackwell, Oxford, 123-151.

Marazziti D, Cassano GB (1997) Neuroscience: Where is it heading? Biol Psychiat 41: 127-129.

Meltzoff A, Moore MK (1977) Imitation of facial and manual gestures by human neonates. Science 198:75-78.

Meltzoff A, Moore MK (1989) Imitation in newborn infants: exploring the range of gestures imitated and the underlying mechanisms. Developmental Psychol. 25: 954-962.

Merleau-Ponty M (1945) Phénomenologie de la perception. Gallimard, Paris. Engl. Transl. by Colin Smith (1996) Phenomenology of perception. Humanities Press, New York.

Nagel T (1974) What is it like to be a bat? The Philosophical Review 83: 435-450.

Parnas J, Bovet P (1995) Research in psychopathology: epistemologic issues. Compr Psychiat 32: 1-15.

Plessner H (1975) Die Stufen des Organischen und der Mensch. De Gruyter, Berlin.

Rizzolatti G, Fadiga L, Gallese V, Fogassi L (1996) Premotor cortex and the recognition of motor actions. Brain Res Cogn Brain Res 3: 131-141.

Schmitz H (1965) System der Philosophie. Vol. II/1: Der Leib. Bouvier, Bonn.

Spitzer M, Weisker I, Maier S, Hermle L, Maher BA (1994) Semantic and phonological priming in schizophrenia. J Abnorm Psychol 103: 485-494.

Steimer-Krause E, Krause R, Wagner G (1990) Interaction regulations used by schizophrenic and psychosomatic patients: studies on facial behaviour in dyadic interactions. Psychiatry 53:209-228.

Straus E (1956) Vom Sinn der Sinne. Springer, Berlin Göttingen Heidelberg.

Varela FJ (1996) Neurophenomenology. A methodological remedy for the hard problem. J Consciousness Studies 3: 330-349.

Varela FJ (1996a) The specious present : A neurophenomenology of nowness. In Petitot J, Roy JM, Pachoud B, Varela FJ (eds) Naturalizing phenomenology: Contemporary issues in phenomenology and cognitive science, pp 266-314. Stanford Univ Press.

Zahavi D, Parnas J (1998) Phenomenal consciousness and self-awareness: A phenomenological critique of representational theory. J Consciousness Studies 5: 687-705.

11: R.D. Laing: An appraisal in the light of recent research
Richard P. Bentall

R.D. Laing: An appraisal in the light of recent research
Richard P. Bentall

"Schizophrenics have more to teach psychiatrists about the inner world than psychiatrists their patients."

R.D. Laing (1967)

In recent times, attempts to explain and treat the psychoses (conditions in which the individual experiences hallucinations and delusions, and is said to be in some sense 'out of touch' with 'reality') have mostly been guided by a set of assumptions made by psychiatrists in the late nineteenth and early twentieth centuries. Following the work of Emil Kraepelin (1899/1990) and others who attempted to classify these conditions into categories such as 'schizophrenia' and 'manic depression', it has been widely assumed that there is a clear dividing line between psychotic illness and sanity, and that there is not one type of psychotic illness but several discrete types. Following the work of Karl Jaspers (1913/1963, 1913/1974) and later authorities such as Kurt Schneider (1959), it has been assumed that psychotic experiences are beyond understanding in psychological terms, so that psychiatrists need only attend to the form rather than the content of the experiences related by their patients. These assumptions have constituted a paradigm (henceforth, the Kraepelinian paradigm), in the exact sense of the term outlined by the philosopher Thomas Kuhn (1970) — they have formed a theoretical framework that has rarely been explicitly articulated but which has guided scientific research and the construction of theoretical models, which in turn have constrained the choice of treatments offered to patients. In modern times, this paradigm has been realized in the form of diagnostic handbooks such as the American Psychiatric Association's Diagnostic and Statistical Manual (DSM; A.P.A., 1994) and the World Health Organization's International Classification of Diseases (W.H.O., 1992); in the expenditure of huge amounts of money in efforts to discover the genetic and neurobiological origins of the psychoses, and in psychiatric services that rely on medication as the main form of intervention and which have neglected the psychological needs of their patients.

As Kuhn pointed out, scientific paradigms can be extremely difficult to question, mainly because their core assumptions seem self-evidently true (thereby requiring no justifications) to the majority of people working in the relevant field. This is certainly true in the case of the Kraepelinian paradigm, which has now dominated psychiatric research and practice for more than a hundred years. Nevertheless, a number of critics have, at different times, challenged its hegemony and have offered alternative understandings of psychotic behaviour.

The Scottish 'anti-psychiatrist' Ronald Laing, an insightful but troubled clinician and theorist whose work was rooted in psychoanalysis and existential philosophy, was for a time one of the most prominent critics of the Kraepelinian approach. His influence in the 1960s and 1970s extended well beyond psychiatry and clinical psychology, because his ideas resonated with the emerging counter-culture, in which parental and government authority were distrusted, and in which many young people were attempting to explore new values, new forms of art and music and alternative life styles. However, despite (or perhaps because of) this success, Laing ultimately failed to establish an alternative account of the psychoses that could be widely accepted by his medical colleagues. Like other critics of the period (for example the American psychiatrist Thomas Szasz, 1960, 1979, who argued that 'mental illness' is a self-contradictory concept; see Bentall, 2004) Laing provoked considerable hostility from his professional colleagues, and was eventually dismissed as eccentric and irrelevant to the main agenda of the psychiatric profession. It can even be argued that, paradoxically, Laing helped perpetuate the Kraepelinian paradigm, as the authors of influential third edition of the DSM (biological psychiatrists who explicitly styled themselves as 'neoKraepelinians', cf Klerman, 1978) were partly motivated by a desire to defend the approach against the anti-psychiatry movements, which they believed threatened the very existence of their profession.

However, the eventual triumph of the neoKraepelinians, and the demise of Laing's influence, has not been the end of the story. In the last decade, the Kraepelinian paradigm has come under renewed criticism, this time from researchers interested in explaining the unusual behaviour and experiences of patients. Most of those contributing to this critique have been clinical psychologists and psychiatrists who have been involved in the development of cognitive-behavioural interventions for hallucinations, delusions and other types of psychotic complaints. Unlike Laing's critique, this new attack shares the scientific values claimed by traditional psychiatry, but uses research evidence to show that the Kraepelinian paradigm fails as a framework for either accounting for psychotic experiences or guiding clinical activity. My purpose in writing this essay is to contrast this new critique with Laing's of more than three decades ago. I will not attempt to provide a comprehensive summary of Laing's ideas about psychosis; to do so would be difficult because these ideas are complex, his writing is sometimes opaque, and at different times he advanced hypotheses that, if not exactly contradictory, were hardly consistent with each other. Instead, I will highlight five main themes that emerge from Laing's work, and address the extent to which they are echoed in the more recent work conducted by psychological investigators.

The scientific validity of Kraepelinian diagnoses

For Laing it was self-evident that the Kraepelinian paradigm is unable to address the complex experiences of individuals who are labeled ' schizophrenic'. Although he never offered a detailed analysis of the scientific limitations of the Kraepelinian approach, it is clear that he was aware of them. For example, in their preface to the second edition of *Sanity Madness and the Family*, Laing and his colleague Aaron Esterson (1969) remarked that:

> "If anyone thinks that 'schizophrenia' is fact, he would do well to read critically the literature on 'schizophrenia' from its inventor Bleuler to the present day. After much disbelief in the new disease more and more psychiatrists adopted the term, though few English or American psychiatrists knew what it meant, since Bleuler's monograph, published in 1911, was not available in English till 1950. But though the term has now been generally adopted as psychiatrists trained in its application, the fact it is supposed to denote remains elusive. Even two psychiatrists from the same medical school cannot agree on who is schizophrenic independently of each other more than eight out of ten times, at best; agreement is less than that between different schools, and less again between different countries. These figures are not in dispute. But when psychiatrists dispute the diagnosis there is no reliable count of

appeal. There are at present no objective, reliable, quantifiable criteria — behavioral or neurophysiological or biochemical — to appeal to when psychiatrists differ".

In this passage, Laing and Esterson appear to be referring to what I have elsewhere described as 'the great classification crisis in psychiatry' (Bentall, 2003) — the realisation that psychiatric diagnoses were being used so haphazardly, that they were almost useless for either research or clinical purposes. This crisis came to a head in the mid-1970s, when it was found that the systematic differences existed in the way that diagnoses were being used in different countries (with US psychiatrists being much more willing to so diagnose patients as schizophrenic than their UK counterparts; cf. Cooper et al., 1972) and with the discovery that agreement between independent clinicians in the same country diagnosing the same patients was often not strikingly better than chance (Spitzer & Fliess, 1974). It was these discoveries that led to the development and eventual publication of the third edition of the DSM (American Psychiatric Association, 1980), which contained detailed operational criteria for a wide range of psychiatric conditions. Following the publication of this handbook, prominent self-styled neoKraepelinians pronounced that acceptable levels of diagnostic reliability (technically defined in terms of inter-clinician agreement) were now achievable (Hyler, Williams, & Spitzer, 1982) and that the problems of psychiatric classification had at last been solved (Klerman, 1986). Recent critiques of the Kraepelinian paradigm, for example by Mary Boyle (1990) and myself (Bentall, 2003), have questioned these claims.

The reliability data from the DSM field trials have been exhaustively analysed by Kirk & Kutchins (1992), who point out that these experiments have been designed in such a way that they give estimates of reliability that far exceed those achievable in routine clinical practice. This is because the participating clinicians have typically received special training, and have used lengthy, structured diagnostic interview schedules that have ensured that symptom information has been collected in a uniform manner. However, even under these exacting conditions, Kirk and Kutchins found that most diagnoses failed to meet the level of reliability defined in advance as acceptable (a value of 0.7 using the kappa statistic for measuring agreement above chance level). In an experiment designed to examine the levels of reliability achieved when clinicians are allowed to collect relevant clinical information in different ways, (McGorry et al., 1995), found that, when any two out of four methods (three different kinds of structured interviews and interview by a team who negotiated a consensus diagnosis) were compared, kappa values varied between 0.53 and 0.67. Full agreement between all four procedures was achieved for only 27 out of the 50 patients who participated in the study.

Matter become more complicated still when it is remembered that the DSM system constitutes only one of the many sets of diagnostic criteria proposed by researchers at one time or another. Brockington (1992) compared a number of definitions of schizophrenia as applied to clinical data collected from a group of patients attending Netherne Hospital in London, finding that the number who were schizophrenic varied between 163 and 19 according to the definition used. In a similar comparison of three sets of diagnostic criteria as applied to over 700 patients, (Van Os et al., 1999) again found striking differences, so that the number of schizophrenia patients varied from 268 (38.0%) using Feighner et al.'s (1972) Research Diagnostic Criteria and 387 (54.8%) according to the tenth addition of the International Classification of Disease.

Other critics of the Kraepelinian paradigm have pointed out that reliability, even if achievable, is no guarantee of the scientific validity of diagnoses (Bentall, 1990). By way of illustrating this point, it is possible to think of an imaginary syndrome (Bentall's disease), which consists of a meaningless combination of symptoms (say, red hair, ownership of a large number of Pink Floyd albums, and a history of summer colds), which could be diagnosed with a high degree of reliability. Validity can only be assessed by determining whether diagnoses pick out patients with similar, naturally occurring clusters of symptoms with similar aetiologies, which have similar outcomes, and which respond to similar treatments. Suffice it to say here that there is no evidence that the diagnosis of 'schizophrenia' identifies a naturally occurring cluster of symptoms — indeed, schizophrenia symptoms seem to fall into at least three independent clusters of positive symptoms (hallucinations and delusions), symptoms of cognitive disorganization (including disordered speech) and negative symptoms (anhedonia, flat affect, avolition) (Andreasen, Roy, & Flaum, 1995: Liddle, 1987). Nor does it seem that the diagnoses pick out patients with a common and unique genetic aetiology (Crow, 1991: Crow, 1997), or with a common poor outcome as supported by Kraepelin (Bleuler, 1978: Ciompi, 1984). Perhaps more alarming for clinicians, the only trial in which drug treatment (antipsychotic, mood stabilizer, both or neither) was randomly assigned to psychotic patients irrespective of their diagnoses found that DSM diagnoses were very poor predictors of drug response (Johnstone, Crow, Frith, & Owens, 1988).

Overall, then, it would seem that Laing's scepticism about the value of Kraepelinian diagnoses was more than justified. However, the implications drawn by Laing and modern researchers have been different. Recent critics of the Kraepelinian paradigm have sought a new framework for developing a scientific account of psychosis that does not depend on broad diagnostic categories, and have hit on the strategy of studying the psychological processes involved in particular complaints (what psychiatrist have traditionally 'symptoms'). This approach has now become so well established that it has begun to attract counter-critiques from neoKraepelinians (Mojtabia & Rieder, 1998). For Laing, by contrast, at least in his later writings, the failure of the Kraepelinian paradigm meant that psychotic experiences could not be understood as properties of people, but as consequence of certain kinds of social relations.

The intelligibility of psychotic communication

The claim that *the psychoses are intelligible*, both in the sense that the experiences and behaviour of psychotic patients have meaningful content, is probably Laing's most important contribution. This attitude comes over very clearly in a striking passage from *The Divided Self* in which Laing (1960) quotes Kraepelin (1905) presenting an apparently thought disordered patient to a group of medical students:

> "The patient I will show you today has almost to be carried into the room, as he walks in a straddling fashion on the outside of his feet. On coming in, he throws off his slippers, sings a hymn loudly, and then cries twice (in English), 'My father, my real father!' He is eighteen years old, and a pupil of the Oberrealschule (higher-grade school), tall, and rather strongly

built, but with a pale complexion, on which there is very often a transient flush. The patient sits with his eyes shut, and pays no attention to his surroundings. He does not look up even when he is spoken to, but he answers beginning in a low voice, and gradually screaming louder and louder. When asked where he is, he says 'You want to know that too? I tell you who is being measured and is measured and shall be measured. I know all that, and could tell you, but I do not want to.' When asked his name, he screams, 'What is your name? What does he shut? He shuts his eyes. What does he hear? He does not understand; he understands not. How? Who? Where? When? What does he mean? When I tell him to look he does not look properly. You there, just look! What is it? What is the matter? Attend: he attends not. I say, what is it,? Why do you give me no answer? Are you getting impudent again? How can you be so impudent? I'm coming? I'll show you! You don't whore for me. You mustn't be smart either; you're an impudent, lousy fellow, such an impudent lousy fellow I've never met with. Is he beginning again? You understand nothing at all, nothing at all; nothing at all does he understand. If you follow now, he won't follow, will not. Are you getting still more impudent? Are you getting impudent still more? How they attend, they do attend,' and so on. In the end, he scolds in quite inarticulate sounds...."

Although Kraepelin goes on to assert that the patient, "has not given us a single useful piece of useful information. His talk was... only a series of disconnected sentences having no relation whatever to the general situation", Laing found the patient's behaviour very easy to comprehend:

"What does the patient appear to be doing? Surely he is carrying on as dialogue between his own parodied version of Kraepelin, and his own defiance rebelling self. 'You want to know that too? I tell you who is being measured and is measured and shall be measured. I know all that, and I could tell you, but I do not want to.' This seems to be plain enough talk. Presumably he deeply resents this form of interrogation, which is being carried out before of lecture room of students. He probably does not see what it has to do with the things that must be deeply distressing him. But these things would not be 'useful information' to Kraepelin except as further 'signs' of a 'disease'...

Now it seems clear that this patient's behaviour can be seen in at least two ways... One may see his behaviour as 'signs' of a 'disease'; one may see his behaviour as expressive of his exsistence... What is the patient's experience of Kraepelin? He seems to be tormented and desperate. What is he 'about' in speaking and acting in this way? He is objecting to be measured and tested. He wants to be heard."

Thus, in Laing's work the psychotic patient is portrayed as attempting to engage in meaningful communication about his experience. To take another example, this time from *The Politics of Experience*:

"To regard the gambits of Smith and Jones [two patients whose apparently incoherent conversation he has recorded and reported] as due primarily to some psychological deficit is rather like supposing that a man doing a handstand on a bicycle on a tightrope 100 feet up with no safety net is suffering from an inability to stand on his own two feet." (Laing, 1967)

In fact, Laing's observations about psychotic speech anticipated the results of modern research into thought disorder (which is better constructed as a communication disorder, as there is no evidence that reasoning is abnormal in the thoughts of disordered patients, cf. Andreasen, 1982). In a series of studies, Harrow and Prosen (1978, 1979) recorded the thought disordered speech of patients and then, at a later date, sensitively interviewed them about what they had said. They found that patients could often give a coherent account of their previously unintelligible speech, and that the apparently thought-disordered content reflected the 'intermingling' or intrusion of emotionally salient ideas, usually concerning distressing experiences earlier in life. Subsequent studies by other investigators have confirmed that the speech of thought/communication disordered patients is perfectly intelligible under most circumstances, but becomes unintelligible only when the patient is discussing emotionally salient topics (Docherty, Evans, Sledge, Seibyl, & Krystal, 1994; Docherty, Hall, & Gordinier, 1998; Haddock, Wolfenden, Lowens, Tarrier, & Bentall, 1995). Interestingly in the light of the argument that complaints rather than diagnoses should be the focus of research, this seems to be as true of the speech of patients diagnosed as suffering from 'manic depression' as it is of the speech of patients diagnosed as suffering from 'schizophrenia' (Tai, Haddock, & Bentall, 2004).

Laing and modern critics of the Kraepelinian system differ about the origins of this intelligibility. As Peter Sedgwick (1972) pointed out in early commentary on Laing's work, although in *The Divided Self*, "the disturbed state is an attribute, at least in large part, of the individual who presents himself as a patient", Laing quickly abandoned this position, and went on to claim that psychotic behaviour should be understood entirely in terms of the social context. Therefore, whereas in *The Divided Self* a set of psychological mechanisms underlying the experience of 'schizophrenia' is proposed — woven out of concepts borrowed from psychoanalysis and existential philosophy - this is not the case in the accounts of psychosis offered in *The Politics of Experience* or (with Esterson) in *Sanity, Madness and the Family*. Recent investigators, by contrast, have not doubted that there is something intrinsically odd in the way that psychotic patients speak, and have argued that the unintelligibility occurs because patients, when under emotional stress, find it difficult to adjust their speech to meet the perceived needs of the listener. This difficulty, in turn, is attributed to various cognitive deficits, for example, working memory limitations (Goldberg & Weinberger, 2000), the patients' difficulty in distinguishing between their own speech and their own thoughts (Harvey, 1985) or their inability to understand the mental state of the other person involved in the conversation (Sarfati, Hadt-Bayles, Besche, & Widloecher, 1997; Sarfati & Hardy-Bayle, 1999).

Thought/communication disorder is not the only psychotic complaint that has been studied by recent critics of the Kraepelinian paradigm. For example, research evidence has been collected to show patients with delusions tend to 'jump to conclusions' while weighing evidence relating to their beliefs (Garety & Freeman, 1999) and that those with persecutory beliefs tend to have abnormal style of explaining threatening events, attributing them to the actions of others, possibly to avoid loss of self-esteem that would be consequent on blaming the self (Bentall, Corcoran, Howard, Blackwood, & Kinderman, 2001). Recent research has also shown auditory hallucinations result from an inability to monitor the source of experiences, so that self-directed inner speech is attributed to agents external to the self (Bentall, 2000) and that passivity of experiences reflects a difficulty in monitoring intentional behaviour (Blackmore et al., 2000). The negative symptoms of 'schizophrenia' have been less intensively studied, although there is evidence that they involve both the exercise of negative affect (Blanchard, Bellack, & Mueser, 1994) and also a difficulty in communicating affect by means of facial expressions (Berenbaum & Oltmanns, 1992).

It should be noted that not all those studies of the psychology of particular complaints are critical of the Kraepelinian approach. Some (especially American) psychologists regard the discovery of the cognitive mechanism involved in 'symptoms' as supplementary to the attempt to find a biological explanation for 'schizophrenia'.

It is important to note that the identification of these kinds of psychological mechanism does not put in doubt the meaningfulness of the experiences concerned. On the contrary, psychotic experiences seem all the more intelligible, once the relevant mechanisms are known. For example, the paranoid worldview of the deluded patient becomes easier to understand when it is realized that the patient is avoiding attributing negative events to the self, and the dreadful, critical voices that sometimes torment hallucinating patients become more understandable when it is realized that the patients, suffering from crushingly low self-esteem, are speaking to themselves. The main advantage of this kind of understanding over intrusive appreciation of the patient's worldview as advocated by Laing is that it leads to tangible therapeutic strategies, based on individuality-tailored psychological formulations of the patient's difficulties, which are in turn informed by the psychological evidence (Morrison et al., 2003).

The arbitrariness of sanity

Laing's observation that psychosis is intelligible led him to conclude that the distinction between psychosis and sanity is almost meaningless. This idea comes over most clearly in The Politics of Experience, (Laing, 1967) in which he observes that, "The perfectly adjusted bomber pilot may be a greater risk to society than the hospitalized schizophrenic deluded that the Bomb is inside in him". This is why, for Laing, the process of psychiatric diagnosis is a political event:

"A feature of the interplay between psychiatrist and patient is that if the patient's part is taken out of context, as is done in the clinical description, it might seem very odd. The psychiatrist's part, however, is taken as the very touchstone for our common-sense view of normality. The psychiatrist, as ipso facto sane, shows that the patient is out of contact with him. The fact that he is out of contact with the patient shows that there is something wrong with the patient, but not with the psychiatrist." (Laing, 1967)

Recent psychological research has addressed the distinction between psychosis and sanity in a slightly different, less radical way. Beginning in the 1970s, personality theorists in both the United States (Chapman, Chapman, & Raulin, 1976; Chapman, Edell, & Chapman, 1980) and in Britain (Claridge, 1987) began to argue for a continuum between psychosis and normal functioning, partly because questionnaire studies (mostly conducted with undergraduate students) found that a surprising number of ordinary people were willing to report psychotic phenomena such as transitory hallucinatory experiences or bizarre beliefs. (It subsequently emerged that these reports fell into three main types — unusual experiences, subjective cognitive difficulties and introverted anhedonia — that corresponded to the main clusters of psychotic complaints reported by patients; cf Bentall, Claridge, & Slade, 1989; Claridge et al., 1996). Although psychiatrists initially ignored these observations, analyses of data from large-scale epidemiological studies (in which random population samples were given psychiatric interviews) confirmed that many more people experience psychotic phenomena than might be expected from psychiatric admission data. For example, in the Epidemiological Catchment Area Study of 18,000 US citizens, it was found that between 11% and 13% of those interviewed had experienced hallucinations meeting the DSM criteria (Tien, 1991). In a similar study of over 7,000 Dutch citizens, it was found that 1.7% of those interviewed had experienced 'true' hallucinations but that a further 6.2% had experienced hallucinations that were judged to be not clinically relevant because they did not occasion distress. In the same study, 0.3% were found to have 'true' delusions but 8.7% were judged to have delusions that were not clinically relevant for the same reason. (van Os, Hanssen, Bijl, & Ravelli, 2000). Overall, it would seem that about ten times more people experience psychotic states than receive a diagnosis of 'schizophrenia'.

Of course, this discovery raises the important question of why some people become patients whereas others avoid becoming enmeshed with psychiatric services. Modern research has shown that it is usually not psychotic experiences *per se* but catastrophic beliefs about those experiences (Morrison, 2001), the fear that they are more powerful than the self (Honig et al., 1998) and represent omnipotent forces (Birchwood, Meaden, Trower, Gilbert, & Plaistow, 2000), and the consequent emotional distress (van Os et al., 2000) that led the patient to the clinic. (It is for this reason that cognitive behavioural psychotherapists advocate 'normalising' psychotic experiences as an essential element of the psychological treatment of psychosis, cf Kingdon & Turkington, 1991).

For Laing, by contrast, the decision about whether the individual becomes a patient or not is seen as largely external to the individual − a conspiracy between the medical profession and family members designed to invalidate the patient's experience. This conspiracy is possible precisely because the Kraepelinian diagnostic system leads the clinician to ignore the social context in which the patient's behaviour occurs. (It may be that this conspiratorial view of diagnosis is less easily accepted today partly because modern clinicians often find themselves as gatekeepers, limiting access to scarce psychiatric beds. Under these circumstances, psychiatrists sometimes require quite a lot of persuading before they will concede that a person is mentally ill.)

Sanity, madness and the family

It was Laing's conviction that psychosis can only be understood in its social context that led him to study the families of psychotic patients. Although his book with Aaron Esterson (1969) provoked considerable hostility from his psychiatric colleagues, mainly because it failed to meet their preferred scientific standards and lacked a control group, Laing and Esterson claimed that they had not aimed to show that the families of psychotic patients were different from other families, but that psychotic beginners and experiences are understandable once the family is known. To some extent this claim may have been disingenuous; as Sedgwick (1972) has noted, Laing and Esterson originally planned to write a second volume dealing with the families of healthy children, which would have made a comparison inevitable.

Whatever the truth about this matter, it is doubtful whether anyone could read the accounts given by Laing and Esterson of families like the Abbotts, the Golds and the Kings, and welcome these people as neighbours. They are portrayed as manipulative, controlling and suffocating at every turn; locked in a desperate struggle to maintain their identities by sacrificing those of their 'mentally ill' daughters. In the case of the Abbotts, for example, the reader is led to regard their daughter Maya's paranoid illness as a reaction to their refusal to recognise her growing autonomy, a refusal that extended to flatly contradicting Maya's own account of her thoughts and feelings. Therefore,

> "In respect of depersonalisation, catatonic and paranoid symptoms, impoverishment of affect, autistic withdrawal and auditory hallucinations, confusion of 'ego boundaries', it seems to us, in this case, more likely that they are the outcome of her inter-experience and interaction with her parents. They seem to be quite in keeping with the social reality in which she lived." (Laing & Esterson, 1969)

Within psychiatry, the negative reaction to this kind of portrayal — which was seen as victimizing the long-suffering and greatly burdened parents of the mentally ill — created a climate of opinion in which it became almost taboo to consider the role of family dynamics in psychosis, or indeed in any other psychiatric condition (Johnstone, 1999). Ironically, this occurred just as firm evidence emerged that family relationships could affect the *course* of a psychotic disorder, so that children returning from hospital to live with 'high expressed emotion' parents (parents who are critical and over-protective, arguably similar in some ways to some of the parents described by Laing and Esterson) were shown to be at much higher risk of relapse than children who returned to live with 'low expressed emotion' parents (who accept their children's unusual behaviour and respect their autonomy) (Bebbington & Kuipers, 1994; Vaughn & Lefft, 1976). This apparent contradiction between scientific ideology and compelling data has led some researchers to assert, without evidence, that although families may influence the chance of recovery after the onset of illness, "We consider that families do not exert a *causal* influence" (Kuipers, Birchwood, & McCreadie, 1992).

Not surprisingly, in this climate research into the aetiological role of the social environment has been scarce. Nevertheless, the limited evidence that has been collected suggests that families may sometimes play a casual role in the development of psychotic complaints, but also that their behaviour towards their children is only part of a complex network of influences. For example, Singer & Wynne (1965a, 1965b) found that thought/ communication disorder in children is associated with 'communication deviance' (a style of speech that is persistently vague, fragmented or contradictory) in parents — the greater the communication deviants in the mentally well parents the greater the severity of the thought/communication disorder in their 'schizophrenic' children. That this is not merely a genetic effect has emerged from an adoption study conducted by Tienari and colleagues in Finland, in which it was shown that the adopted away (and hence genetically vulnerable) offspring of 'schizophrenic' parents were more likely to develop thought/ communication disorder than the adopted away offspring of non-'schizophrenic' parents, but only when raised by adoptive parents who exhibited high levels of communication deviants (Wahlberg et al., 1997).

Other aspects of family relationships have also been highlighted in longitudinal research. For example, in the Copenhagen high-risk study, it was found that reports of dysfunctional family relationships in healthy adolescence at high genetic risk (because one or more parent had been diagnosed as suffering from 'schizophrenia') predicted the later development of psychosis (Schiffman et al., 2002). In a very large cohort study of children born in Finland, it was found that the risk of psychosis at twenty-six years of age was raised by a factor of four if the mother, during pregnancy, had described the child as unwanted (Myhrman, Rantakallio, Isohanni, & Jones, 1996). To be sure, these findings might be explained in other ways (perhaps the mothers of 'schizophrenia' patients themselves suffer from a mild form of genetically determined psychosis) but the most likely explanation is that certain types of family dynamics affect the development of the psychological processes that underlie complaints such as hallucinations and abnormal beliefs. (See Bentall, 2003, for a more detailed discussion of the relevant evidence).

Despite these findings, the picture of patients' families that emerges from recent research is much less damning than the portrait painted by Laing and Esterson. It is now recognised that, when parents fail to provide their children with optimum child-rearing experiences, it is usually because they are struggling with their own psychological difficulties, which in turn may reflect their own childhood experiences (Diamond & Doane, 1994, Paley et al., 2000). Moreover, even the most damaging action by parents may results from good motives (as when the high expressed emotion parent is over-protective out of love) or may at least be understandable (as when a parent, almost crushed by a burden of guilt, externalises her negative feelings towards herself in the form of criticism directed at her child).

When recent investigators have addressed the role of the environment in the development of psychosis, they also acknowledged that the family may not be the only influence of importance. It seems that, for example, early exposure to inner city environments (Mortensen et al., 1999), experiences of radical discrimination (Boydell et al., 2001), victimisation (Mirowsky & Ross, 1983) and trauma (Mueser et al., 1998), can all increase the risk that the developing child will develop hallucinations and paranoid beliefs. Further understanding of the origins of psychosis will undoubtedly require a much richer description of the environment than Laing or even more recent researchers have been able to offer, and exploration of how different kinds of influences interact with biological endowment to affect the development of the psychological processes that give rise to unusual experiences and behaviour.

Psychosis as a transcendental, healing experience

In much of Laing's work, psychosis was seen as some kind of problem, either as a form of distress in itself (*The Divided Self*) or as the mark of some kind of rupture in social relationships (*Sanity Madness and the Family*). In *The Politics of Experience*, however, Laing (1967) offers a more startling portrayal of madness, in which the psychotic, in response to the intolerable pressures associated with modern social relationships, embarks on some kind of inner voyage. Under optimum circumstances (such as those which Laing attempted to offer the residents of Kingsley Hall, his therapeutic community) the journey would be healing, and the traveller might be expected to return more integrated, at one with herself, and better able to tolerate the contradictions of modern society. Laing's description of this kind of journey is shrouded in 'mysticism:'

"What is entailed then is:
(i)   a voyage from outer to inner,
(ii)   from life to a kind of death,
(iii)   from going forwards to going back,
(iv)   from temporal movement to standstill,
(v)   from mundane time to aeonic time,
(vi)   from the ego to the self,
(vii)   from being outside (post-birth) back into the womb of all things, and then subsequently a return voyage from,

    (1)   inner to outer,
    (2)   from death to life,
    (3)   from the movement back to a movement once more forward,
    (4)   from immortality back to mortality,
    (5)   from eternity back to time,
    (6)   from self to a new ego,
    (7)   from a cosmic foetalization to an existential rebirth"

Laing's only detailed account of a psychotic episode of this sort concerns a 'ten-day voyage' undertaken by a sculptor, Jesse Watkins, twenty-seven years before *The Politics of Experience* was published. However, a more detailed, autobiographical account of a similar, but more protracted voyage into psychosis was subsequently published by Mary Barnes, a nurse who later became an artist (Barnes & Berke, 1973, see also Schatzman, 1972). The fact that both of these case studies involve people who were highly creative provides the only discernable point of contact between this phase of Laing's work and recent research.

The idea that there maybe a positive side to psychosis is not unique to Laing. Indeed, speculation about an association between madness and creativity can be traced back as far as the ancient Greeks (Brod, 1997). In recent times, researchers have attempted to test this association in various ways. For example, some have shown that patients with a diagnosis of 'schizophrenia' score highly on psychological measures of creativity (Keefe & Magaro, 1980). Others have attempted to measure psychological symptoms in usually creative people and their relatives, typically finding high rates of psychosis, although more often meeting the criteria for 'manic depression' than 'schizophrenia' (Post, 1996; Simonton, 1994). However, perhaps the most impressive study that has addressed this issue was conducted by Karlsson (1984), who examined the professional status of relatives of schizophrenia patients admitted to hospital in Iceland between 1851 and 1940. Using available records to enable a comparison with the general population, he showed that the first-degree relatives of the patients significantly more often entered creative occupations.

To the mind this of this writer, therefore, the connection between psychosis and creativity is proven. However, this does not mean that we should accept Laing's romantic notion of a kind of super-sanity, willingly entered into by people who are too sensitive to endure the contradictions and inauthenticity of life in the capitalist world. The problem with psychosis is that it is more often a curse than a benefit; it robs more people of the ability to cope with stress and dysfunctional relationships than it provides others with alternative, viable ways of being in the world. Perhaps the best evidence that this is so, is that more than one in ten patients successfully arrange their own departure from this life by suicide.

Without a doubt, Laing's greatest contribution was to make his readers change their point of reference in order to see the world from the viewpoint of the patient defined as psychotic. He achieved this aim with language that was at times powerful and polemical and, at other times, opaque and steeped in existential philosophy that is perhaps alien to the Anglo-Saxon, scientifically educated mind. He supported his arguments with vivid case studies that demonstrated an unusual ability to empathise with people in severe psychological distress, whose behaviour seemed bizarre and irrational to others. And yet, his long-term influence on mainstream psychiatry has been at the best very limited. There are several reasons why this was the case.

Although Laing the man is beyond the scope of this essay, it is fair to describe him as troubled and, at times self-destructive.

His predilection for alcohol became legendary and, at times, reduced him to an embarrassing level of incoherence in public places (Clay, 1996). These attributes were not those of the successful guru; nor did they inspire his professional colleagues. More importantly, perhaps, Laing's work failed to deliver a proven, alternative way of managing the distress of people who would otherwise avail themselves of conventional treatments. Of course, this does not mean that Laing's ideas about providing psychotic people with a safe refuge were worthless; the only scientific attempt to test the effectiveness of this kind of approach in fact produced encouraging results (Mosher, 1999). However, Laing either failed to see the need to evaluate alternative strategies for working with psychosis, or lacked the skills to do so.

By contrast, modern clinical psychologists and psychiatrists who are critical of the Kraepelinian paradigm have believed it essential to conduct scientific tests of their theories. Furthermore they have used their understanding of the psychological mechanisms involved in hallucinations and delusions to develop novel cognitive-behavioural interventions, which have been evaluated in clinical trials. The results of these trials can fairly be described as promising (Pilling et al., 2002). This growing body of knowledge about the origins and treatment of psychosis is more scientific and more philosophically coherent than any of the approaches that preceded it. It is therefore much harder to dismiss. Perhaps, finally, we are witnessing the demise of the Kraepelinian monolith.

references

American Psychiatric Association. (1980). *Diagnostic and statistical manual of mental disorders* - 3rd Edition. Washington, DC: Author.
American Psychiatric Association. (1994). *Diagnostic and statistical manual for mental disorders* - 4th edition. Washington, DC: Author.
Andreasen, N.C. (1982). Should the term 'thought disorder' be revised? *Comprehensive Psychiatry, 23*, 291-299.
Andreasen, N.C., Roy, M.A., & Flaum, M. (1995). Positive and negative symptoms. In S.R. Hirsch & D.R. Weinberger (Eds.), *Schizophrenia* (pp. 28-45). Oxford: Blackwell.
Barnes, M., & Berke, J. (1973), *Mary Barnes: Two accounts of a journey through madness*. London: Penguin.

Bebbington, P.E., & Kuipers, E. (1994). The predictive utility of expressed emotion in schizophrenia. *Psychological Medicine*, 24, 707-718.

Bentall, R.P. (1990). The syndromes and symptoms of psychosis: Or why you can't play 20 questions with the concept of schizophrenia and hope to win. In R.P. Bentall (Ed), *Reconstructing schizophrenia* (pp. 23-60). London: Routledge.

Bentall, R.P. (2000). Hallucinatory experiences. In E. Cardena & S.J. Lynn & S. Krippner (Eds.), *Varieties of anomalous experience: Examining the scientific evidence* (pp. 85-120). Washington, DC: American Psychological Association.

Bentall, R.P. (2003). *Madness explained: Psychosis and human nature.* London: Penguin.

Bentall. R.P. (2004). Sideshow?: Schizophrenia as construed by Szasz and the neoKraepelinians. In J. Schaler (Ed.), *Szasz under fire*. Chicago: Open Court.

Bentall, R.P., Claridge, G.S., & Slade, P.D. (1989). The multidimensional nature of schizotypal traits: A factor-analytic study with normal subjects. *British Journal of Clinical Psychology*, 28, 363-375.

Bentall, R.P., Corcoran, R., Howard, R., Blackwood, R., & Kinderman, P. (2001). Persecutory delusions: A review and theoretical integration. *Clinical Psychology Review*, 21, 1143-1192.

Berenbaum, H., & Oltmanns, T.F. (1992). Emotional experience and expression in schizophrenia and depression. *Journal of Abnormal Psychology*, 101, 37-44.

Birchwood, M., Meaden, A., Trower, P., Gilbert, P., & Plaistow, J. (2000). The power and omnipotence of voices: Subordination and entrapment by voices and significant other. *Psychological Medicine*, 30, 337-344.

Blanchard, J.J., Bellack, A.S., & Mueser, K.T. (1994). Affective and social correlates of physical and social anhedonia in schizophrenia. *Journal of Abnormal Psychology*, 103, 719-728.

Blakemore, S.J., Smith, J., Steel, R., Johnstone, E.C., & Frith, C.D. (2000). The perception of self-produced sensory stimuli in patients with auditory hallucinations and passivity experiences: Evidence for a breakdown in self-monitoring. *Psychological Medicine*, 30, 1130-1131.

Bleuler, M. (1978). *The schizophrenic disorders.* New Haven: Yale University Press.

Boydell, J. van Os, J., McKenzie, J., Allardyce, J., Goel, R., McCreadie, R.G., & Murray, R.M. (2001). Incidence of schizophrenia in ethnic minorities in London: Ecological study into interactions with environment. *British Medical Journal*, 323, 1-4.

Boyle, M, (1990). *Schizophrenia: A scientific delusion.* London: Routledge.

Brockington, I. (1992). Schizophrenia: Yesterday's concept. *European Psychiatry*, 7, 203-207.

Brod, J.H. (1997). Creativity and schizotypy. In G.S. Claridge (Ed.), *Schizotypy: Implications for illness and health.* Oxford: Oxford University Press.

Chapman, L.J., Chapman, J.P., & Raulin, M.L. (1976). Scales for psychical and social anhedonia. *Journal of Abnormal Psychology*, 85, 374-382.

Chapman, L.J., Edell, E.W., & Chapman, J.P. (1980). Psychical anhedonia, perceptual aberration and psychosis proneness. *Schizophrenia bulletin*, 6, 639-653.

Ciompi, L. (1984). Is there really a schizophrenia?: The longterm course of psychotic phenomena. *British Journal of Psychiatry*, 145, 636-640.

Claridge, G., McCreery, C., Mason, O., Bentall, R.P., Boyle, G., & Slade, P.D. (1996). The factor structure of ' schizotypal' traits: A large replication study. *British Journal of Clinical Psychology*, 35, 102-115.

Claridge, D.S. (1987). The schizophrenias as nervous types revisited. *British Journal of Psychiatry*, 151, 735-743.

Clay, J. (1996). *R.D. Laing: A divided self.* London: Hodder and Stoughton.

Cooper, J.E., Kendell, R.E., Gurland, B.J., Sharpe, L., Copeland, J.R.M., & Simon, R. (1972). *Psychiatric diagnosis in New York and London: Maudsley Monograph No. 20.* Oxford: Oxford University Press.

Crow, T. (1991). The failure of the binary concept and the psychosis gene. In A. Kerr & H. McClelland (Eds.), *Concepts of mental disorder: A continuing debate.* London: Gaskell.

Crow, T.J. (1997). Current status of linkage for schizophrenia: Polygenes of vanishingly small effect of multiple force positives? *American Journal of Medical Genetics (Neuropsychiatric Genetics)*, 74, 99-103.

Docherty, N.M., Evans, I.M., Sledge, W.H., Seibyl, J.P., & Krystal, J.H. (1994). Affective reactivity of language in schizophrenia. *Journal of Nervous and Mental Disease*, 182, 98-102.

Docherty, N.M., Hall, M.J., & Gordinier, S.W. (1998). Affective reactivity of speech in schizophrenia patients and their nonschizophrenic relatives. *Journal of Abnormal Psychology*, 107, 461-467.

Feighner, J.P., Robins, E., Guze, S.B., Woodruff, R.A., Winokur, G., & Munoz, R. (1972). Diagnostic criteria for use in psychiatric research. *Archives of General Psychiatry*, 26, 57-63.

Garety, P., & Freeman, D. (1999). Cognitive approaches to delusions: A critical review of theories and evidence. *British Journal of Clinical Psychology*.

Goldberg, T.E., & Weinberger, D.R. (2000). Thought disorder in schizophrenia: A reappraisal of older formulations and an overview of some recent studies. *Cognitive Neuropsychiatry*, 5, 1-19.

Haddock, G., Wolfenden, N., Lowens, I., Tarrier, N., & Bentall, R.P. (1995). The effect of emotional salients on the thought disorder of patients with a diagnosis of schizophrenia. *British Journal of Psychiatry*, 167, 618-620.

Harrow, N., & Prosen, M. (1978). Intermingling and the disordered logic as influences on schizophrenic thought. *Archives of General Psychiatry*, 35, 1213-1218.

Harrow, M., & Prosen, M. (1979). Schizophrenic thought disorders: Bizarre associations and intermingling. *American Journal of Psychiatry*, 136, 293-296.

Harvey, P. D. (1985). Reality monitoring in mania and schizophrenia: The association between thought disorder and performance. *Journal of Abnormal Psychology*, 92, 368-377.

Honig, A., Romme, M. A. J., Ensink, B. J., Escher, S. D. M. A, C., Pennings, M. H. A., & DeVries, M. W. (1998). Auditory hallucinations: A comparison between patients and nonpatients. *Journal of Nervous ad Mental Disease*, 186, 646-651.

Hyler, S., Williams, J., & Spitzer, R. (1982). Reliability in the DSM-III field trials. *Archives of General Psychiatry*, 39, 1275-1278.

Jaspers, K. (1913/1963). *General psychopathology* (J. Hoenig & M. W. Hamilton, Trans.). Manchester: Manchester University Press.

Jaspers, K. (1913/1974). Casual and 'meaningful' connexions between life history and psychosis. In S. R. Hirsch & M. Shepard (eds.), *Themes and variations in European psychiatry: An anthology* (pp. 81-93). Bristol: John Wright & Sons.

Johnstone, E. C., Crow, T. J., Frith, C. D., & Owens, D. G. C. (1988). The Northwick Park 'functional' psychosis study: Diagnosis and treatment response. *Lancet*, ii, 119-125.

Johnstone, L. (1999). Do families cause 'schizophrenia'?: Revisiting a taboo subject. *Changes*, 77-90.

Karlsson, J. L. (1984). Creative intelligence in relative of mental patients. *Hereditas*, 100, 83-86.

Keefe, J. A., & Margaro, P. A. (1980). Creativity and schizophrenia: An equivalence of cognitive processing. *Journal of Abnormal Psychology*, 89, 390-398.

Kingdon, D. G., & Turkington, D. (1991). Preliminary report: The use of cognitive behaviour therapy and a normalizing rationale in schizophrenia. *Journal of Nervous and Mental Disease*, 179, 207-211.

Kirk, S. A., & Kutchins, H. (1992). *The selling of DSM: The rhetoric of science in psychiatry*. Hawthorne, NY: Aldine de Gruyter.

Klerman, G. (1986). Historical perspectives on contemporary schools of psychopathology. In T. Milton & G. Klerman (Eds.), *Comtemporary directions in psychopathology: Towards DSM-IV*. New York: Guilford Press.

Klerman, G. L. (1978). The evolution of a scientific nosology. In J. C. Shershow (Ed.), *Schizophrenia: Science and practice* (pp. 99-121). Cambridge, Mass.: Harvard University Press.

Kraepelin, E. (1899/1990). *Psychiatry: A textbook for students and physicians. Volume 1: General psychiatry*. Canton, MA: Watson Publishing International.

Kraepelin. E. (1905). *Lectures in clinical psychiatry* (revised 2nd ed.). London: Bailliere, Tindal and Cox.

Kuhn, T. (1970). *The structure of scientific revolutions* (2nd ed.). Chicago: Chicago University Press.

Kuipers, L., Birchwood, M., & McCreadie, R.D. (1992). Psychosocial family intervention in schizophrenia: A review of empirical studies. *British Journal of Psychiatry*, 160, 272-275.

Laing, R.D. (1960). *The divided self.* London: Tavistock Press.

Laing, R.D. (1967). *The politics of experience and the bird of paradise.* London: Penguin Press.

Laing, R.D., & Esterson, A. (1969). *Sanity, madness and the family: Families of schizophrenics, 2nd edition.* London: Tavistock.

Liddle, P.F. (1987). The symptoms of chronic schizophrenia: A reexamination of the positive-negative dichotomy. *British Journal of Psychiatry*, 151, 145-151.

McGorry, P.D., Mihalopoulous, C., Henry, L., Dakis, J., Jackson, H.J., Flaum, M., Harrigan, S., McKenzie, D., Kulkarni, J., & Karoly, R. (1995). Spurious precision: Procedural validity of diagnostic assessment in psychotic disorders. *American Journal of Psychiatry*, 152, 220-223.

Mirowsky, J., & Ross, C.E. (1983). Paranoia and the structure of powerlessness. *American Sociological Review*, 48, 228-239.

Mojtabai, R., & Riede, R.O. (1998). Limitations of the symptom-orientated approach to psychiatric research. *British Journal of Psychiatry*, 173, 198-202.

Morrison, A.P. (2001). The interpretation of intrusions in psychosis: An integrative cognitive approach to hallucinations and delusions. *Behavioural and Cognitive Psychotherapy*, 29, 257-276.

Morrison, A. P., Renton, J. C., Dunn, H., Williams, S., & Bentall, R. P. (2003). *Cognitive therapy for psychosis: A formulation-based approach.* London: Brunner-Routledge.

Mortensen, P. B., Pedersen, C. B., Westergaard, T., Wolfahrt, J., Ewald, H., Mors, O., Andersen, P. K., & Melbye, M. (1999). Effects of family history and place and season of birth on the risk of schizophrenia. *New England Journal of Medicine*, 340, 603-608.

Mosher, L.R. (1999). Soteria and other alternatives to acute psychiatric hospitalization. *Journal of Neurosis and Mental Disease*, 187, 142-149.

Mthrman, A., Rantakallio. P., Osohanni, M., Jones, P., & al., e. (1996). Unwantedness of pregnancy and schizophrenia in the child. *British Journal of Psychiatry*, 169, 637-640.

Pilling, S., Bebbington, P., Kuipers, E., Garety, P.A., Geddes, J.R., Orbach, G., & Morgan. (2002). Psychological treatments in schizophrenia: I Meta-analysis of family intervention and cognitive behaviour therapy. *Psychological Medicine*, 32, 763-782.

Post, F. (1996). Verbal creativity, depression and alcoholism: An investigation of 100 American and British writers. *British Journal of Psychiatry*, 168, 545-555.

Sarfati, Y., Hadt-Bayles, M.C., Besche, C., Widloecher, D. (1997). Attributions of intensions to others in people with schizophrenia: A non-verbal exploration with comic strips. *Schizophrenia Research*, 25, 199-209.

Sarfati, Y., & Hardy-Bayles, M.C. (1999). How do people with schizophrenia explain the behaviour of others? A study of theory of mind and its relationship to thought and speech disorganization in schizophrenia. *Psychological Medicine*, 29, 613-620.

Schatzman, M. (1972). Madness and morals. In R. Orrill (Ed.), *Laing and antipsychiatry.* London: Penguin.

Schiffman, J., LaBrie, J., Carter, J., Tyrone. C., Schulsinger, F., Parnas, J., & Mednick, S. (2002). Perception of parent-child relationships in high-risk families, and adult schizophrenia outcome of offspring. *Journal of Psychiatric Research*, 36, 41-47.

Schneider, K. (1959). *Clinical Psychopathology.* New York: Grune & Stratton.

Sedgwick, P. (1972). R.D. Laing: Self, symptom and society. In R, Orrill (Ed.), *Laing and anti-psychiatry.* London: Penguin.

Simonton, D.K. (1994). *Greatness: Who makes history and why.* New York: Guilford Press.

Singer, M.T., & Wynne, L.C. (1965a). Thought disorder and family relations of schizophrenics III. Methodology using projective techniques. *Archives of General Psychiatry*, 12, 187-200.

Singer, M.T., & Wynne, L.C. (1965b). Thought disorder and family relations of schizophrenics IV. Results and implications. *Archives of General Psychiatry*, 12, 201-212.

Spitzer, R.L., & Fliess, J.L. (1974). A reanalysis of the reliability of psychiatric diagnosis. *British Journal of Psychiatry*, 123, 341-347.

Szasz, T.S. (1960). The myth of mental illness. *American Psychologist*, 15, 564-580.

Szasz, T.S. (1979). *Schizophrenia: The sacred symbol of psychiatry.* Oxford: Oxford University Press.

Tai, S., Haddock, G., & Bentall, R.P. (2004. the effects of emotional salience on thought disorder in patients with bipolar affective disorder. *Psychological Medicine*.

Tien, A.Y. (1991). Distribution of hallucinations in the population. *Social Psychiatry and Psychiatric Epidemiology*, 26, 287-292.

van Os, J., Gilvarry, C., Bale, R., van Horn, E., Tattan, T., White, I., & Murray, R. (1999). A comparison of the utility of dimensional and categorical representations of psychosis. *Psychological Medicine*, 29, 595-606.

van Os, J., Hanssen, M., Bijl, R.V., Ravelli, A. (2000). Strauss (1969) revisited: A psychosis continuum on the normal population? *Schizophrenia Research*, 45, 11-20.

Vaughn C.E., & Leff, J. (1976). The influence of family and social factors on the course of psychiatric illness: A comparison of schizophrenic and depressed neurotic patients. *British Journal of Psychiatry*, 129, 125-137.

Wahlberg, K.E., Wynne, L.C., Oja, H., Keskitalo P., Pykalainen, L., Lahti, I.., Moring J., Naarala, N., Sorri, A., Seitamaa, M., Laksy, K., Kolassa, J., & Tienari, P. (1997). Gene-environments interactions in vulnerability to schizophrenia: Findings from the Finnish Adoptive Family Study of Schizophrenia. *American Journal of Psychiatry,* 154, 355-362.

World Health Organization. (1992). *ICD-10: International statistical classifiction of diseases and related health problems* (10th revision ed.). Geneva: World Health Organization.

part three

therapy

John R. Bola & Loren R. Mosher

Treatment of Acute Psychosis Without Neuroleptics:
Two-Year Outcomes From the Soteria Project
(The American Soteria Project)

Treatment of Acute Psychosis Without Neuroleptics: Two-Year Outcomes From the Soteria Project

John R. Bola [1] and Loren R. Mosher [2]

Abstract

The Soteria project (1971-1983) compared residential treatment in the community with minimal use of antipsychotic medication to "usual" hospital treatment for individuals with early episode schizophrenia spectrum psychosis. Newly diagnosed DSM-II schizophrenia subjects were assigned consecutively (1971-76, N=79) or randomly (1976-79, N=100) to the hospital or Soteria and followed for two years. Admission diagnoses were subsequently converted to DSM-IV schizophrenia and schizophreniform disorder. Multivariate analyses evaluated hypotheses of equal or better outcomes in Soteria on eight individual outcome measures and complete outcome scale in three ways: for endpoint subjects (N=160), for completing subjects (N=129). and for completing corrected for differential attrition (N=129). Endpoint subjects exhibited small to medium effect size trends favouring experimental treatment. Completing subjects had significantly better composite outcomes of a medium effect size at Soteria (+0.47 SD, p=03). Completing subjects with schizophrenia exhibited a large effect size benefit with Soteria treatment (+.81 SD, p=.02), particularly in domains of psychopathology, work and social functioning. Soteria treatment resulted in better two-year outcomes for newly diagnosed schizophrenia spectrum psychosis, particularly for completing individuals and for those with schizophrenia. In addition, only 58 percent of Soteria subjects received any antipsychotic medications during the follow-up period, and only 19 percent were continuously maintained on antipsychotic medications.

Introduction

It is notable that 30 years after its initial design and implementation, and 17 years since completion of data collection, the Soteria project is still producing information relevant to today's treatment of psychosis. Soteria's original aim was to assess whether a specially designed intensive psychological treatment, a relationship focused therapeutic milieu incorporating minimal use of antipsychotic medications for 6 weeks, could produce equivalent or better outcomes in treating individuals newly diagnosed with schizophrenia, compared to general hospital psychiatric ward treatment with antipsychotic medications. Soteria also intended to reduce the proportion of individuals maintained on antipsychotic medications (thereby reducing exposure to drug-induced toxicities), and to reduce the rate at which early-episode clients became chronic users of mental health services. This study is unique in employing a relatively large sample (N=179) of clients newly diagnosed with DSM-II schizophrenia (diagnoses were subsequently converted to DSM-IV schizophrenia and schizophreniform disorder) in a quasiexperimental research design comparing multiple outcomes at two years.

Antipsychotic medications have been the treatment of choice in early episode psychotic disorders for many years (APA 1997; Cole et al., 1966; Lehman and Steinwachs, 1998). However, prescription of conventional antipsychotics carries substantial risk of drug toxicities (Popp and Trezza, 1998) and structural brain changes (e.g. Madsen et al., 1998). While atypical antipsychotics exhibit a more benign short-term side effect profile (Worrel et al., 2000), there has not yet been adequate time observing their effects to rule out emergence of additional long-term toxicities. For example, the recently reported association of atypical antipsychotics with diabetes mellitus (Sernyak et al., 2002) is cause for some concern.

In developing the Soteria approach to treatment, the desire to minimize medication-induced toxicities converged with three additional factors: the recognition of significant rates of recovery without drug treatment in early episode psychosis, the observation that many individuals do not benefit from medications (through drug treatment-resistance and non-compliance), and a valuing of interpersonal care and treatment of the mentally ill.

Rates of recovery without medication are significant, particularly in early episode psychosis. For example, placebo recovery in the acute phase of the early NIMH multi-site trial was approximately 37 percent (Cole et al., 1964), and the placebo treated group had fewer rehospitalizations at one year post-discharge (Schooler et al., 1967). Estimates of placebo response rates in acute schizophrenia range from 10 to 40 percent (Davis et al., 1989; Thornley et al., 2001), with a median of 25 percent (Dixon et al., 1995). Long-term follow-up studies conducted prior to the widespread use of antipsychotic drugs report functional recovery rates above 50 percent (Bleuler, 1978; Ciompi, 1980; Huber et al., 1980).

Not all psychotic individuals benefit from drug treatment. Treatment resistance to conventional antipsychotic agents is estimated at 20-40 percent (Hellewell, 1999). Noncompliance with conventional antipsychotics is estimated at 41-55 percent (Fenton et al., 1997). Improved compliance with atypical antipsychotics is often assumed, but has not yet been established (Wahlbeck et al., 2001).

"Traitement morale", a humanistic trend in the care and treatment of individuals with mental illness, can be traced to Pinel's removing chains from the men in Paris' Bicetre Hospital in 1997. Following in humanistic treatment tradition, Soteria incorporated aspects of moral treatment (Bockhoven, 1963), Sullivan's (1962) interpersonal theory and specially designed milieu at Shepard-Pratt Hospital in the 1920s and the "developmental crisis" notion that growth may be possible from psychosis (Lain, 1967; Menninger, 1959; Perry, 1974).

This is the first report from the entire Soteria sample using multivariate methods to test hypotheses of comparable outcomes over a two-year period. We use two-tailed tests to evaluate hypotheses for each outcome in 3 ways: for endpoint subjects (N=160), for completing subjects (N=129) and for completing subjects adjusted for differential attrition (N=129; Heckman, 1979). Subsequently, we conducted tests for schizophrenia and schizophreniform subjects separately.

Method

Study Design
The Soteria project employed a quasi-experimental treatment comparison using consecutive space-available treatment assignment in the first cohort (1971-1976; N=79) and an experimental design with random assignment in the second cohort (1976-1979; N=100).

Subjects
Subjects were recruited from two country hospital psychiatric emergency rooms in the San Francisco Bay Area. All persons meeting the following criteria were asked to participate: initial

diagnosis of schizophrenia by three independent clinicians (per DSM-II), at least 4 of 7 cardinal symptoms of schizophrenia (thinking or speech disturbances, catatonic motor behaviour, paranoid ideation, hallucinations, delusional thinking other than paranoid, blunted or inappropriate emotion, disturbance of social behaviour and interpersonal relations), judged in need of hospitalization, no more than one previous hospitalization for one week or less with a diagnosis of schizophrenia, ages 15-32, and not married. Emergency room staff psychiatrists made intial diagnoses. Subsequent assessments were made by an independent research team trained to maintain inter-rater reliability (kappa) of 0.80 or better on all measures. Measures were taken at entry, 72 hours (designed to screen out drug-induced psychoses), 6 weeks, 1 and 2 years post-admission. Most follow-up measures were face valid (e.g. work, living arrangements, rehospitalizations, etc.).

Ethnicity of subjects (N=171) were: 80 percent European American, 9 percent African American, and 11 percent other ethnic groups. Sixty-four percent (N=179) were male and 36 percent female. The mean age was 21.7 years (range: 15-32, SD=3.4, N=179), with the average client coming from Hollinghead's lower-middle class (1957; higher score is lower social class; class III is 24-43; mean SES score = 42.3, SD=16.1, range; 11-77, n=159).

Treatments

Soteria was predominantly an extra-medical treatment, employing a developmental-crisis approach to recovery from psychosis. Treatment involved a small, home-like, intensive, interpersonally focused therapeutic milieu with a non-professional staff that expected recovery and related with clients "in ways that do not result in the invalidation of the experience of madness (Mosher and Menn, 1978a, p. 716)." Experimental treatment was provided at two facilities, at Soteria and a replication facility, Emanon. Antipsychotic medications were ordinarily not used during the first six weeks of treatment. However, there were explicit criteria for their short-term use during this period; 76 percent (62 of 82) received no antipsychotic medications during the initial 45-day period. After six weeks, medication prescription decisions were made at a treatment conference that included the client, staff, and the consulting psychiatrist. A manual describing Soteria treatment in greater detail has been published in German (Mosher et al., 1994).

Control facilities were well-staffed general hospital psychiatric units geared towards "rapid evaluation and placement in other parts of the country's treatment network (Mosher and Menn, 1978a, p. 717)." In these units, virtually all subjects (94%; 85 of 90) were treated with continuous courses of antipsychotic medication (average 700 mg. chlorpromazine equivalence per day), and nearly all were prescribed post-discharge medications. Upon discharge, subjects were referred to an extensive array of outpatient services.

Measures
    Eight outcome measures were used: readmission to 24-hour care (yes or no), number of readmissions, days in readmission(s), a global psychopathology scale (Mosher et al., 1971; 1-7, higher is more symptomatic), a global improvement scale (Mosher et al., 1971; coded 1-7, 1=much improvement, 4=no change, 7=much worse), leaving independently or with peers (yes or no), and ordinal measure of working (none, part-time, full-time) and the social functioning subscale of the Brief Follow-up Rating (BFR; Sokis, 1970). For completing subjects (N=129), observations to the two-year follow-up were used. Endpoint analyses (N=160) used observations to the last post-discharge observation.

    Composite outcome scales were created for endpoint and completing subjects from the eight individual outcome measures by converting each to standardized (z) scores oriented with positive values for better outcomes and summing. Missing values were set to the individual's mean score on available standardized measures for 5 percent of missing endpoint and 8 percent of missing completer information. Cronbach's alpha for the endpoint scale was 0.77 and for the completer scale was 0.74. Composite scales were then re-standardized, allowing subsequent analyses to be interpreted in standard deviation (effect size) units (Neter et al., 1996).

    DSM-II schizophrenia subjects with symptoms for at least six months were rediagnosed with schizophrenia (42%; 71 of 169), since the addition of this criterion was the primary change from DSM-II to DSM-III, and has been carried forward into DSM-IV. Subjects not meeting this criterion were rediagnosed with schizophreniform disorder (58%; 98 of 169). A variable approximating days of antipsychotic use during follow-up (between end of experimental control of medication at 45 days and the observation at two years) was created as the proportion of use (0=no use, .33=occasional use, .67=frequent use, 1=continuous use) times the length (in days) of the observation periods and summed (mean (SD) = 327.5). range: 0-685).

Statistical Analysis

In main effect analyses, the influence of experimental treatment on composite outcome and on each outcome measure was estimated in three ways: for endpoint subjects (N=160), for completing subjects (N=129), and for completing subjects statically adjusted for differential attrition (Soteria nonattritions is 83%, 68 of 82; vs. hospital nonattritions of 63%, 61 of 97; Ç2=4.15, df=1, p=.04) and for the length of time in the post-discharge follow-up period, since Soteria's design allowed longer initial treatment stays (mean=548 post-discharge days for Soteria completers vs. 677 for hospital completers, t=5.89, df=128, p=.00).

Due to differential attrition across treatment groups, Heckman's (1979) procedure for correcting attrition bias was used in one set of treatment effect estimates for completers (tables 1, 2, and 3; column 4). This procedure involves three steps: estimating a probit model on nonattrition from baseline variables, calculating a function of the probability that an individual was not lost to follow-up (the inverse mills ratio), and using this function as a covariate in multivariate estimates of treatment effects. The inverse mills ratio from the probit model on nonattrition was assessed for co-linearity with other control variables (Stolzenberg and Relles, 1997; schizophrenia, days in the follow-up period); none was found (the largest correlation was with schizophrenia, Pearson's r= -.06, n.s.). The two-stage Heckman procedure results in a small distortion of standard error estimates through use of an estimated rather than observed inverse mills ratio. Initial efforts to correct the standard errors resulted in only slight p-value changes (in the third decimal place), therefore they were left uncorrected.

These analytic procedures were repeated separately for endpoint (N=63) and completing subjects (N=49) with insidious onset schizophrenia, and for endpoint (N=97) and completing subjects (n=80) with schizophreniform disorder. Subgroup analyses use the same control variables, omitting only the indicator variable for schizophrenia.

In each analysis, estimates were made with the multivariate statistical procedure appropriate for the level of measurement of the dependent variable: ordinary least squares (OLS) regression for interval measures (composite outcome scale, social functioning), a maximum likelihood probit for binary categorical variables (readmission, living independently), an ordered probit for ordered categorical variables (McKelvey and Zavoina, 975; global psychopathology, improvement in psychopathology, working), and a classic tobit for lower truncated interval measures (Tobin's probit; Tobin, 1958; number of readmissions, day in readmission).

Treatment effects from probit models report the difference in the probability of the observed outcome (readmission, living independently) for experimental subjects. Experimental treatment estimates from ordered probability models report the difference in the combined probability of membership in the two best categories of the dependent variable. Effect estimates on work functioning are presented both as the change in the probability of working full-time and as the change in the probability of working at all (working full-time plus working part-time) for experimental subjects. For truncated interval measures (number of readmissions, days in readmission), estimates represent the change in the expected value of the dependent variable associated with experimental treatment (see Breen, 1996, p. 27, eq. 2.18 for the specification). Analyses were conducted in the statistical software packages SPSS and LIMDEP (acronym for LIMited DEPendent variables; Greene, 1998).

Results

Main Effects

Main effects results for endpoint subjects (N=160; table 1, column 2) indicate that experimentally treated individuals had a non-significant two-tenths of a standard deviation better outcomes (+0.17 SD, t=1.07, df=149, n.s., all statistical tests are two-tailed). Experimentally treated endpoint subjects had significantly better outcomes on one of the eight outcomes: an 18 percent higher probability of living alone or with peers (+0.18, z= 1.94, df=147, p=.05).

Marginal Effects of Experimental Treatment on Two-Year Outcomes: Endpoint Subjects (N=160) and Completers (N=129) and Corrected for Attrition (N=129)

Outcome Variable	Endpoint a,c	Completers a,c	Completers Adjusted b,c
Composite Outcome d	.17	.350	.47*
Social Functioning e	.20	.18	.08
Global Psychopathology f	.05	.21*	.20*
Improvement in Psychopathology g	.09	.170	.170
Working h			
Any	.01	.05	.08
Full-time	.02	.04	.07
Living Alone or With Peers i	.18*	.190	.17
Readmission j	-.10	-.05	-.160
Number of Readmissions k	-.30	-.44	-.98*
Days in Readmission l	-.93	-4.6	-23.6

a. Estimates control for schizophrenia/schizophreniform disorder and number of days between initial discharge and 2-year follow-up.
b. Estimates control for schizophrenia/schizophreniform disorder, number of days between initial discharge and 2-year follow-up, and differential attrition by treatment group.
c. Significance tests are two-tailed: □denotes p<10, *denotes p<o5, **denotes P<01.
d. Difference in the composite outcome for Soteria subjects (in standard deviation units).
e. Difference in the probability of membership in the two best categories (having little or no psychopathology).
f. Difference in the probability of membership in the two best categories (having excellent or very good improvement in psychopathology).
g. Difference in the probability of the event occurring (readmission).
h. Difference in the expected value (number of readmissions).
i. Difference in the expected value (days in readmission).
j. Difference in the probability of the event occurring (living alone or with peers).
k. Difference in the probability of events occurring (any work, full-time work).
l. Difference in social functioning (on a 3 point scale).

Results for completers, unadjusted for attrition (N=129; table 1, column 3), indicate that experimentally treated subjects had a third of a standard deviation better composite outcomes (statistical trend, +0.35 SD, t= 1.73, df=124, p=.09), including significantly better outcomes on one of eight measures: a 21 percent higher probability of having no or very low psychopathology scale scores (+0.21, z=2.53, df=103, p=.01).

Main effect results for completers adjusted for attrition (N=129; table 1 column 4) indicate that experimentally treated individuals had nearly one-half standard deviation better composite outcomes (=0.47 SD, t=2.20, df=123, p=.03), and significantly better outcomes on two of eight measures : a 20 percent higher probability of membership in the lowest two psychopathology categories (+0.20, z= -2.17, df=104, p=.03) and nearly one fewer readmission (-0.98, z= -2.37, df=123, p=.02).

Schizophrenia Subjects

Endpoint schizophrenia subjects (N=63; table 2, column 2) had four-tenths of a standard deviation better composite outcomes in Soteria (not statistically significant; (+0.39 SD, t=1.42, df=60, p=.16). this includes significantly better outcomes on three of eight measures: a 34 percent higher probability of membership in the two best psychopathology improvement categories (+0.34, z= -2.16, df=58, p=.03) and six-tenths of a point (on a three point scale) better social functioning (+0.64, t=2.34, df=45, p=.02).

Marginal Effects of Experimental Treatment on Two-Year Outcomes for Schizophrenia Subjects: Endpoint (N=63), Completer (N=49), and Completer Corrected for Attrition (N=49)

(table on opposite page)

a Estimates control for number of days between initial discharge and 2-year follow-up.
b. Estimates control for number of days between initial discharge and 2-year follow-up, and differential attrition by treatment group.
c. Significance tests are two-tailed: ᵒ denotes p<.10, * denotes p<.05, ** denotes p<.01.

d. Difference in the composite outcome for Soteria treatment (in standard deviation units).
e. Difference in the probability of membership in the two best categories (having little or no psychopathology).
f. Difference in the probability of membership in the two best categories (having excellent or very good improvement).
g. Difference in the probability of the event occurring (readmission).
h. Difference in the expected value (number of readmissions).
i. Difference in the expected value (days in readmission).
j. Difference in the probability of the event occurring (living alone or with peers).
k. Difference in the probability if the events occurring (any work, full-time work).
l. Difference in social functioning (on a 3 point scale).

Outcome Variable	Endpoint a,c	Completers a,c	Completers Adjusted b,c
Composite Outcome d	.39	.38	.81*
Social Functioning e	.64*	.67*	.59□
Global Psychopathology f	.34*	.44*	.44*
Improvement in Psychopathology g	.34*	.49**	.48*
Working h Any	.18	.31	.40*
Full-time	.13	.23	.29*
Living Alone or With Peers i	.19	.27	.28
Readmission j	.05	.12	-.21□
Number of Readmissions k	.36	.38	-.92
Days in Readmission l	31.2	34.8	-3.83

Unadjusted for attrition, schizophrenia completers table (table 2, column 3) treated at Soteria had a non-significant four-tenths of a standard deviation better outcomes (+0.38 SD, t= 1.19. df=46, n.s.), and statistically significant benefits on three of eight individual outcomes: a 44 percent higher probability of being in the lowest two psychopathology improvement categories (+0.44, z=-2.13, df=36, p=.03), a 49 percent higher probability of being in the best two psychopathology improvement categories (+0.49, z= -2.75, df=36, p=.01), and two-thirds of a point better social outcomes (+0.67, t=2.53, df=37, p=.02).

Adjusted for differential attrition, completing schizophrenia subjects (N=49; table 2, column 4) had eight-tenths of a standard deviation better composite outcomes when treated at Soteria (+0.81 SD, t= 2.42, df=45, p=.02), and significantly better outcomes on four of eight measures: a 44 percent higher likelihood of having no or nearly no psychopathology (+0.44, z= -2.11, df=35, p=.04), a 48 percent higher likelihood of having excellent or very good psychopathology improvement (+0.48, z= -2.67, df=34, p=.01), and a 40 percent higher probability of working (+0.40, z=2.30, df=40, p=.02).

Schizophreniform Subjects

Schizophreniform endpoint subjects (N=97; table 3, column 2) had a non-significant two-tenths of a standard deviation better outcome at Soteria (+0.19 SD, t=o.92, df=94, n.s.)

Marginal Effects of Experimental Treatment of Two-Year Outcome for Schizophreniform Subjects: Endpoint (N=97), Completing Subjects (N=80), and Completers Corrected for Attrition (N=80)

Outcome Variable	Endpoint a,c	Completers a,c	Completers Adjusted b,c
Composite Outcome d	.19	.33	.34
Social Functioning e	-.10	-.15	-.22
Global Psychopathology f	.03	.08	.07
Improvement in Psychopathology g	.05	.05	.06
Working h			
Any	-.01	-.09	-.09
Full-time	-.01	-.08	-.08
Living Alone or With Peers i	.17	.13	.12
Readmission j	-.19□	-.16	-.20
Number of Readmissions k	-.59□	-.16	-.20□
Days in Readmission l	-.16.4	-30.0	

a. Estimates control for number of days between intial discharge and 2-year follow-up.
b. Estimates control for number of days between initial discharge and 2-year follow-up, and differential attrition by treatment group.
c. Significance test are two-tailed : □denotes p<.10, *denotes p<.05, **denotes p<.01.
d. Difference in composite outcome for Soteria treatment (in standard deviation units).
e. Difference in social functioning (on a 3 point scale).
f. Difference in the probability of membership in the two best categories (having little or no psychopathology).
g. Difference in the probability of membership in the two best categories (having excellent or very good improvement).
h. Difference in the probability of the events occurring (any work, full-time work).
i. Difference in the probability of the event occurring (living alone or with peers).
j. Difference in the probability of the event occurring (readmission)
k. Difference in the expected value (readmissions)
l. Difference in the expected value (days in readmission)

Unadjusted for attrition, completing schizophreniform subjects (N=80; table 3, column 3) had a non-significant one-third standard deviation better composite outcome at Soteria (+0.33 SD, t=1.28, df=77, p=.20) that includes one statistically significant finding, approximately one fewer readmission to 24-hour care (-0.98 readmits, z= -1.98, df=74. p=.05).

Adjusted for attrition , completing schizophreniform subjects (N=80; table 3, column 4) had a non-significant one-third standard deviation better composite outcomes at Soteria (+0.34 SD, t=1.22. df=76. n.s), including significantly better outcomes on one of eight measures, an average of one and one-quarter fewer readmissions (-1.24 readmits, z= -2036, df=76, p=.02).

Post-hoc Analyses

Post-hoc analysis comparing endpoint subjects later lost to follow-up (9 Soteria and 22 hospital subjects) found no composite outcome differences (-0.18 vs. = -0.23, t=.89, df=29, n.s.), indicating that loss of a high functioning subgroup of hospital subjects is not a plausible explanation for observed Soteria treatment benefits.

Investigating whether Soteria acted to reduce medication for all subjects or only for those not medicated during the follow-up period, nonmedicated completers (29 of 68 Soteria, 2 of 61 hospital subjects) were excluded in a comparison of medication use. This comparison found no differences between groups (Soteria mean=421 days vs. hospital mean 437 days, t= -0.42, df=96, n.s.), indicating that experimental treatment does not reduce the duration of medication use for those receiving medications, but only reduces the proportion of individuals being medicated.

Comparison of the proportions of Soteria treated schizophrenia versus schizophreniform subjects not receiving antipsychotic medications during follow-up found no significant difference: 44 percent of schizophreniform (16/36) versus 41 percent of schizophrenia subjects (13/32) were not drug treated (X^2=0.10, df=1, n.s.), indicating Soteria was equally effective in reducing antipsychotic medication use in both groups.

Discussion

Main Findings

Despite some treatment crossover during the follow-up period, strikingly beneficial effects of Soteria treatment are still evident at the two-year follow-up. This is particularly notable because an earlier report of two-year outcomes from the first cohort of this study described more modest benefits (Mosher and Menn, 1978a). These results extend and refine previous reports by including both cohorts and conducting multivariate endpoint and two completing subject analyses. Recall that previously reported (Mosher and Menn, 1978b; Mosher et al., 1995) separate cohort analyses of six-week data showed significant and comparable symptomatic improvement for both groups, despite marked differences in neuroleptic treatment.

Three sets of treatment effect estimates show a pattern of small to medium effect size benefits for Soteria that are larger for completing than for endpoint subjects. This may be partly due to completers having the full two-year period in which to recover. The possibility that a group of higher functioning control subjects might have been lost to follow-up between endpoint and completion turns out not to be an explanation for Soteria benefits, since lost to follow-up endpoint subjects had comparable outcomes in both treatment groups. However, due to higher attrition among the hospital treated subjects, especially among hospital treated schizophrenia subjects, effect estimates for completing subjects unadjusted for attrition are likely to contain a bias. Therefore the third set of treatment effect estimates uses a statistical procedure developed by Nobel Laureate James Heckman (2000 in Economics) to more accurately estimate the effect of Soteria treatment on a new sample of similar clients. Adjusting for differential attrition, completing subjects treated at Soteria had nearly one-half of a standard deviation better composite outcome scores than the usual treatment group (table 1, column 4), a "medium" effect size (Cohen, 1987) that is both statistically and practically significant. Soteria treated subjects also had lower psychopathology scores, and fewer readmissions than hospital treated subjects.

When considering schizophrenia subjects separately, results indicate even more favorable outcomes in the Soteria treated group. Adjusted for differential attrition, these individuals have significantly better composite outcomes of a large effect-size (Cohen's 1987, "large" effect size =0.80), despite not being more frequently medicated in Soteria than schizophreniform subjects.

What Can Account for these Findings?

These favorable findings from Soteria call for some explanation. We therefore examined possible explanations in three areas: analytic methodology, components of treatment, and similarities between Soteria and factors hypothesized as responsible for favorable developing country outcomes in World Health Organization studies (Jablensky et al., 1992; Leff et al., 1992).

Analytic Methodology

The more favorable results in the present analyses seem partly due to the larger sample and more contemporary statistical methods. We have noted several important variables both related to outcomes and different across treatment groups (schizophrenia, length of post-discharge follow-up period, and attrition). The contrast between these and previously reported results highlights the importance of including in statistical analyses relevant control variables that are: 1) scientifically related to study design (length of follow-up period; Wyatt, 1991), 2) theoretically related to outcome (schizophrenia; Cohen and Cohen, 1983), or 3) may affect the generalizabilty of results (differential attrition rates; Heckman, 1979).

To illustrate this point, control variables from the regression on composite outcome were added one at a time, using completing subjects (N=129; table 1, compare to row 1). When only experimental treatment was included in the regression, the effect size estimate (regression coefficient, in standard deviation units) for experimental treatment was 0.12 and not statistically significant (t=0.66, df=127, p=.51). This is analogous to the commonly used, and perhaps overly simplistic, two-group t-test used in earlier reports. When the variable for length of the follow-up period was added, the effect size estimate for experimental treatment became 0.32 (t=1063, df=126, p=011). Adding the variable for schizophrenia (and its missing value indicator), the effect size estimate for experimental treatment became 0.35 (table 1, row 1, column 3; t=1073, df=124, p=.08). Finally, adding the indicator for the probability of non-attrition, the effect size estimate for experimental treatment became, as reported here, 0.47 (table 1, row 1, column 4; t=2.20, df=123, p=.03). Thus it appears that previous reports from Soteria have underestimated the benefits of experimental treatment through omission of important control variables. In sum, we view these multivariate analytic methods as more appropriate than previously used bivariate methods, and as producing relatively unbiased estimates of the effectiveness of Soteria treatment.

Treatment Components

A number of therapeutic ingredients in Soteria treatment have been suggested by Mosher (2001) as likely sources of benefit, and include: 1) the milieu, 2) attitudes of staff and residents, 3) quality of relationships, and 4) supportive social processes.

Milieu: Differences between experimental and hospital milieus were assessed with the Moos Ward Atmosphere (WAS) and Community Orientated Program Environment Scales (COPES; Moos, 1974). Significant differences were found on 8 of 10 sub-scales, notably favouring the experimental milieu on involvement, support and spontaneity (Wendt et al., 1983).

Attitudes: Soteria staff was significantly more intuitive, introverted, flexible, and tolerant than hospital staff (Hirshfeld et al., 1977). Soteria's atmosphere was imbued with the expectation that recovery from psychosis was to be expected (Mosher, 2001).

Therapeutic relationships: Perhaps the most important therapeutic ingredient in Soteria emerged from the quality of relationships that were formed, in part because of the additional treatment time allowed. Within staff-resident relationships, an integrative context was created to promote understanding and the discovery of meaning within the subjective experience of psychosis. Residents were encouraged to acknowledge precipitating events and emotions, to discuss and eventually place them into perspective within the continuity of their life and social network.

Social networks: The role of social networks in providing direct support and buffering stress for individuals with psychotic disorders has been well documented (Buchanan, 1995). Social support has been positively correlated with favourable outcomes (Erikson et al., 1998). Psychotic individuals tend also to have diminishing social support networks (Cohen and Sokolovsky, 1978). To address this deficit, the Soteria project provided a surrogate family for clients in residence, and client-centered post-discharge social network grew up de novo. The result was peer support for community reintegration (e.g., peers helped to organize housing, education, work and social life) and an ongoing source of social support.

Supportive social processes: Social processes were influenced by a number of aspects of the program (Mosher, 2001): the creation of a family-like atmosphere, an egalitarian approach to relationships and household functioning, and an environment that respected and tolerated individual differences and autonomy.

Cultural Factors

Evident contrasts between Soteria and hospital treatment cultures brings to mind the superior outcomes in developing countries for first-episode schizophrenia in World Health Organization (WHO studies (Jablensky et al., 1992; Leff et al., 1992; Whitaker, 2002). There are many plausible similarities between Soteria and the supportive and collectivist social processes frequently hypothesized for better developing country outcomes. The second WHO study also reported a 43 percent lower proportion of individuals maintained on antipsychotic medications in developing countries (16% vs. developed countries 59%; Jablensky et al., 1992).

Study Limitations

This study has a number of limitations that restrict the validity and generalizability of these findings. One limitation arises from the inclusion of some second episode clients (35%, 63 of 179 had been previously hospitalized) and requiring both poor prognosis characteristics of being young and unmarried. Thus, this sample can be considered to be of somewhat poorer prognosis than one representative of only first-episode schizophrenia spectrum disorders.

Another limitation arises from the lack of explicit comparability between the rediagnosis of schizophrenia used here (DSM-II schizophrenia *and* an insidious onset of symptoms for six months or more), and a DSM-IV diagnosis of schizophrenia. However, diagnostic criteria in the Soteria study were quite rigorous, requiring agreement from three independent clinicians, and since all were deemed in need of hospitalization, impaired functioning can be assumed.

Attrition of 28 percent gives rise to concern for the sample's representativness. This is accompanied by concern for a possible bias in the treatment effect estimate due to greater attrition in the hospital (37%) than the experimental group (17%). As detailed above, statistical methods to control for attrition bias in estimating treatment effects were used (Heckman, 1979), but these methods certainly do not replace missing subjects.

It is possible that the use of independent raters not blind to treatment could have introduced a measurement bias. While financial limitations precluded the use of blind reviewers, raters were independent of the project, rotated across conditions, and were trained to maintain high inter-rater reliability on the few measures that required rater judgment.

An additional limitation derives from the quasi-experimental nature of the study. While second cohort subjects were randomly assigned to treatment, first cohort subjects were assigned using a consecutive space available decision rule. This raises the question of group comparability. Although we did not find statistical evidence of between group differences at baseline, there were clearly some differences. Differences tended to favour the hospital group, particularly with an initially lower proportion of insidious onset schizophrenia subjects that became significantly different by follow-up (addressed via statistical control). However, similar results have been noted in comparing findings from experimental and quasi-experimental designs (Shadish and Ragsdale, 1996), especially when controlling for between-group differences.

Clinical Implications

On the whole, these data argue that a relationally focused therapeutic milieu with minimal use of antipsychotic drugs, rather than drug treatment in the hospital, should be a preferred treatment for persons newly diagnosed with schizophrenia spectrum disorder. We think that the balance of risks and benefits associated with the common practice of medicating nearly all early episodes of psychosis should be reexamined. In addition, the search, begun earlier, for treatment response subtypes in schizophrenia spectrum disorders (Carpenter and Heinrichs, 1981), particularly for individuals not benefiting from antipsychotic medications, should be resumed (Bola and Mosher, in press a & b).

In many minds, and in clinical practice guidelines for schizophrenia (APA, 1997; Frances, Docherty and Khan, 1996; Lehman and Steinwachs, 1998), the question of whether to administer antipsychotics in all early episodes is answered affirmatively, and discussion of alternate interventions is thereby closed. We regard this closure of inquiry as premature. Current Scandinavian projects involving in-home family crisis intervention, avoiding use of hospitals and neuroleptics, and providing continuity of teams and approach over an extended period have shown highly promising results in the treatment of newly diagnosed psychosis (Lehtinen et al., 2000). The Scandinavian results, Ciompi's Soteria replication (Ciompi et al., 1992, 1993), and the findings reported here, indicate that, contrary to popular views, minimal use of antipsychotic medications combined with specially designed psychosocial intervention for individuals newly identified with schizophrenia spectrum disorders is not harmful, but appears to be advantageous.

In a well-known reanalysis of mostly first-episode schizophrenia spectrum studies comparing antipsychotic medications versus psychosocial and/or milieu treatment, Wyatt (1991) concluded: "early intervention with neuroleptics in first-break schizophrenic patients increases the likelihood of an improved long-term course" (p. 325). This conclusion has contributed to enthusiasm for efforts to prevent psychosis through "early intervention" in the prodromi, often with low-dose atypical antipsychotic medications. However, most of the studies reviewed by Wyatt (1991) were of a pre-experimental (mirror-image) design that does not control many threats to internal validity (Carpenter, 1997). In fact, a preponderance of the few available quasi-experimental or experimentally designed early episode studies in which one group was initially not medicated (Schooler, 1967; Carpenter et al., 1977; Rappaport et al., 1978; Mosher and Menn, 1978a; Ciompi et al., 1992 & 1993; Lehtinen et al., 2000) show better long-term outcomes for the unmedicated subjects. In concert with the fuller presentation of Soteria results here, these studies suggest that specially designed psychosocial intervention combined with minimal medication use may be an effective treatment strategy in early episode schizophrenia spectrum psychosis.

references

American Psychiatric Association (1997) Practice guidelines for the treatment of patients with schizophrenia. *American Journal of Psychiatry*, **154**, 1-63.

Bleuler ME (1978) The long-term course of schizophrenic psychosis. In *The nature of schizophrenia: new approaches to research and treatment* (eds L. C. Wynne, R. L. Cromwell, & S. Matthysse), pp. 631-636. new York: John Wiley and Sons.

Bockhoven (1963) *Moral treatment in American psychiatry*. New York: Springer.

Bola JR & Mosher LR (in press a) Predicting drug-free treatment response in acute psychosis from the Soteria project. *Schizophrenia Bulletin*.

Bola JR & Mosher LR (in press b) Clashing ideologies or scientific discourse? *Schizophrenia Bulletin*.

Breen R (1996) *Regression models: Censored, sample selected, or truncated data.* Quantitative applications in the social sciences, pp. 80, Beverly Hills: Sage.

Buchanan J (1995) Social support and schizophrenia: A review of the literature. *Archives of Psychiatric Nursing,* **9,** 68-76.

Carpenter WT & Heinrichs DW (1981) Treatment-relevant subtypes of schizophrenia. *The Journal of Nervous and Mental Disease,* **169,** 113-119.

Carpenter WT, McGlashan TH & Strauss JS (1977) The treatment of acute schizophrenia without drugs: An investigation of some current assumptions. *The American Journal of Psychiatry,* **134,** 14-20.

Carpenter WT (1997) The risk of medication-free research. *Schizophrenia Bulletin,* **23,** 11-18.

Ciompi L (1980) Catamnestic long-term study on the course of life and aging of schizophrenics. *Schizophrenia bulletin,* **6,** 606-618.

Ciompi L, Duwalder HP, Maier C, Aebi E, Trutsch K, Kupper Z & Rutishauser C (1992) The pilot project "Soteria Berne": Clinical experiences and results. *British Journal of Psychiatry,* **161,** 145-153.

Ciompi L, Kupper Z, Aebi E, Duwalder HP, Hubschmidt, Trutsch K & Rutishauser C (1993) [The pilot project "Soteria Berne" in treatment of acute schizophrenia patients: II. Results of a comparative prospective follow-up period over 2 years] Das Pilot-Projekt "Soteria Berne" zur Behandlung akut schizophrener: II. Ergebnisse der vergleichenden prospektiven Verlaufsstudie uber zwei Jahre. *Nervenartz,* **64,** 440-450.

Cohen CI & Sokolovsky J (1978) Schizophrenia and social networks: Ex-patients in the inner city. *Schizophrenia Bulletin,* **4,** 546-560.

Cohen J (1987) *Statistical power analysis for the behavioural sciences* (Revised edn). Hillsdale, N.J.: Lawrence Erlbaum Associates.

Cohen J & Cohen P (1983) *Applied multiple regression/correlation analysis for the behavioural sciences,* pp. 545 (2nd edn). Hillsdale, NJ: Lawrence Erlbaum Associates.

Cole JO, Klerman GL, Goldberg SC & NIMH PSC Group (1964) Phenothiazine treatment in acute schizophrenia. *Archives of General Psychiatry,* **10,** 246-261.

Cole JO, Goldberg SC & Davis JM (1966) Drugs in the treatment of psychosis: Controlled studies. In *Psychiatric drugs: Proceedings of a research conference held in Boston* (ed. P. Solomon), pp. 152-180. New York: Grune and Stratton.

Davis JM, Barter JT & Kane JM (1989) Antipsychotic drugs. In *Comprehensive Textbook of Psychiatry* (eds H. I. Kaplan & B. J. Sadock), pp. 1591-1626. Baltimore: Williams and Wilkins.

Dixon LB, Lehman AF & Levine J (1995) Conventional antipsychotic medications for schizophrenia. *Schizophrenia Bulletin,* **21,** 567-557.

Erickson DH, Beiser M & Iacono WG (1998) Social support predicts 5-year outcome in first-episode schizophrenia. *Journal of Abnormal Psychology,* **107,** 681-685.

Fenton WS, Blyer CR & Heinssen RK (1997) Determinants of medication compliance in schizophrenia: Empirical and clinical findings. *Schizophrenia Bulletin*, **23**, 637-651.

Frances A, Docherty JP & Kahn DA (1996) The expert consensus guidelines series: Treatment of schizophrenia. *Journal of Clinical Psychiatry*, **57**, 5-58.

Greene WH (1998) *LIMDEP:* Version 7.0 user's manual, pp. 925 (revised edn). Plainview, N. Y.: Econometric Software Inc.

Heckman JJ (1979) Sample selection bias as a specification error. *Econometrica*, **47**, 153-161.

Hellewell JS (1999) Treatment-resistant schizophrenia: Reviewing the options and identifying the way forward. *Journal of Clinical Psychiatry*, **60**, 14-19.

Hirschfeld RMA, Matthews SM, Mosher LR & Menn AZ (1977) Being with madness: Personality characteristics of three treatment staffs. *Hospital and Community Psychiatry*, **28**, 267-273.

Hollingshead AB (1957) *Two factor index of social position.* New Haven: August Hollingshead.

Huber G, Gross G, Schuttler R & Linz M (1980) Longitudinal studies of schizophrenic patients. *Schizophrenia Bulletin*, **6**, 592-605.

Jablensky A, Sartorius N, Ernberg G, Anker M, Korten A, Cooper JE, Day R & Bertelsen A (1992) Schizophrenia: Manifestations, incidence, can course in different cultures. A World Health Organization ten-country study. *Psychological Medicine*, **Monograph Supplement 20**, pp.97.

Laing RD (1967) *The politics of experience.* New York: Ballantine.

Leff J, Sartorius N, Jablensky A & Korton A (1992) The international pilot study of schizophrenia: Five-year follow-up findings. *Psychological Medicine*, **22**. 131-145.

Lehman AF & Steinwachs DM (1998) The schizophrenia patient outcomes research team (PORT) treatment recommendations. *Schizophrenia Bulletin*, **24**, 1-10.

Lehtinen V, Aaltonen K, Koffert T, Rakkolainen V & Syvalahti E (2000) Two-year outcome in first-episode psychosis treated according to an integrated model. Is immediate neuroleptisation always needed? *European Psychiatry*, **15**, 312-320.

Madsen AL, Keidling N, Karle A, Esbjerg S & Hemmingsen R (1998) Neuroleptics in progressive structural brain abnormalities in psychiatric illness [Research letters]. *Lancet*, **352**, 784-785.

McKelvey RD & Zavoina W (1975) A statistical model for the analysis of ordinal level dependent variables. *Journal of Mathematical Sociology*, **4**, 103-120.

Menninger K (1959) *A psychiatrist's world: the selected papers of Karl Menninger*, pp. 931. New York: Viking Press.

Moos RH (1974) *Evaluating treatment environments: A social ecological approach.* New York: John Wiley.

Mosher LR (2001) Soteria-California and its successors: Therapeutic ingredients. In *Wieso wirke Sotoria? – eine ungewohnliche Schizophreniebehandlung unter der Lupe (Why does Soteria work-an unusual schizophrenia therapy under examination).* Eds L. Ciompi, H. Hoffman, & M. Broccard, pp. 13-41. New York and Berne, Switzerland: Huber,

Mosher LR Hendricks V & Participants SP (1994) Dabeisein: Das manual zur Praxis in der Soteria (Treatment at Soteria House: A manual for the practice of interpersonal phenomenology). In *Psychososoziale Arbeitshilfen 7:* (ed. D. Ford). Berlin: Psychiatrie-Verlag.

Mosher LR & Menn AZ (1978a) Community residential treatment for schizophrenia: Two-year follow-up. *Hospital and Community Psychiatry,* **29,** 715-723.

-(1978) Enhancing psychosocial competence in schizophrenia: Preliminary results of the Soteria project. In *Phenomenology and treatment of schizophrenia* (eds W.E. Fann, I.C. Carcan, A Pokorney et al), pp. 371-386. Jamaica, N.Y.: Spectrum Publications.

Mosher LR, Pollin W & Stabenau R (1971) Identical twins discordant for schizophrenia: Neuroleptics findings. *Archives of General Psychiatry,* **24,** 422-430.

Mosher LR, Vallone R & Menn A (1995) the treatment of acute psychosis without neuroleptics: Six-week psychopathology outcome data from the Soteria project. *The International Journal of Social Psychiatry,* **41,** 157-173.

Neter J, Kutner MH, Nachtsheim CJ & Wasserman W (1996) *Applied linear statistical models* (Fourth ed). Chicago: Irwin.

Perry JW (1974) *the far scale of madness,* pp. 177 pp. Englewood Cliff, NJ: Prentice Hall.

Popp SM & Trezza GR (1998) Side effects of and reactions to psychotropic medications. In *Emergencies in mental health practice* (ed P.M. Kleespies), pp. 279-311. New York: Guilford.

Rappaport M, Hopkins HK, Hall K, Belleza T & Silverman J (1978) Are thee schizophrenics for whom drugs may be unnecessary or contraindicated? *International Pharmacopsychiatry,* **13,** 100-111.

Schooler NR, Goldberg SC, Boothe H & Cole JO (1967) One year after discharge: Community adjustment of schizophrenic patients. *The American Journal of Psychiatry,* **123,** 986-995.

Shadish WR & Ragsdale K (1996) Random versus nonrandom assignment in controlled experiments: Do you get the same answer? *Journal of Consulting and Clinical Psychology,* **64,** 1290-1305.

Sokis DA (1970) A brief follow-up rating: *Comprehensive Psychiatry,* **11,** 445-459.

Stolzenberg RM & Relles DA (1997) Tools for intuition about sample selection bias and its correction. *American Sociological Review,* **62,** 494-507.

Strauss JS & Carpenter WT (1978) the prognosis of schizophrenia: Rationale for a multidimensional concept. *Schizophrenia Bulletin*, **4**, 56-67.

Sullivan HS (1962) *Schizophrenia as a human process*. New York: Norton.

Thornley B. Adams CE & Awad G (2001) Chlorpromazine versus placebo for schizophrenia. *The Cochrane Database of Systematic Reviews*, **2**.

Tobin J (1958) Estimation of relationships for limited dependent variables. *Econometrica*, **26**, 24-36.

Wahlbeck K, Tuunainen A, Ahokas A & Leucht S (2001) Dropout rates in randomized antipsychotic drug trails. *Psychopharmacology*, **155**, 230-233.

Wendt RJ, Mosher LR, Matthews SM & Menn AZ (1983) A comparison of two treatment environment for schizophrenia. In *The principles and practices of milieu therapy* (eds J.G. Gunderson, O.A. Will, & L.R. Mosher), pp. 17-33. New York: Jason Aronson Inc.

Whitaker R (2002) *Mad in America: Bad science, bad medicine, and the enduring mistreatment of the mentally ill*. Cambridge, MA: Perseus Books.

Worrel JA, Marken PA, Beckman SE & Ruehter VL (2000) Atypical antipsychotic agents: A critical review. *American Journal of Health-System Pharmacy*, **57**, 238-258.

Wyatt RJ (1991) Neuroleptics and the natural course of schizophrenia. *Schizophrenia Bulletin*, **17**, 325-351.

notes

[1] Department of Social Work. University of Southern California, MRF-222, Los Angeles, CA 900089-0411, USA. Send reprint request to Dr. Bola.

[2] Soteria Associates, 2616 Angell Ave., San Diego, CA 92122

acknowledgements

The authors would like to thank Leonard S. Miller, Ph.D., UC Berkely, and Jim Mintz, Ph.D., UCLA, for their help with statistical consultations, and John M. Davis, M.D., University of Illinois, for critique of an earlier version of this manuscript.

Portions of this paper were presented at the World Psychiatric Association's International Congress in Madrid, Spain on October 2, 2001.

13: The Legacy of Kingsley Hall II

Luc Ciompi

The Soteria-Concept. Theortical Bases And Practical
13-Year Experience With A Milieu-Therapuetic
Appraoch To Acute Schizophrenia
(The Swiss Soteria Bern Project)

The Soteria-Concept. Theoretical Bases And Practical 13-Year Experience With A Milieu-Therapeutic Approach To Acute Schizophrenia

Luc Ciompi

I am very sorry not to be able to participate at this commemoration, having other unavoidable obligations at the same time. Ronald Laing's thinking and work had a deep influence on mine mainly through our pilot-experience "Soteria Berne" — a therapeutic community for acute schizophrenics which replicated a first similar experience created by Loren Mosher and Alma Menn in San Francisco. What follows are extracts of a lecture on his project which I delivered in 1997 before the Japanese Society for Psychiatry and Neurology in Tokyo.

In addition to general clinical experience and knowledge, our approach to the treatment of schizophrenia is also grounded on our own research on the long-term evolution of the illness, and on the resulting concept of affect-logic which tries to understand normal and pathological mental functioning through the analysis of constant and inseparable interactions between emotional and cognitive components, or feeling and thinking. My presentation of this approach will be subdivided in the following three parts:

- Firstly, I will outline the empirical and theoretical bases of "Soteria-Berne".
- Secondly, our practical experiences with this concept will be reported.
- And thirdly, I will draw some practical and theoretical conclusions.

1. Empirical and theoretical bases

The Greek work "Soteria" means something like "salvation", or "protection". It was chosen by Loren Mosher and Alma Menn as the name for a new community-based milieu-therapeutic approach to acute schizophrenia that they inaugurated in the seventies in San Francisco. Despite the fact that our own theoretical background was (and is) quite different from Mosher's and Menn's, and that we also introduced certain modifications of their initial proceedings, we wanted to testify our indebtedness for their pioneering work by adopting the same name.

Mosher's and Menn's point of departure was Ronald Laing's Kingsley Hall therapeutic community in London, where Mosher had spent a year in 1966. Laing was a leading exponent of the so-called "antipsychiatric" movement of the sixties that criticised the traditional medical, hospital-centered and mainly drug-orientated treatment of psychotic phenomena. On the basis of his observations at Kingsley Hall and his own clinical experience, Loren Mosher, a well known researcher in the field of schizophrenia, proposed an alternative approach that was essentially grounded on a psychodynamic-psychotherapeutic understanding of psychotic phenomena. His claim was that human closeness with the psychotic patient ("being with"), based on an adequate psychodynamic understanding in a small, supporting and protective non-hospital setting where neuroleptic drugs were not, or only very parsimoniously, used, could have similar, or even better, therapeutic effects than the traditional hospital-based methods. In several carefully controlled studies, Mosher and co-workers could, in fact, show that comparatively at least similar, and, on the subjective level, often better, results were obtained by the proposed approach, with much lower doses of neuroleptics and also lower cost (Mosher et al 1975, 1978, 1995,). Despite this evidence, the research project "Soteria San Francisco" was eventually closed in the early nineties for lack of financial support. A number of Soteria-like experiments were, however, carried on in the US and elsewhere.

Our own empirical background and approach was, as mentioned before, quite different. On the one hand, systematic follow-up research that we did in Lausanne, Switzerland during the sixties and early seventies had showed, in surprising accordance with previous and succeeding studies by Bleuler in Zurich, Switzerland and Huber and co workers in Bonn, Germany, that long-term evolution of schizophrenia was considerably more variable, more favorable and, especially, more dependent on environmental and psychosocial influences than hitherto believed (Bleuler 1972; Ciompi et al 1976; Huber et al 1979, 1980; Ciompi

1980; see also Harding 1987a and b; Ogawa et al 1987, McGlashan 1988). On the other hand, extensive psychoanalytical and family-centered investigations provided new insight into the individual and social dynamics of outbreak and further evolution of the psychosis (Bateson et al 1956; Singer et al 1978; Benedetti 1982, 1983; Leff et al 1982, 1985). In addition, the development of new techniques of social and vocational rehabilitation proved that innovative approaches based on community-centered half-way institutions could develop a remarkable therapeutic potential (Ciompi et al 1978, 1979; Ciompi 1985; Ciompi 1988).

Figure 1

Three-phase-model of schizophrenia
(Ciompi 1982/1988)

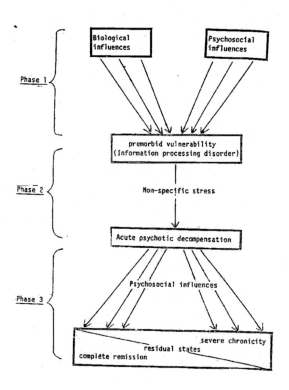

The concept of affect-logic, that grew out of a synthesis of these ingredients, lead to a comprehensive psycho-socio-biological model of the long-term evolution of the schizophrenic psychosis in three phases (figure 1), based on the notion of vulnerability (Zubin et al 1977; Ciompi 1982; Nuechterlein at al 1984). According to this model, in a *first phase* which lasts from conception until the outbreak of psychosis, a particular vulnerability - or information processing disorder, oversensibility, ego weakness, as it might also be called according to different methods of investigation — is gradually built up by circular interactions between unfavorable biological and psychosocial factors such as genetic or perinatal damages, inconsistent rearing conditions and other traumatisms, contradictory and confusing family communication patterns. Their common denominator is that they all lead to unstable structuration of important affective-cognitive systems of reference generated through experience — or functionally integrated feeling-thinking-behaving programs, as I also call them — that form the basic "building blocks of the psyche" according to the concept of affect-logic.

In the *second phase*, characterized by the outbreak of manifest psychosis, this vulnerable coping system is critically overtaxed by additional biological or psychosocial stressors, amongst them, alone or in combination, hormonal changes and developmental problems related to adolescence and early adulthood, drug abuse, leaving home, professional difficulties, mating, childbirth, etc..

During the *third phase*, long-term evolution, the above-mentioned variability of evolution can be explained by the changing interplay of different personality structures and other genetically pre-established variables with current stressful or protective environmental influences, such as family attitudes (in particular the so called high express emotions), socioeconomic and cultural conditions, institutional factors, and therapeutic, preventive and rehabilitative measures (cf Leff et al 1982, 1985; Cavanaugh 1992; Ciompi et al 1976, 1978, 1979; Ciompi 1982,1988,1995).

During each phase of the illness, affective factors play an essential role, according to the concept of affect-logic. One central characteristic of the above-mentioned further developments of this concept since 1982, concerns a more precise analysis of the organising and integrating effects that basic affective states continually exert on cognitive functions, and that I call "operator effects" (an operator is a force that acts on a variable and changes it). Overt or secretly underlying affected states of variable intensity, such as fear, rage, sadness, joy continually influence the focus of attention, the selection and hierarchy of cognitive contents, the way we store and reactivate cognitive material from memory (according to the well established notion of state-dependent memorization, cf. Overton 1964; Koukkou et al 1986), and how we eventually combine them into a context-related whole. In other words, affects constantly function as outstandingly important reducers of cognitive complexity, thus creating a specific "fear-logic", "anger-logic", "sadness-logic", "joy-logic", "love-logic", "erotic logic", and so on, according to context and dominating affective state. This is, however, only clearly apparent when emotions are particularly intense. In everyday routine, in contrast, where cognitive activity follows semi-automatised habitual patterns characterised by flexible affects of relatively low intensity, these effects are less evident, but nevertheless constantly at work on an unconscious or only marginal conscious level. Moreover, increasing affective tension is also capable of provoking sudden nonlinear shifts from one global feeling-thinking-pattern to another, e.g. from love-logic to hate-logic, from fear-logic to rage-logic, or, in vulnerable individuals, from a common everyday logic to a psychotic type of mental functioning.

It is not possible to go into more details concerning the empirical and theoretical bases of the concept of affect-logic. Let me just add that this theory is largely supported by current neurophysiologic findings on affect-generating cerebral structures and their close connections with cognitive (and also hormonal, sensory motor, expressive and behavioural) regulations (Ploog 1989; Gainotti 1989; Derryberry et al 1982; LeDoux 1993; Panksepp 1993). Modern choastheoretical notions about the nonlinear dynamics of complex biological and neuronal systems, too, are fully integrated (see below). An elaborated presentation of the current state of the theory of affect-logic and its practical applications will soon be published in German, under the title "The emotional bases of thinking; outline of a fractal affect logic" (Ciompi 1997e), and a Japanese translation is, to my pleasure, already underway. One of the main conclusions of this most recent synthesis is that the already-mentioned ubiquitous operator effects of emotions on cognition are of high relevance for understanding the dynamics not only of many psychological and psychosocial everyday processes but also of psychopathology in general, and of schizophrenia in particular. Apart from their already-mentioned overtaxing effects in phase 2 or the described evolutionary model of schizophrenia, they also contribute to a premorbid vulnerability (phase 1) by generating the mentioned instability of crucial important feeling-thinking-behaving programs such as, in particular, the mental representation of self and others (self- and object-representations in the psychoanalytic sense) that guide all interpersonal behaviour. And in phase 3, destabilising effective stressors (especially under form of the the above mentioned high expressed emotions) are among the best observed factors that are statistically related to psychotic relapses. The protective effects of an emotionally stable and supportive milieu, on the other hand, will be addressed in the next section.

2. Practical and therapeutic consequences

One important consequence of this new understanding is, in fact, the demand for a therapeutic environment which reduces tension and increases security as much possible, quite similar to the Mosher and Menn approach. Traditional hospital-centred procedures are, however, in many respects rather anxiety-provoking instead of anxiety-reducing (e.g. by violent and non-transparent admission practices, large, loud, promiscuous and often violent admission-wards, privation from personal atmosphere and belongings, lack of adequate information for patients and family, lack of security-inducing personal and conceptual continuity as a consequence of frequent changes from one ward and therapeutic team to another, and so on). All this often leads to a further exacerbation of psychotic fears and symptoms that can only be reduced by higher doses of neuroleptic drugs. The following *eight therapeutic principles* provided the basis for an alternative approach in our pilot-project "Soteria Berne":

1.   Instead of treating acute psychotic patients in a traditional closed hospital setting, we admit them in a small, open, friendly, and quite normal family-like house with garden located in the midst of the community and offering a pleasant living space for 6-8 patients and, continuously, at least two nurses.

2.   During the most acute state, the patient is never alone, but is accompanied round the clock by a specially selected and

trained staff member whose only task is to calm him down, not so much by doing something but rather by silent or talking "being-with", sometimes also by simple common activities such as handcraft, drawing, plaiting, by soft foot-massage, by walking or running together, or by other activities according to personal intuition and responsibility. This first and most intensive phase of care takes place mainly in a calm and stimulus-protected so-called "soft room" where patients and nurse live constantly together for several days and nights, or even for weeks. The "soft room" thus becomes a womblike protective environment where frightening and, sometimes, angry or ecstatic psychotic experiences can be outlived and, gradually, overcome with help of a solid parental figure and "mentor".

3. Personal and conceptual continuity is assured by a small and closely collaborating team consisting of nine members that are backed by two part-time doctors and work in overlapping 48 hour-shifts, so that at least two staff-persons can continually be present. Staff members are carefully selected for their complementary personal qualities and life experiences: they have different ages and professions, are approximately half male and half female, and approximately half have a specifically psychiatric background, and half a different professional education that may provide alternative (and perhaps more "normal") understanding of life problems including psychosis. To each patient, two staff-members (usually a man and a woman) are specially assigned as personal coordinators and "persons of reference". For half a day per week, all staff members meet to exchange information and coordinate therapeutic proceedings. Fortnightly, the team gets an external supervision by an experienced psychotherapist, and about monthly, it meets for an hour of "intervision", that is for a common review of managing problems and team dynamics. In addition, two day-long "retreats" that offer time and space for a more fundamental self-critique are organized per year.

4. Close collaborative relations based on personal trust, frequent visits and extensive exchanges of information are from the first day systematically built up with family members and other important persons of reference. In addition, educational-style discussion evenings are offered monthly for family members and other close persons.

5. Great emphasis is given to providing, at every formal or informal occasion, information which is clear, complete and convergent as possible on the illness itself, its evolutionary risks and chances, the methods of treatment and relapse prevention, the current state of scientific knowledge and ignorance etc. to

patients, family members, and also to professionals, including the staff-members themselves.

6.   Concrete therapeutic aims and priorities concerning future housing and work are systematically formulated for each patient in an early phase of treatment. Negotiating (not just prescribing) realistic aims with the patient himself and his family has, implicitly, an important family-therapeutic dimension, because it often allows, for instance, intergenerational or interpersonal boundaries, mutual responsibilities, and areas of privacy to be clarified. Particular attention is also given in this context to create for everybody who is involved (patients, relatives, important persons of reference, staff members, family doctors, etc) both realistic hopes *and* an adequate consciousness of possible risks (e.g. for relapses) for the future.

7.   Neuroleptic medication is used selectively in states of otherwise uncontrollable tensions; of critical psychological events, or of openly threatening relapses. Dosages remain low in the sense of current low-medication strategies (Herz et al 1982; Carpenter 2983, Herz 1996). Medication is only given in agreement with the patient himself and often also his family, and controlled self-medication is encouraged whenever possible.

8.   Post-care and relapse-prevention techniques are, whenever possible, systematically implemented over at least two years, with the help of external therapists and community-based institutions, with a special weight on educating patient and family members on individual-specific prodromi of relapses, and possible preventative measures.

Despite continuous minor adaptations over the years, these eight therapeutic principles have basically remained the since the implementation of Soteria Berne in spring 1984, that is 13 years ago. They are largely similar to Mosher's initial practice; main differences concerning, however, the composition of staff in our project (not lays only, but also professionals), the adopted techniques of family work, rehabilitation, relapse prevention, and, to some extent, also the use of low-medication and targeted-medication strategies. Therapeutic skills of staff members for managing psychosis in such a setting have, of course, considerably increased with growing experience. Whereas completely drug-free treatments were quite frequent at the beginning, early low and targeted medication strategies have eventually become more frequent, thus lowering the risk of a time-induced fixation of therapy-resistant psychotic patterns of feeling, thinking and behaving. Activities such as house-keeping, cooking, gardening, shopping and so on that strengthen the contact with everyday realities and simultaneously also lower the overall cost, were systematically included in the therapeutic programs right from the beginning. Different day-structuring ego-therapeutic, art-therapeutic and music-therapeutic activities were eventually introduced in addition, when it became clear that the therapeutic program was, initially, not sufficiently structured especially for patients who were no longer severely psychotic. Formal social and vocational rehabilitation, as well as different types of individual, group or family treatments carried our by external agencies were, whenever possible for technical reasons, flexibly combined with part-time care in Soteria itself during a phase of transition before leaving the community. When psychotic relapses occur, former patient are readmitted at Soteria Berne; and a number of them have been included in different evaluative research programs — among them a systematic 2-year matched pair comparison with traditional methods — on which information will be given below. In addition, friendly informal contacts continue for years with many former patients and their relatives, providing non-systematic follow up information on long-term evolutions that has, however, not yet been fully exploited in formal research.

Practical experience and research

Our experience with this approach has many different aspects, among them objective and subjective ones, short-term and long-term aspects, and also more patient-related, family-related, staff-related or society-related aspects. It is, of course, not possible to discuss them all here. Two points of particular interest however shall be selected for a more detailed presentation. The first one concerns phenomenological aspects and subjective experiences of staff, patients and family members that have been explored, mainly by the method of participant observation (cf. Aebi et al 1993), and the second one will deal with some of the main results of our evaluative research. (Ciompi et al. 1991, 1992, 1993).

Concerning *phenomenology and subjective experience*, the unique field of observation provided by the fact that our staff lives 24 hours a day, and for 48 hours continually, in close personal contact with minimally medicated psychotic patients and their families, has certainly considerably increased, and also changed, our understanding of the enigma of psychosis. First of all, we learnt that the boundaries between "normality" and "psychosis" are extremely flexible in such a situation. Psychotic states and symptoms change not only from day to day, but from hour to hour, and even from moment to moment according to the current situation. They are highly dependent on environmental influences, and especially on the immediate basic emotional state of staff members and other patients. Increasing emotional tension, irritation, or ambiguity of communication almost invariably intensifies psychotic disturbance, whereas lowering tension, genuine calm, clarity and respectful friendliness decreases them. Too much change, confusion, noise and stimulus overload (e.g. from visits, television, invasive music, newspapers, too complex or too heavy discussions, etc.) has the same unfavorable effect. Emotional contact with the healthy parts of the personality remains usually possible even across highly psychotic states; and maintaining this contact proves extremely helpful in the long run, even though seemingly ineffective at the time. Authenticity and reliability of communication are among the most powerful therapeutic tools, just as are maintaining hope and confidence that things will change again despite extreme current difficulties. The main attitude of staff members confronted with the terrifying fears and odd thoughts of the acutest psychotic phase should closely resemble the calming, securing and "holding" attitude (Winnicott, 1965) of a good mother that supports her ill child caught in high fevers with heavy nightmares. This, of course, implies not only not only warmth and proximity, but also the ability to maintain an adequate distance and keep one's mind cool, when things become too hot. Similarly, the unavoidable limits of personal presence and closeness and, above all, the final necessity of separation from an "ideal parent" which may be identified with the therapeutic community must be kept in mind, and clearly signified, right from the beginning. Exactly the same simultaneously open and firm, authentic and sympathetic, understanding and reality-orientated attitude has proved useful, mutatis mutandis, with family members and with other persons of reference. In summary, anxiety and fear certainly appear as the emotional core-symptoms of psychosis on all relevant levels (patient and family, and even professionals and society in general), and these emotions also play a central role, as I believe and will further discuss below, in the genesis of psychotic thinking and behaving.

The *evaluative research* was mainly done in two studies, the first on concerning immediate outcomes without a control group, and the second one comparing the outcomes of Soteria patients after two years with carefully matched controls coming from four different hospital settings in Switzerland and Germany. From these studies, the following findings are of particular interest:

Firstly, by using a German version of the well known "Ward Atmosphere Scale" (WAS) by Moos (1974), it was verified that the therapeutic atmosphere in Soteria differed significantly from the atmosphere in four traditional control institutions (figure 2, Ciompi et al 1993). Main differences concern greater emotional closeness and more warmth and spontaneity of patient-staff relations in Soteria, and less hierarchy, order and control.

Figure 2

WARD ATMOSPHERE : SOTERIA vs. CONTROL GROUPS

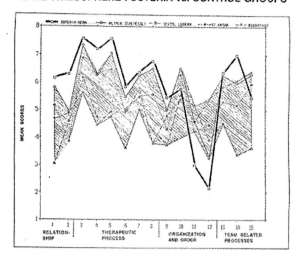

Secondly, immediate results on the four "axes" of psychopathology, housing situation, work situation, and global outcome were very good or good in about 2/3 of the first 56 treated cases (figure 3). Statistically, women and less medicated patients had a significantly better outcome respectively than men, and patients receiving higher doses of neuroleptics (Ciompi et al 1991). This latter and, at first hand, quite surprising finding should not be overinterpreted, however, as an indicator for a superiority of drug-free treatment, because only the most severely disturbed and, milieu therapy-resistant patients received higher doses of neuroleptics, according to the above mentioned treatment rules. The main result of this first study is, therefore, the confirmation that acute psychotic patients with schizophrenia spectrum disorders (full schizophrenia in 38 out of 56 cases according to DSM III criteria, 14 schizophreniform psychosis, 3 unclear) can in fact be successfully treated in a Soteria-like setting, as claimed by Mosher et al (1978, 1995).

Figure 3

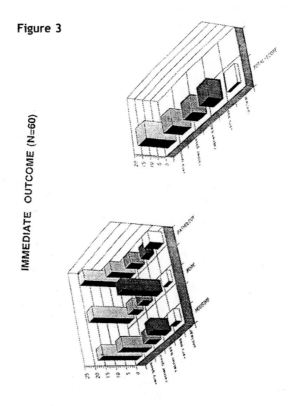

Thirdly, our comparative study revealed no significant differences between Soteria patients and controls, two years after the first admission, concerning the same four axes, and, in addition, the relapse rates. Significant differences existed on the contrary, concerning daily doses of neuroleptic medication that were about 3-5 times lower in Soteria (figure 4 and 5), and also concerning the average duration of institutional care which was 6 months in Soteria, versus 3 months in the control setting (Ciompi et al 1993). This longer duration was mainly related to the fact that initially, we systematically tried to include full social and vocational rehabilitation into the Soteria treatment, for reasons of personal and conceptual continuity. But longer duration means also higher costs, as average daily costs were exactly the same in Soteria in the control setting — an economically not acceptable difference which could, however, be fully corrected by eventually displacing the main period of rehabilitation towards less expense part-time institutions and thus limiting the duration of stay in Soteria to three months only, on average.

Figure 4

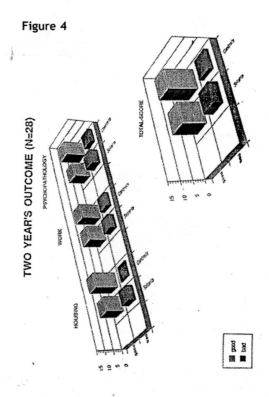

Figure 5

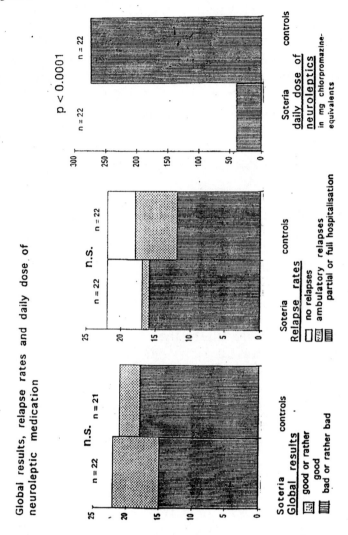

Global results, relapse rates and daily dose of neuroleptic medication

Globally, our evaluation confirms that with much lower doses of neuroleptic medication and without higher costs, similar 2-year results can be obtained with the Soteria approach, as with traditional drug-centered hospital treatments. In addition, casuistic observations and follow-up information over the last 13 years suggest that many former Soteria patients have had a considerably better long term evolution than usual. Advantages seem to be mainly located on the subjective and innerpsychic level, in particular concerning a less traumatic subjective impact of the psychotic experience and the subsequent institutional measures. Feelings of personal value and identity, too, seem better preserved, allowing for a better eventual integration of the psychotic experience into the whole personal life history. Even clearly maturing effects related to psychotic crisis and its psychodynamic elaboration in Soteria could be sometimes be observed, especially when post-care was adequately prolonged, after discharge, by rehabilitative measures and a sufficiently long individual-centred or family-centred psychotherapy.

Conclusions and further implications

In summary, we were able to fully confirm Mosher's observations that in an open Soteria-like environment, acute schizophrenia can be as successfully treated as in a traditional hospital setting, but with much lower doses of neuroleptics and without higher costs. Some findings even suggest better results in the long run, especially on the subjective and psychodynamical level. How can this be explained?

In my opinion, an explanation is mainly possible on the basis of an affect-centred understanding of the dynamics of the human psyche in general, and of the dynamic of psychotic states in particular, along the lines conceptualized above. The theory of affect-logic leads, in fact, to hypothesis — which is extensively discussed in my already mentioned book on "The emotional basis of thinking"(Ciompi 1887e) — that neuroleptics do not directly influence cognitive functions, but act primarily on emotions by their impact on the affect-regulating limbic and paralimbic structures which, secondarily, then influence cognitive functions and behaviour. Similar but more differentiated, because more closely context-related, problem-centred and personality-adapted effects of emotions on thinking and behaving can, however, also be obtained in a natural way, as showed by the Soteria experience. Somewhat provocatively, it might therefore be concluded that lasting human support in an emotionally relaxing, protecting and empathic milieu has the same effects on psychosis as neuroleptic medication, but without the corresponding short-term and long-term side-effects.

An additional unconventional conclusion on the same lines is the hypothesis that schizophrenia too, and not only mania or depression, may basically be an "affective psychosis" of, however, a quite particular kind (cf Ciompi 1997d and e). This at first sight probably surprising idea, too, is based on the mentioned organising — or, at critical levels, pathologically disorganizing — operator effects of emotions on cognitive functions: whereas under normal conditions, affective-cognitive interactions and their effects on thinking show an optimal average flexibility and adaptability to changing contexts, these interactions become pathologically one-sided, in opposite directions, in mania and melancholia, where euphoric or melancholic emotional connections are rigidly attributed to perceptions and thoughts of all kinds. In acute schizophrenia, on the contrary, the functional links between affects and cognitions become too loose and unstable. This, in turn, leads to a highly dysfunctional discontinuity of cognitive and behavioural activities with, sometimes, extreme degrees of ambivalence. Already Eugen Bleuler, the father of the concept of schizophrenia, considered a pathological "loosening of associations" as a pathogenic core phenomenon of this enigmatic illness (Bleuler 1911). He also already postulated a central importance of affective dynamics for psychopathology in general (Bleuler 1926). Another outstanding German-speaking psychopathologist, Werner Janzarik (1959, 1988), developed, since the fifties, quite similar ideas in the framework of his concept of "structural dynamics". Recent clinical as well as neuropsychological and neuropathological findings, among them the already-mentioned circular relations between limbic-paralimbic and prefrontal areas as well as the growing evidence of abnormalities in just these areas in schizophrenics point in the came direction (Bogerts 1985, 1995; Buchsbaum 1990). Recent spectroelectronencephalographic findings, too, that show a predominant role of anxiety (and sometimes also aggression) in all kinds of schizophrenic states, including chronic states characterised by so called "flattened emotions" (Machleidt et al 1989; Machleidt 1992), speak for an affect-centered schizophrenia hypothesis.

Further support for an affect-centered understanding both of normal and pathological psychodynamics is provided by the chaos-theoretical approach of mental functioning that we have systematically developed on a theoretical level, and partly also confirmed by empirical research, during the last years (Ambühl et al 1992; Tschacher et al 1997; Ciompi 1989, 1997a, b, e). In this view, basic emotions such as fear, rage, sadness, joy etc. have attractor-like effects on cognitive functioning, and normal as well as psychotic states can be understood as so-called dissipative structures in the sense of Prigogine et al (1983) which are organized and integrated by the dominant emotional "tuning". They correspond, in fact, to global patterns of affective-cognitive functioning that are characterized by a specific distribution of affective connotations among the relevant cognitions. Under certain conditions, sudden non-linear changes, or so-called bifurcations, toward globally different, namely psychotic (paranoid, hebephrenic, catatonic, etc) patterns of affective-cognitive functioning can occur after a more or less long period of intense fluctuations. Of particular importance is the fact that critically increasing affective tensions, that are related to the affective-cognitive stressors mentioned above in the framework of our 3-phase schizophrenia model, may be understood, from the chaos-theoretical point of view, as so-called control parameters in the sense of Haken (1982, 1983) which furnish the energy needed for the observed overall shifts toward globally different (that is, psychotic) dynamic pattern of functioning. Formerly peripheral delirious ideas, on the other hand, can be understood as newly emerging so-called order parameters that eventually reorganize (or enslave", as Haken calls this phenomenon) the whole mental and behavioural field in a new way, after a critical period of instability.

Both for clinical practice and for research, it follows from all this that much more attention than has so far been the case should in future be paid to affective factors, and especially to the emotional atmosphere of therapeutic settings and proceedings of all kinds. Results of drug trials, too, remain biased, as long as this important variable is not adequately controlled. Just like patients with acute heart injury or decompensated diabetes, acute schizophrenics, too, need specialised intensive care in small therapeutic settings which are properly adapted to their particular needs. Only in such an environment does it become possible to combine adequately the complementary effects of modern psychotherapeutic, sociotherapeutic and pharmacotherapeutic, approaches into a differentiated instrument that corresponds to the complexities of a severe psychosis.

I therefore hope that Soteria-like institutions will multiply in the future. This is also necessary to deepen our experience and further explore the many research questions that still remain open, among them especially the long-term evolutions and the exact nature of the self-repairing forces that are at work in favorable cases. Just in German-speaking countries, about 20 Soteria-like projects are currently in preparation, and at least one other "Soteria" is already functioning in — Frankfurt an der Oder, Germany. In addition, certain components of the Soteria approach, for instance the so-called "soft room", have been introduced quite successfully into several conventional hospital settings. At another symposium in Berne in October of this year, we will try to obtain an overview of the rapidly expanding Soteria scene in Germany and elsewhere.

bibliography

Aebi, E., Ciompi, L., Hansen, H.: Soteria im Gespräch. Ueber eine alternative Schizophreniebehandlung, Psychiatrie-Verlag, Bonn 1993

Ambühl, B., Dünki, R.M., Ciompi, L.: Dynamical systems and the development of schizophrenic symptoms. In: Tschacher, W., Schiepek, G., Brunner, E.J. (eds.): Self-organization and clinical psychology. Springer, Berlin, Series in Synergies 58: 195-203, 1992

Bateson, G., Jackson, D.D., Haley, J., Weakland, J.W.: Sind schizophrene Psychosen dissipative Strukturen? Die Hypothese der Affektlogik. Vieweg. Wissenschaftstheorie, Wissenschaft und Philosophie 43, Braunschweig/Wiesbaden, 191-217, 1997

Benedetti, G. Klinische Psychotherapie. Huber, Bern-Stuttgart-Wien 1982

Benedetti, G.: Todeslandschaften der Seele. Vandenhoeck und Ruprecht, Göttingen, 1983

Bleuler, E.: Dementia praecox oder die Gruppe der Schizophrenien. In: Aschaffenburg, G. (Hrsg.): Hanndbuch der Psychiatrie, specieller Teil, 4. Abt. 1. Hälfte. Deuticke, Leibzig, 1911

Bleuler, E.: Affektivität, Subjektivität, Paranoia. Carl Marhold, Halle, 1926

Bleuler, M.: Die schizophrenen Geistesstörungen im Lichte langjähriger Kranken - und Familiengeschichten. Thieme, Stuttgart 1972

Bogerts, B.: Schizophrenien als Erkrankungen des limbischen Systems. In: Huber, G. Hrsg.): Basisstudien endogener Psychosen und das Borderline-Problem. Schattauer, Stuttgart, 1985

Bogerts, B.: Hirnstrukturelle Untersuchungen an schizophrenen Patienten. In: Leib, K., Riemannn, D., Berger, M. (Hrsg.): Biologischpsychiatrische Forschung. Fischer, Stuttgart-Jena-New York 1995, pp. 125-144

Buchsbaum, M.S.: Frontal lobes, basal ganglia, temporal lobes – Three sites for schizophrenia? Schizophrenia Bulletin 16: 377-378, 1990

Carpenter, W.T., Heinricks, D.W.: Early intervention time limited, targeted pharmacotherapy in schizophrenia. Schizophr. Bull. 9: 533-542, 1983

Ciompi, L.: Catamnestic long-term studies on the course of life of schizophrenics. Schizophrenia Bull. 6: 606-618, 1980

Ciompi, L.: Affektlogik. Ueber die Struktur der Psyche und ihre Entwicklung. Ein Beitrag zur Schizophrenieforschung. Klett-Cotta, Stuttgart, 1982 (In English: The psyche and schizophrenia. The bond between affect and logic. Harvard University Press, Cambridge/Mass. (USA) and London (GB), 1998)

Ciompi, L. (Hrsg): Sozialpsychiatrische Lernfälle. Aus der Praxis – für die Praxis. Bonn, 1985

Ciompi, L.: Zur Integration von Fühlen und Denken im Licht der Äffektlogik". Die Psyche als Teil eines autopoietischen Systems. Springer, Berlin-Heidelberg-New York-Tokyo, Psychiatrie der Gegenwart, Bd !: S. 373-410, 1986

Ciompi, L.: Learning from outcome studies. Toward a comprehensive biological-psychological understanding of schizophrenia. Schizophrenia Research 1: 373-384, 1988

Ciompi, L.: The dynamics of complex biological-psychosocial systems. Four fundamental psycho-biological mediators in the long-term evolution of schizophrenia. Brit. J. Psychiatry 155: 15-21, 1989

Ciompi, L: Affects as central organising and integrating factors. A new psychosocial/biological model of the psyche. Brit. J. Psychiat. 159: 97-105, 1991

Ciompi, L.: Affect logic: an integrative model of the psyche and its relations to schizophrenia. Brit. J. Psychiatry 164: 51-55, 1994

Ciompi, L.: Der Einfluss psychosozialer Faktoren in der Schizophrenie. Theoretische und praktisch-therapeutische Konsequenzen. Schweiz. Arch. Neurol. Psychiat. 145: 207-214, 1995

Ciompi, L.: Sind schizophrene Psychosen dissipative Strukturen? – Die Hypothese der Affektlogik. In: Schiepek, G., Tschacher, W. (Hrsg.) Selbstorganisation in Psychologie und Psychiatrie. Springer, pp. 191-127. 1997a

Ciompi, L.: Non-linear dynamics of complex systems: the chaos-theoretical approach to schizophrenia. Hogrefe & Huber, Seattle-Toronto-Bern-Göttingen, 18-31, 1997b

Ciompi, L.: The concept of affect logic. An integrative psycho-socio-biological approach to understanding and treatment of schizophrenia. Psychiatry 60: 158-170, 1997c

Ciompi, L.: Is schizophrenia an affective disease? The hypothesis of affect-logic and its implications for psychopathology. In: Flack, I.F., Laird, H.D. (eds). Emotions in psychopathology: theory and research. Oxford University Press, pp. 473-495, 1997d

Ciompi, L. die emotionalen Grundlagen des Denkens. Entwurf einer fraktalen Affektlogik. Vanderhoeck und Ruprecht, Göttingen 1997e

Ciompi, L., Müller, C.H.: Lebensweg und Alter der Schizophrenen. Eine katamnistische Langzeitstudie bis ins Alter. Springer, Berlin-Heidelberg-New York, 1976

Ciompi, L., Dauwalder, H.P., Agué, C.: Ein Forschungsprogramm zur Rehabilitation psychisch Kranker. II. Querschnittsuntersuchung einer Population von chronischen Spitalpatienten. Nervenarzt 49: 332-338, 1978

Ciompi, L., Dauwalder, H.P., Agué, C.: Ein Forschungsprogramm zur Rehabilitation psychisch Kranker. III. Längsschnittuntersuchungen zum Rehbilita-tionserfolg und zur Prognostik. Nervenartz 50: 366-378, 1979

Ciompi, L., Dauwalder, H.P., Maier, Ch., Aebi, W., Trütssch, K., Kupper, Z., Rutishauser Ch.: Das Pilotprojekt "Soteria Bern" zur Behandlung akut Schizphrener. I. Konzeptuelle Grundlagen, praktische Realisiering, Klinische Erfahrungen., Nervenartz 62: 2428-435, 1991

Ciompi, L., Dauwalder, H.P., Maier, Ch., Aebi, W., Trüzsch, K., Kupper, Z., Rutishauser, Ch.: The pilot project "Soteria Berne". Clinical experiences and results., Brit. J. Psychiat. 161: 145-153, 1992

Ciompi, L., Kupper, Z., Aebi, E. Dauwalder, H.P., Hubscmid, T. Trütsch, K., Rutishauer, Ch.: Das Pilotprojekt "Soteria Bern" zur Behandlung akut Schizophrener. II. Ergebnisse der verleichenden prospektiven Verlaufstudie über zwei Jahre., Nervenarzt 64: 440-450, 1993

Derryberry, D., Tucker, D.M.: Neural mechanismes of emotion., J. of Consulting and Clinical Psychology 60: 329-338, 1992

Gainotti, G.: Features of emotional behaviour relevant to neurobiology and theories of emotions. In: Gainotti, G. & Caltagirone, C, (eds.): Emotions and the dual brain. Springer, Berlin-Heidelberg-New-York-London-Paris-Tokyo-Hong-Kong, pp. 9-27, 1989

Haken, H.: Evolution of order and chaos. Springer, Berlin, 1982

Haken, H.: Synergetics. An introduction, Springer, Berlin, 1990

Harding, C.M. Brooks, G.W., Ashikaga, T., Strauss, J.S., Breieà, A.: The Vermont longitudinal study of persons with severe mental illness. I. Methodology study sample and overall status 32 years later. Am. J. Psychiatry 144: 716-726, 1987a

Harding, C.M., Brooks, G.W., Ashikaga, T., Strauss J.S., Breieà, A.: The Vermont longitudinal study of persons with severe mental illness. II. Long term outcome of subjects who retrospectively met DSM-III criteria for schizophrenia., Am. J. Psychiatry 144: 727-737, 1987b

Herz, M.I., Prodromalsymptome, intermitterende Medikation und Rezidvprophylaxe bei Schizophrenie. In: Böker, W., Brenner, H.D. (Hrsg). Integrative Therapie der Schizophrenie. Huber, Bern, pp. 264-277, 1996

Herz, M.I., Stymanski, H.V., Simon, J.C.: Intermitted medication for stable schizophrenic outpatients: An alternative to maintenance medication. Am. J. Psychiat. 139:918-922, 1982

Huber. G., Gross, G., Schüttler, R.: Schizophrenie. Eine verlaufs- und sozialpsychiatrische Langzeitstudie. Springer, Berlin-Heidelberg-New York, 1979

Huber, G., Gross, G., Schüttler, R. et al.: Longitudinal studies of schizophrenic patients. Schizophrenia Bulletin 6: 592-605, 1980

Janzarik, W.: Dynamische Grundkonstellationen in endogenen Psychosen. Springer, Berlin-Göttingen-Heidelberg, 1959

Janzarik, W.: Strukturdynamische Grundlagen der Psychiatrie. Enke, Stuttgart, 1988

Kavanagh, D.J.: Recent developments in expressed emotion and schizophrenia. Brit. J. Psychiat. 160: 601-620, 1992

Kimura, B.: Zwischen Mensch und Mensch. Strukturen japanischer Subjektivität. Wiss Buchgesellschaft, Darmstadt, 1995

Koukkou, M., Mansake, W.: Functional states of the brain and schizophrenic states of behaviour. In: Shagass, C., Josiassen, R.C., Roemer, R.A. (eds.): Brain Electrical Potentials and Psychopathology. Elsevier Science Publishing, Amsterdam, pp. 91-114, 1986

LeDoux, J.E.: Emotional networks in the brain. In: Lewis, M., Haviland, J.M.: Handbook of emotions. Guilford Press, New York, London, 109-118, 1993

Leff, J., Kuipers, L., Berkowitz, R., Eberlein-Vries, R., Sturgeon, D.: A controlled trial of social intervention in the families of schizophrenic patients. Brit. J. Psychiat. 141: 121-134, 1982

Leff, J., Vaughn, C.: Expressed emotions in families. Its significance for mental illness. Guilford Press, New York-London 1985

Machleidt, W.: typology of functional psychosis – A new model on basic emotions. In: Ferrero, F.P., Haynal, A.E., Sartorius, N. (eds.): Schizophrenia and effective psychoses. Nosology in contemporary psychiatry. John Libbey CIC., pp. 97-104, 1992

Machleidt. W., Gutjahr., Mügge, A: Grundgefühle. Phänomenologie Psychodynamik EEG-Spektralanalytik. Springer, Berlin, 1989

McGlashan, T.H.: A selective review of recent North American long-term follow-up studies of schizophrenia., Schizophrenia Bull 14: 515-542, 1988

Moos, R.: Evaluating treatment environments. A social exological approach. Wiley, New York 1974

Mosher, L.R., Menn, A.J., Matthews, S.: Evaluation of a home based treatment for schizophrenics., Am J Ortopsychiat. 45: 455-467, 1975

Mosher, L.R., Menn, A.J.: Community residential treatment for schizophrenia: two-year follow-up data., Hospital and Community Psychiatry 29: 715-723, 1978

Mosher, L.R., Vallone, R., Menn, A.: The treatment of acute psychosis without neuroleptics: new data from the Soteria project: Six-week psychopathology outcome data from the Soteria project., Internat. J. of Social Psychiatry: 157-173, 1995

Nuechterlein, K.H., Dawson, M.E.: A heuristic vulnerability/stress model of schizophrenic episodes., Schizophrenia Bulletin 10: 300-312, 1984

Ogawa, K, Miya M., Watarai, A., Nakazawa, M., Yuasa, S., Uténa, H.: A long-term follow-up study of schizophrenia in Japan – with special reference to the course of social adjustment. Brit. J. Psychiat. 151: 758-765, 1987

Overton, D. A.: State-dependant of "dissociated" learning produced with Pentobarbital Journal of Competitive and Physiological Psychology: 57: 3-12, 1964

Panksepp, J.: Neurochemical control of moods and emotions from amino acids to neuropeptides. In: Levis, M., Haviland, M.J. (eds): Handbook of emotions. New York, London, 87-107, 1993

Plogg, D.: Human neuroethology of emotion., Progr. Neuro-Psychopharmacol. & Biolog. Psychiat. 13: 15-22, 1989

Prigogine, I., Stengers, I.: Order of our chaos. Heinemann, London 1983

Singer, M.T., Wynne, L.C., Toohey, B.A.: Communication disorders in the families of schizophrenics. In: Wynne, L.C., Cromwell, R.L. & Matthysse, S. (eds.): The nature of schizophrenia. Wiley, New York-Chichester-Brisbane-Toronto. 1978

Tschacher, W., Scheier, C. Hashimoto, Y.: Dynamical analysis of schizophrenia courses. Biological Psychiatry: 41: 428-437, 1997 Wing, J.K., Brown, G.W.: Institutionalism and schizophrenia. A comparative study of three mental hospitals 1960-1968. University Press, Cambridge 1970

Winnicott, D.W.: The maturational processes and the facilitating environment. International University Press, New York 1965 /Dts: Reifungsprozesse und fördernde Umwelt, Kindler, München 1974

Zubin, J., Spring, B.: Vulnerability – a new view on schizophrenia. J. Abnorm. Psychology 86: 103-126, 1977

14: Seeking Asylum: R.D. Laing and the Therapeutic Community

Robin Cooper

Seeking Asylum: R.D. Laing and the Therapeutic Community

Robin Cooper

−1−

Two kinds of difficulty may beset the person attempting, in a brief presentation, to convey the salient features of some or other field of enquiry. One arises where the inherent complexities or technicalities of the subject matter are such as to resist any easy assimilation — perhaps this would be the case were I to be talking about the latest developments in particle physics or genetics. The other kind of difficulty, the one I confront here, and I think the greater difficulty, is that of doing justice to an idea which is, at heart, quite simple. Laing's conception of asylum is like this.

> "People didn't have to *do* anything", he says. "They were living under the same roof, and making a life together, on an ad hoc day-by-day basis. There were no formal duties. Simply sharing the same situation, sharing a kitchen, sharing the arrangements to buy food."

How can I ask you, for example, to take seriously the idea that the most consummate helpfulness may not require anyone "having to do anything", without my seeming to demonstrate utter simplemindedness, if not complacency, or smugness.

Two different inflections of the argument for places of asylum can be found in Laing's writings. Firstly, there is the ethical case. If a person does not wish things to be done to him, in the name of psychiatry, therapy or whatever, and however "well-intentioned" they may be, that person should be entitled to decline the intervention.

"Asylum" for such a person may be a matter of enabling a place to become available where he is allowed to be, without interference or, "treatment", and permitted to suffer or go through whatever confronts or besets him. It is worth noting that public concern seems to bear much more upon the question of *our* need for protection from *them*.

Laing's concern here is to do with treating a person *as a person*, however abject his circumstances; treating him or her with the full respect to which a person is entitled, which includes allowing him or her the dignity of being left alone. Laing here would be very much in accordance with the spirit of Robert Burns' "a man's a man for a' that" which is inscribed so deeply into the Scottish psyche. There but for the grace of God go I. Throughout the pages of Laing's writings there calls out a simple plea, not for more and more ever more sophisticated methods of treatment, but for more ordinary human decency.

Secondly, there is what might be termed — with some reservations — the *clinical* argument in favour of benign non-interference, and of letting the "illness" run its course. Laing was very aware of the irony whereby the psychiatrist ordinarily is not permitted to witness the unfolding natural history of "the schizophrenic process", insofar as this process invariably will be frozen by the powers of anti-psychotic medications. It was at any rate part of my training — no, not even my training, my *pre-training* — to play a part in the team which — not just once or twice — let the illness, in its acute form, run its perilous course. *One* of the aims of Laing's "asylum" was to generate and explore conditions where this might come feasible.

—2—

Laing's best known exploration of the practicalities of creating a place of "asylum" was, of course, Kingsley Hall. This followed his much earlier "experiment", putting his case for "asylum" to the test at Gartnaval Hospital. Whilst Kingsley Hall was clearly inspired by that kind of revulsion which exclaims in desparation: "there must be some other way", it was by no means simply set up out of blind well-intentionedness. A very great deal of theoretical labour had already prepared the way for Kingsley Hall, as readers of The Divided Self, written nearly ten years earlier, will be aware.

> "In our experimental places", states Laing "we've tried to do without "roles". I'm not sure that not doing without the roles really improves matters or is possible. That's not the essential of the thing. It's experimenting with social form so that we

can find within the context of our social system and the best sanctuary, wherein *a nexus of relationships* can subsist."

Kingsley Hall's experimentation with social form was an attempt to create a place where people could meet upon common ground. "So I'm just going to say," states Laing, in words of praiseworthy simplicity, "that I'm going to treat this person on equal terms to me. If he behaves in a way that is insufferable to me, I'll deal with that accordingly."

In particular Kingsley Hall attempted to cultivate the common ground of *living together*. One of the ways of approaching the idea of common ground might be by thinking about what it can mean to eat at the same table, and partake in various rituals which might accompany this, and which lead us in turn to reflect upon companionship and friendship, conviviality and hospitality, and the settings and circumstances conducive to these. The notion of common ground, as I understand the term, is furthermore inseparable from freedom: freedom to find one's voice, speak one's mind, to move and be moved. Common ground also requires us to think about the individual responsibilities entailed in its stewardship.

−3−

Laing spoke of Kingsley Hall as an experiment, and as such he regarded it as having been "inconclusive". "Under the circumstances" he writes, "its seemed to me that you could call it a draw, in a way, as far as it went... The thing is still in progress". Laing regarded some of the expectations placed upon Kingsley Hall as having been hopelessly unrealistic. "A lot of people" he says, referring to the unfair comparisons drawn between the Kingsley Hall initiative, and the far-reaching, legally enshrined national reforms associated with Basaglia in Italy, "talk about using this household, a *small scale strategy*, as an alternative way of addressing the whole domain of psychiatry."

It would, nonetheless, be fair to say that, as an experiment, it was somewhat flawed. It displays, for example, something of what psychologists have come to recognize as the "Hawthrone Effect": where the inherent self-consciousness of an experiment itself modifies the situation and distorts the data. Very much in the public eye, Kingsley Hall (in the words of one commentator "the Havana of the schizophrenic revolution") was in some respects hyper self-conscious, so that, according to some accounts, the most "ordinary" social niceties somehow became proscribed under the tyranny of "authenticity". What Kingsley Hall perhaps failed to address and to generate was something we might call "ordinary unselfconscious human habitat". It created some real possibilities for the cultivation of *common ground* between persons who might otherwise find themselves radically segregated, but this, ironically, seemed to take place at the expense of *common sense*. The collective abandonment of ordinary social niceties as a sub-cultural norm is here, I think, a violation of common sense, and indicates some degree of failure to appreciate to what degree common sense holds us together. Laing clearly recognizes this:

> "I couldn't negotiate with what I thought was a complete loss of common sense... If there weren't enough people who had that common sense, it wouldn't work..."

Laing makes no great claims that Kingsley Hall provided any definitive answer to anything.

I thought to myself that Kingsley Hall was certainly not a roaring success. But it is providing lessons that we can learn from anything, even if it simply shows that this particular way of doing it is not the way that it is going to work. That should percolate through, and maybe lessons can be learned.

"I was", he says "sadder and hopefully wiser". He speaks of his contribution of "harmlessness and compassion" which at the same time failed to find - and we should carefully savour these words — a *"tactical, workable, pragmatic, operational, down-to-earth, nitty gritty sort of thing that could work for other people"*. This is where we now turn.

—4—

We start where the human being resides — in a dwelling. Instead of "asylum" we have come, since the days of Kingsley Hall — and very significantly influenced by the late Dr. Hugh Crawford — to speak much more of *dwelling*, and of the *hospitality* of dwelling. Since Kingsley Hall — which played host to the rich and famous — we have become much more interested in *the ordinary*, and in *ordinary* human dwellings. "Asylum" is not ordinary; for most of *us*, asylum is for *them*. There is an oppositionality to the notion of asylum, which might encourage us to address ourselves too much to the tyranny *of the other*. But dwelling is much more to do with us. With all of us — and I don't need to remind you how insistent Laing was that we should worry much less about them — much more about us.

The concept of dwelling is important in a phenomenological philosophy, and occupies a significant and quite explicit place in the philosophy of Heidegger, Levinas, and Bachelard. The resonances which the word sounds in the writings of these thinkers have important bearings upon the way we approach our community households. We do not have the time here to go into all that. We must note, that with the introduction here of *dwelling* a difficulty arises. Because from this point on, the way that we conceptualize what we are on about no longer translates readily into the prevailing idioms of caring for, or treating the mentally ill. We find ourselves in a different epistemology. In keeping with this, we speak a different language. Or rather, we speak ordinary language, for we find in ordinary language, and the accumulated wisdom contained in ordinary language, all that we need to say. We do not eschew psychiatric language as part of some carefully contrived anti-stagmatist or "anti-psychiatry" posture, but much more pragmatically because it is of no great use to us. Ordinary language works well enough to describe and bring into view the sort of things which we find ourselves addressing.

Our concerns are with the vicissitudes, transitions and variations of human life. Included within the vicissitudes of ordinary life are its errings. Our conception of error — of losing one's way — is not that of malfunction and maladjustment; nor do we think here of broken things to be repaired. Neither do we see help as something to applied like force, within a structure of means and ends; helpfulness rather is more akin to the masterly inactivity which is responsible attentiveness to the situation.

When a person comes to one of our households, we have neither interest in, or need for, *paperwork*. There is, for example, no need for a person approaching one of our houses with an interest in moving in, to be accompanied by whatever psychiatric record he or she may have accumulated, since this information quickly becomes redundant in the business of getting to know one another. The people who live in our communities in any case become very sophisticated in their assessments and appraisals of others. Any dealings arising at the interface between the household and administrative bureaucracy (for example social services) maybe be minimal, and quite unobtrusive.

People who come to our houses (seeking asylum, if you like) do so because, as they make clear, they have something to go through, or to *weather*. The things that they have to go through, are human things, which include human fears, terrors and weaknesses. The most fitting place to go through or *suffer* human things — is in a human place. This is what Laing re-iterates throughout his entire writings. A human place for human things. Some of you will remember the stories which Laing would tell with such dark irony, as human places in the world, and our faith in our own capacity to nurture and trust these, seem to recede. Where would *you* rather die, Laing asks: in a hospital ward whilst the television is on, or in the slums of Benares?

—5—

The dwelling is the foremost human place. It is where we start from — the birthplace of consciousness and of civilization. Not just chronologically but *epistemologically* — this is one of the lessons of phenomenology. All our knowledge about the world presupposes and takes for granted an original being at home in it. "There is no dearth of abstract philosophers..." says Gaston Bachelard, "who know the universe before they know the house, the far horizon before the resting place, whereas the real beginnings... if we study them phenomenologically, will give concrete evidence of the values of inhabited space..."

But "the values of inhabited space" tend for the most part to be taken quite for granted, in rather the same way as we take for granted the lived body, and the lived world towards which the phenomenologists draw our attention. The contours of the dwelling place, the place to which all other places bear reference, are in many ways the sort of things which we take for granted, precisely because they are so day to day, so commonplace, so ordinary.

Helmut Plessner, in his essay *With Different Eyes*, writes:

> The world of the familiar and conventional is the self-evident, but this kind of understanding is a meaningful experience only when it is fought for and won. Only when it is won can it be called one's own. But for this new understanding to be won, the first familiarity has to have been lost, and life does not always do us the painful service of removing us from our familiar milieu.

This, as the Scottish poet Alasdair Maclean puts it, is the heavenly jest at the heart of all earthly paradises: you have to leave them to recognize them.

Here, Plessner articulates the project of phenomenology — to show us the world as it comes into being for us. To bring us back to our senses. Our approach to asylum, to households and communities, is profoundly informed by this call "to the things themselves". Indeed, we could very fairly say that our households *are* a kind of phenomenological practice. If I had to recommend just one text to provide guidance to the "therapeutic community", I don't think I could choose better than *The Phenomenology of Perception*. "What is phenomenology?" asks Merleau-Ponty, in his memorable preface to that work. "It is a philosophy for which the world is always already there before reflection begins... and all its effort are concentrated upon reachieving a direct and original contact with the world, and endowing that contact with philosophical status..."

—6—

But sometimes life *does* do us the painful service of removing us from our familiar milieu. The people who come to our households do so because they find themselves, in one way or another, isolated; alienated or disarticulated from *ordinary human belonging*. We could just as readily describe these disarticulations in terms of homelessness. Not homelessness in the sense of not having a roof over their heads (which is hardly ever the case) but rather in the way in which they do not enjoy that freedom of movement which is *being at home* in the world.

We all recognize experiences of not being at home in the world, in one way or another. Particular kinds of (extreme) disarticulation from the interpersonal world, and of not being at home in the world, we call madness. If this meeting had been held in the last century, it would probably have been convened under the auspices of the Royal College of Alienists.

It is not too difficult to offer some forms of translation between the categories of psychiatric or psychoanalytic diagnosis, and the phenomenological particularities of not being at home in the world. We would find ourselves describing some typical structures of the world of the obsessional, the world of the hysteric, the world of the schizophrenic. We would be describing the situations of persons who have lost their hold on the world, in very particular ways.

"Such a person", writes Laing, in *The Divided Self*, "is not able to experience himself "together with" others or "at home in " the world, but, on the contrary, he experiences himself in despairing aloneness and isolation."

—7—

Being at home in the world is a kind of *knowing one's way about*. But it is not primarily an intellectual knowing, for it crucially implies a *freedom to move* in some domain or other, which is more akin to sure-footedness. This is true even when it is a matter of being at home in the ideas of a particular thinker. If I am at home in, say, the ideas/the writings of Freud, I am free to move in this, it gives me an idiom in which I can speak, and which is now my own. It is perhaps easiest to think of being at home in terms of a particular field of play (e.g. the sailor is at home at sea, it is an element in which he moves freely). The footballer on the field, the dancer on the dance floor. It is very important, also, to think of the importance of *language* in knowing one's way about. Finding one's way, and finding one's voice seem to belong together inseparably.

Consider this illustration of habitation and living space, which I take from Goffman.

Patients who had been on a given ward for several months tended to develop personal territories in the day room, at least to the degree that some inmates developed favourite sitting or standing places and would make some effort to dislodge anybody who usurped them. Thus on one continued treatment ward, one elderly patient was by mutual consent accorded a free-standing radiator; by spreading paper on top, he managed to be able to sit on it, and sit on it he usually did. Behind the radiator he kept some of his personal effects, which further marked off the area as his pace. A few feet from him, in a corner of the room, a working patient had what amounted to his 'office', this being the place where staff knew they could find him when they wanted him. He had sat so long in this corner there was a soiled dent in the plaster wall where his head usually came to rest.

This evocative little account illustrates something of the centrality in our lives of taking up a place and making it our own, and the importance of this to human *dignity*. It makes us reflect upon inhabitation, which is our hold on the world, and its spaces. It rather clearly brings into view circumstances which do not lend themselves to a free inhabitation, within which, nonetheless, some patients are able to carve out for themselves some little pockets of free space in what essentially is occupied territory. It is of the utmost relevance, then, to be able to ponder upon *spaces which invite us to come out of ourselves*, to use Bachelard's fine phrase. It is also of the utmost relevance to be able to think of those gestures which point to, beckon towards, and open up these spaces.

"She thinks this house is her own", exclaims one of the members of the community, in exasperation. But why not! What hell are we talking about where the place that one inhabits is not " one's own"? What many people, of course, have difficulty in understanding, and in negotiating, are the distinctions between possessive and non-possessive ownership, and the fundamental issues of boundary which arise here. It is rather akin to the distinction — which can give rise to so much confusion and misery — between the self as an entity to be sought, and as a possibility to be realized in relation with another. Again, it is rather like human belonging, which is existential, not possessive: I belong to Glasgow and Glasgow belongs to me.

–8–

From the very beginning, when the infant is cradled in his mother's arms, the world becomes open by the gestures which we make to one another. In a gestural choreography, which has very little to do with the objectifications of "body language", we beckon, invite, repel, open and close, often in nuances of infinite subtlety.

But in a household, such as I am thinking of, these gestures, these lived intentionalities do not take the form of some kind of naked face-to-face confrontations. This is one place – one, I think, among many – where we would part company with some of the prevailing "therapeutic community" ideas, where, for example, the community is regarded as some kind of round the clock, 24-hour, ongoing therapy group. The gestures which arise in living together entirely change their meaning if they come to be subsumed as means towards the overarching goal of "therapy". They are contextualised in living together, *textured* in the stuff of living together, and living together is not a means to some end. Part of what makes a place feel lived in, alive, and conducive to being alive, are these textures and the meanings which are inscribed within them.

"Persons are not simply in front of one another; they are along with each other around something", writes Levinas, "it is through participation in something common, in an idea, a common interest, a work, a meal, in a 'third man' that contact is made". It is this "around something", the very substance of it, and the spirit in which we are around it, which is so important to our understanding of household community.

A person in one of our houses was saying the other day how she sometimes (quite often, in fact) feels so frightened of any dealings with others that she retreats to her room, where she remains in states of very considerable anxiety. As she stays there, the sounds of the house waft up to her. They hold her, they place her. We probably can imagine, without too much difficulty, something of the complex chorus of concordant and discordant meanings that the house sings out. We could think of this as just one modality of what I would call the textures of a household, into which the person (even the person who withdraws) becomes woven. This is the household, to use Winnicott's unforgettable phrase, "going on being".

A dwelling is shaped or takes shape; like a path it traces our intentions. It is shaped by our concerns — what we have time for — and our concern in turn takes shape within the dwelling. Concern is dispositional, and refers to that towards which, and the manner in which, we are disposed, inclined or drawn. "Concern" is not of course something which can be switched on at will - it belongs, we might say, with a generative rather than an administrative order. Our households simply attempt to cultivate, through talking, through thoughtfulness and tentativeness, an ambiance within which individuals' concerns — their concern, and their lack on concern — may show.

—9—

The gestural discourse between persons finds its most intricate articulation in language.

It is very appropriate to think of the household and its ambiance of concern in terms of its *conversation*. Conversation *belongs*. What is said, what can and what cannot be said, depends very much upon *where* it is said. It depends upon the spirit of the place. Here I am particularly concerned with conversation which belongs and takes place at home, with what we might call an *abiding conversation*, and the ways in which such conversation is textured. The conversation opens and closes, ebbs and flows, stays and moves on, becomes stuck, becomes freed. It opens up and is extended, as hospitality. A person proposing to join the community approaches, stands at the threshold of, and finds the words to enter this conversation.

Home is where you don't have to get it right. Silliness, foolishness, weakness and vulnerability belong there. So of course do the furies. We would want to stress, over and over again, the importance of error and of losing one's way, as the possibility of finding it, and of a culture which is hospitable to these things. "Don't for heaven's sake be afraid of talking nonsense", says Wittgenstein. "But you must pay attention to your nonsense."

−10−

Our houses are just like any other houses in the street. They're are like any other households where (predominantly) young people live together, getting on with their business in their own way. Some of the members of the household will have work, or studies, of one sort or another, typically most do not. If they don't want to get up in the morning, they don't have to. If their chosen sphere of inactivity extends to not wanting to wash up, or rinse the bath, clean the toilet or shop etc. then this will have to be negotiated with the others, as presumably it is in all sorts of ways, in households throughout the land.

But there is a difference between this house and the ones next door. Unlike the situation in most other houses in the street, one or more psychotherapists visit these community households, regularly, three or more times a week. Our households would not be possible without this. How could you expect people to go through the hell of living together, without very substantial encouragement? This doesn't mean that the house is now transformed into a clinic, where everything is in the service of analysis. It doesn't mean that the house is no longer a place where ordinary living comes first. The therapeutic presence, however, not only makes a difference; it radically alters the situation, by introducing psychotherapeutic self-consciousness, under the spell of transference, into the home.

−11−

There is another difference between these houses and the ones next door. The households gather in a certain name (e.g. the Philadelphia Association) and are an important part of the broader "community" of the Philadelphia Association. This constitutes a kind of *facilitating network* without whose help they could not have come into being. Without this 'backing' the household would hardly have the weight to obtain what a small group of individuals otherwise might not (e.g. a property), the know-how to administer that which needs administration, and the experience, broader perspective, and most importantly the colleagueship to draw upon when it comes to weathering the inevitable difficulties. In that most interesting era of American psychiatry, the era of moral treatment, the *ethnic community* provided an excellent example of a facilitating network which mediated between the therapeutic communities which sprang up, and the broader society. Indeed, it was largely because of the erosion of ethnic cohesiveness that these early "therapeutic communities" began increasingly to die out.

Our network makes it possible for our houses offer a rather unique kind of opening to the community at large, which does not fall readily into some pre-existing contemporary social paradigm. In the households — which are not half-way houses — hospitality takes root — this is why we might call them radical.

—12—

Over the thirty years which have passed since Kingsley Hall, many things which bear upon the life of our communities have changed. No such experiment would be tolerated today. Nevertheless, these three decades, with their different climates and influences, have seen some 20 Philadelphia Association community households — each with their quite different styles and idiosyncrasies — arise. We currently have 3 households in London, two of which are owned by the P.A. The third is made available by a housing association.

The concept, as I keep saying, is simple. We don't seem to do any harm to anyone. We cost practically nothing, since we incur none of the expenses associated with "residential care". There are many needs, we hardly need reminding, that we do not begin to answer, but upon a very small scale we can claim to fulfil the modest hopes set out at the beginning, of finding a tactical, pragmatic, workable way of going about things, which for the most part we enjoy, and find worthwhile. In thinking of these hopes, I recall the words of Michael Foot, in his plea, in a speech delivered in 1983, for "a civilized, compassionate home of freedom, and all the untidiness that freedom encourages and protects".

It will not come as a surprise to hear that the climate within which we work today is not particularly conducive to the cultivation of these small scale sanctuaries of untidiness, and we are constantly reminded of how delicately balanced is the matter of their survival. No matter how closely we approximate to being self-financing, and not needing to ask very much from anyone, we could not manage without some central government grants. So far as we can, we abide by the maxim that if you sup with the devil, you need a long spoon. We nonetheless become increasingly subject to bureaucratic controls. Although "caring" is not our style, we are subject to Regulations of Care. Persons who move into our households are required, for example, to read, and sign a statement indicating that they have read and understood our "complaints procedure". So the culture of litigation seeps into our work, and its inevitable corrosions. We are required to fulfill admissions policies. Health and safety procedures can of course make excellent sense, but can a household not become too safe, too healthy? Unheard of in the days of Kingsley Hall, the members of our communities are required to enter into formal agreement whereby they then have a tenanted entitlement to their room. This can make getting rid of someone who may no longer subscribe to the ethos of the house very problematic. It is a long way away from Laing's "if he behaves in a way that is insufferable from me, I'll deal with that accordingly...".

All of this tends to make us cautious. We become preoccupied with safety, and cover, and we become timid, afraid of risk.

Perhaps more disturbing is the "voluntary servitude" increasingly being self-imposed by the "caring professions", and which is transforming the culture within which therapy, of one sort or another, is practised. We have seen how the professionalization of psychotherapy has changed the nature of the whole field in all sorts of subtle, and not so subtle, ways. Now we await the forces of standardization and regulation to reach into the home. The Association of Therapeutic Communities, our relation towards which has been at best ambivalent, proudly proclaims in its recent newsletter that:

> In the last two years, we have begun a re-organization of the Association and its activities. With an active research group, the initiation of a Register of Therapeutic Community Practitioners, the beginnings of an established European Network, and some basic thinking about Therapeutic Community training and accreditation, the Association is thinking about representing TC work nationally.

We might ponder the reflection to which Martin Heidegger again and again, in different ways, returns. According to the Safranski Biography, the last words which Heidegger committed to paper, a couple of weeks before his death:

> There is a need for contemplation whether, in the age of a uniform technological world civilization, there can still be such a thing as home.

*****

notes

Talk given at Conference R.D. Laing Psychiatrist – Philosopher, under the auspices of the Royal College of Psychiatrists, London January 9th 1999

Of related interest, see also Cooper, Robin (1997) *What we take for granted*, Free Associations Vol.6, No.4

Cooper, Robin. (1989) *Dwelling and the Therapeutic Community* in Thresholds between Philosophy and Psychoanalysis. Papers from the Philadelphia Association Free Association Books. London

Cooper, Robin (1991) *Can Community be Planned?* Talk given to 18th Annual Conference, Friends Hospital, Philadelphia. Journal of Therapeutic Communities Vol.12 No.4

15: Laing and Psychotherapy

John M. Heaton

Laing and Psychotherapy

John M. Heaton

This paper is divided into two parts. First I will give a brief account of Laing's background in psychotherapy and his position in it for those who are not familiar with his work. Then I will discuss his concept of experience which is central to his thought on psychotherapy and his critique of modern society.

His Background: Laing trained in psychiatry in Glasgow and did his National Service in the army as a psychiatrist. He became interested in severely disturbed people and practised a psychotherapy chiefly inspired by his reading in phenomenology. He admired practitioners like Harry Stack Sullivan and John Rosen who introduced direct analysis; he was impressed that they talked in ordinary language to psychotics. Then he came to London to the Institute of Psychoanalysis where he trained with the middle group, having Charles Rycroft as his analyst and Winnicott and Marion Milner as his supervisors. His analysis was "undramatic" and according to him he soon realised "the name of the game" so presumably he conformed, perhaps rather strange in view of his childhood which, on his own account, was very disturbed. My own impression from talking to Laing was that he was disappointed with his experience at the Institute, but he certainly had a thorough grounding in psychoanalysis which influenced him deeply.

While training at the Institute, Laing was a registrar at the Tavistock for 6 years. He became very disillusioned with them, and I think they with him. He had a lot of sympathy with the argument that the Maudsley dealt with really ill people, but the Tavistock was a sort of dilettante outpost that dealt with normal middle class people. He was unhappy at not working in a hospital and only seeing people well enough to attend outpatients. However he did run groups for "border-line" patients at the Tavistock and learned a lot of the contempory work on psychotherapy. After he left the Tavistock he worked in private practice for the rest of his life.

Perhaps his main objection to the Tavistock was that the therapists there were in the state that Kierkegaard described as: 'The despair which is ignorant of being despair, or the despairing ignorance of having a self and an eternal self' (Kierkegaard 1989 p.73). They had no concept of man as spirit. There had to be something wrong with their patients and they saw it as their job to find it. There was a spiritlessness about the Tavistock that I think drove Laing to despair. A form of despair incidently also described by Kierkegaard — the despair of wanting in despair to be oneself, a form of defiance. It is clear from his first book *The Divided Self* and from conversations with him that Kierkegaard's *The Sickness unto Death* influenced his thought about the schizoid state more than any other book. His critique of 'normality' is based on Kierkegaard and one can see this influence in much of his writing.

His Psychotherapy: Absolutely central to Laing's thought and practice is that psychotherapy involves a relationship between persons, and he was concerned all his life in working out the implications of this. Now, persons are embodied beings and not bodies plus minds; he was scathing of any psychotherapeutic theory or practice that studied minds apart from bodies or bodies apart from minds; or the pretence of uniting them by means of a hyphen: psycho-somatic. He agreed with Aristotle in his *Politics (Bk1.2)* who stated that man is a political animal and that *man is the only animal who has the gift of speech. And whereas mere voice is but an indication of pleasure or pain, and is therefore found in other animals, the power of speech is intended to set forth the expedient and inexpedient, and therefore likewise the just and the unjust. And it is characteristic of man that he alone has any sense of good and evil, of just and unjust, and the like, and the association of living beings who have this sense makes a family and a state.*

The voice can cry out in pleasure or in pain as in infancy but human speech is articulated and has to be learned and can be written down. It is the ability to be articulate that is central to human being.

Now all this was fundamental to Laing and we can take each of Aristotle's statements and directly apply them to Laing's thought.

Persons are embodied: There are two ways that Laing developed this. He was very interested in gesture and the way our bodies communicate using the codes and classification systems of body symbolism which illustrate how political and social categories shape the decoration, perceptions and dispositions of the body. He was a friend and admirer of Ray Birdwhistell, an anthropologist who pioneered kinesics, the study of gestures and their meaning with the use of sound cameras and tape recorders. Laing would vividly describe the gestures of students, lecturers and sometimes colleagues and speculate on their meaning. The way words are spoken can be more revealing than the words themselves.

His concern with the body was also manifest in his interest in Yoga and the martial arts, and he would often recommend their practice as well as practising them himself. In no way did he think of the practice of psychotherapy as a purely mental exercise; he would, for example, advise patients who had a bad posture or some other body ailment to take up Yoga or some other body therapy.

Psychiatrists of course would rightly claim that they are very concerned about the body in that they study the brain and influence it with an increasingly powerful arsenal of drugs. But as far as psychotherapy is concerned it is the lived body that is important and this is influenced and empowered by the cultural principles that organise society as well as biological principles. For example it is very difficult for us to understand the gestures of someone from a very distant culture. Injunctions as insignificant as: 'Stand up straight' or 'Don't hold your knife in your left hand' reflect a whole political philosophy which can be largely unconscious (Bourdieu 1977 p.94).

Politics — Man is a political animal: Two of Laing's books have politics in the title: *The Politics of Experience* and *The Politics of the Family*. Again and again he emphasised that to understand people it is no good retiring into oneself and introspecting one's mind, observing one's so called inner world. As Louis Sass (1994) has argued it is the schizophrenic who is the extreme example of one who enters within himself to try and reach a solipsistic self sufficiency. For Laing it is *the relation between persons that is central in theory, and in practice* (Laing 1967 p.42). He was thus critical of the Cartesian tradition; Descartes was one of the first and most influential to articulate the division of mind from body and he had his basic insight by retiring by himself into a poule or stove heated room for some days.

Laing's interest in games theory and the various strategies that people develop to cope in families is another example of the political emphasis in his thought. His belief that the behaviour of the schizophrenic is better understood as *a special strategy that a person invents in order to live in an unliveable situation* (Laing 1967 p.95) is another example. These are attempts to get out of the 'malfunction' perspective of much psychotherapy which tends to address and treat the individual and his/her inner world, without taking into account that we are all situated in a practical space in which we live our lives and have to develop ways of coping with the difficulties we meet. It is this insight into practical space that is the source of Laing's interest in couples, the family, groups, communities, and society at large.

What Laing was trying to do was to create a shift not in what is seen, but in the way you see it. To see people behaving in certain ways as schizophrenic is one way of seeing them. But it is not the only way, for a different way of seeing brings different things into view; a confusion of Sir Martin Roth (1986) who criticised Laing for talking as if he had never been to a psychiatric outpatients and seen people who were obviously schizophrenic. The Laingian reply was that if you have been trained to look in a certain way then you will construe things according to how you have been taught to see them. So a psychiatrist will see schizophrenics. But this is not the only way of seeing people. At one time one may have seen the same people as possessed by demons, others would see them as people suffering a great deal of mental pain, or one might just see one's old Dad in a terrible state. It all depends on one's training, what one is asked to do etc. But it is fundamental to the concept of a person that they can be seen and see in different ways, as the structure of human perception.

Another political dimension of Laing's thought was his interest in power. He studied Foucault closely and was responsible for the translation of some of his books. To both thinkers power is present in all human relations and is not good or bad as such but of course can be, and is frequently misused; they were opposed to the liberal dictum of Lord Acton that all power corrupts and absolute power corrupts absolutely. Laing was interested in demystifying power not in the absurd project of getting rid of it; he was perfectly aware and not ashamed of the fact that he had a considerable amount of power — to get his books published, to take on or reject students, for example. Demystifying power is important in psychotherapy since some people think that because one is a doctor one can have them certified and bundled off to hospital; or alternatively that one can save them from the consequences of crazy actions. To make the law clear can be very helpful to some and Laing would do this. At a more sophisticated level he argued that psychiatric and psychoanalytic knowledge is not so impersonal and value free as it is often made out to be; there are complicated political forces at work in all societies which encourage and reward some forms of knowledge and discourage others.

Psychiatry, he thought, more than any other branch of medicine, is necessarily influenced by political forces. And by politics he meant much more than the amount of money the government is prepared to spend on psychiatry. The sort of dazed protest that one gets from some psychiatrists at the changes in psychiatric practice produced by politicians is the result of them ignoring the political dimension of most psychiatry. The failure of psychiatrists to think through the political dimension of their practice has left them at the mercy of politicians. To hide one's head in the 'inner world' as many psychoanalysts do or in the mechanisms of the brain as many psychiatrists do is an avoidance of an essential dimension of the care of mental suffering.

Laing was concerned with the study of people in situations especially people in a social crisis. Crucial to this is his insight that *no one in the situation knows what the situation is* (Laing 1971 p.31). *The situation has to be discovered* (p.33). The stories people tell about the situation which includes the 'patient', parents, spouses, children, social workers, doctors; do not tell us simply and unambiguously what the situation is. These stories are a significant part of the situation but there is no *a priori* reason to believe or disbelieve a story because someone tells it. The history of a situation is a sample of it, one person's way of defining it. It is vitally important for the psychiatrist not to construe the situation in terms of a few psychiatric myths, for resorting to one mythology or other is precisely what people do when confronted with a frightening and confusing situation.

To study a situation one has to enter it and try and keep a clear head, for critical situations are usually confusing to all concerned. One then finds one is involved in a process for the situation changes as soon as one has entered it. Each interpretation is an act of intervention that changes the situation, which thus invites another interpretation. So a movement of deliberation, negotiation and engagement is started which hopefully leads to a desirable conclusion for all. It is not the imposition of one person's demands on others; it is political and not managerial.

Laing was scathing of the tendency to label people schizophrenic on just a few minutes' interview in outpatients as if this label conveyed much understanding. It may be easy for an experienced person to spot various signs and symptoms but the central question to him was the nature of the social situation that the person lived in which drove the person to respond in the way they did. And of course the situation in outpatients is also a social situation for all concerned as he showed beautifully in his discussion of Kraepelin's catatonic patient at the beginning of *The Divided Self* (Laing 1960 p.29) .

The Talking Cure: Aristotle's remarks about the difference between the mere voice and articulated speech is central to all psychotherapy which is a talking cure. Freud was perfectly clear that psychotherapy involves a movement away from being ruled by the pleasure principle to the ability to judge what is or is not expedient, the just and unjust. As Laing put *it: Psychotherapy is an obstinate attempt of two people to recover the wholeness of being human through the relationship between them (*Laing 1967 p.45). He emphasised that it is two human beings that are in a relationship and so language, how we address one another, patterns of communication, the good and the bad, are central. He was always concerned that justice must be seen to be done by all concerned as far as possible in the treatment of mental disorder because justice is a basic characteristic of our humanity.

Ritual: One of the ways in which Laing was far ahead of his time was his insight into the importance of ritual in psychotherapy.

Ritual is used by all societies as a powerful means of dealing with and preventing social conflicts. It is a means of integrating the society and the individual both externally and internally. It is central to culture as a means of reconciling ourselves to nature and the natural violence within human beings. Rituals themselves are a way of constructing power relations and a way of empowering some and disempowering others. Symbolic systems, such as particular ritual patterns encode, and therefore promote particular social patterns. Ritual is basic to Foucault's notion of the constitution and exercise of power because of the way in which power involves the body and strategy. The social body is the micronetwork of power relations. And by social body he means the shifting network of power relations between a man and a woman, between the members of a family, between a master and his pupil, between everyone who knows and everyone who does not (Foucault 1980 p.187).

Ritual is not necessarily seen as a form of control by its participants. Thus a devout Roman Catholic will not feel controlled by the Mass but empowered by it whereas someone trying to free themselves from Catholicism may feel it is an instrument of coercion. Revolutions such as the Russian revolution of 1917 tried to do away with ritual but it has been shown they merely substituted a new lot of rituals for the old ones.

Ritual is basic to psychotherapy and probably more basic than story telling for there is a ritualistic aspect to story telling, and in the healing rituals of many societies story telling plays a little part. Freud and most psychoanalysts overlooked the importance of ritual as they were too much under the influence of the Enlightenment, and thus understood ritual to be mere superstition and only recognised debased forms of it as obsessional rituals. In the last 50 years anthropologists have understood ritual to be a key focus in the study of culture. Few people now hold the beliefs of the Enlightenment. Ritual is not to do with truth and falsehood as is science. It is more a strategy of social action, probably basic to man and many animals, and is a way of empowering or disempowering people.

Laing was interested in all sorts of psychotherapy partly because of his interest in ritual and what makes an efficacious psychotherapeutic ritual. It is often easier to see the ritualistic aspect of therapies that one does not practise oneself. He was interested in Shamanism as numerous anthropologists have shown that it is a very effective therapy in certain types of what we would call mental disorder. I should add that he did not claim to be a Shaman himself. He was perfectly aware that psychotherapy is very culture specific for its effectiveness; at root it is a cultural therapy for a cultural disorder in contrast, for example, to surgery. Surgery has been mostly developed in Western cultures but its effectiveness is not culturally specific; a heart transplant would be perfectly effective if done by a surgeon on someone whose culture was completely foreign to him.

Man, one could say is not only a political animal or a featherless biped but is also a creature that has a natural impulse for ritual and this has an important part to play in psychotherapy and Laing was a pioneer in its study.

Experience: Laing frequently used the notion of experience and it is central to his thought. But, as is well known in philosophy, the notion of experience is a very tricky one as it has many meanings; almost every philosopher who uses it gives it his own special meaning.

To anyone brought up in the Anglo-American tradition one thinks of the standard empiricist doctrine that all knowledge originates from experience and that nothing is in the intellect that was not first in sense. This gives it an epistemological flavour as it is assumed that there is an unproblematic foundation of knowledge which is given in experience and this is usually identified with sense experience, from which all knowledge is assumed to be derived and against which all theoretical interpretations must be tested. Hence the importance of observation and experiment in science. The threat to scientific progress is then seen as undisciplined interpretations arising from rationalist intuitions or unreflective dictates of custom and tradition.

Of course the bugbear of this view of the development of knowledge is mathematics; mathematics is essential to science but depends on axioms and proofs and not sense experience. Freud, who considered himself an empiricist, completely ignored mathematics with disastrous results to psychoanalysis. For the conceptual confusions in psychoanalysis are much more like the confusions in the foundations of mathematics studied by philosophers such as Frege and Wittgenstein than confusions due to lack of knowledge in the empirical sciences which require more experiment and observation. Laing, like Lacan and Bion, was one of the few psychotherapists to have some understanding of this. Hence his interest in mapping, games, rules and metarules. But he was in this as in much else, a pioneer but also something of an amateur.

For example for a time he was much enamoured of Gregory Bateson's explanation of the double bind theory in terms of

Russell's theory of types. But the theory of types had been shown to have fatal difficulties in the 1920s.

But Laing had a much more robust concept of experience than the standard empiricist one. He was a great admirer of David Hume whom he mentions several times with approval in Bob Mullan's *Mad to be Normal* (1995) and I often discussed Hume with him. It is easily forgotten that Laing was proud of his Scottish roots and so naturally was familiar with Hume and the Scottish Common Sense school of Thomas Reid. If people were more familiar with these Scottish roots then much of Laing's intellectual itinerary would become clearer.

Experience does not necessarily mean the sense data epistemology of modern empiricism with which Hume has been identified by many English academics. That abstract notion of experience is a barbarism of refinement to use Hume's term; it occurs when reflection becomes separated from common life, instantiating the view from nowhere; the thinker becomes radical and absolute or so he thinks.

Experience for Hume as well as for Laing is the enjoyment through conversation of the deeply established customs and conventions of a way of life, the domain of participation. To quote Hume: *And indeed, what could be expected from Men who never consulted Experience in any of their reasonings, or who never search'd for that experience, where alone it is to be found, in common Life and Conversation* (Hume 1996 p.2). He goes on to stress that the participation of women is essential to achieving the sort of humane self-knowledge that the conversation of common life makes possible.

Both Laing and Hume argued that the human world is understood through social participation in contrast to the world of the physical sciences which we learn about by limiting ourselves to observation and theorising. One might ask how does experience teach? We derive our judgments from experience but experience cannot direct us to derive anything from it. However, inherent in the notion of experience is the idea of multiple instances, repeatable occurences. So we can learn from experience but what we learn could have been otherwise and so experience could not teach without a context of human life with its customs and ways.

Psychoanalysis studies a particular way of participation, with its customs, rules and techniques. But to generalise this and assume that it is the best way of studying human nature and, worse still, to try and force its study into the methods of the physical sciences is to fall victim to a false philosophy. Human beings participate with one another in many different ways and so there are many different ways of getting to know and understand the human world.

I think this is one reason why Laing always retained some regret for leaving the mainstream of psychiatry. For psychiatry studies people in mental pain in all sorts of situations — inpatients, outpatients, their home and with their family, in prisons and the community not just under the constraints of consulting room psychoanalysis.

To quote Laing:

If human beings are not studied as human beings, then this once more is violence and mystification.

A little later referring to some contemporary writing on the family and the individual:

Gone is any sense of possible tragedy, of passion. Gone is any language of joy, delight, passion, sex, violence. The language is that of the boardroom. No more primal scenes, but parental coalitions; no more repression of sexual ties to parents, but the child 'rescinds' its Oedipal wishes... There is frequent reference to security, the esteem of others. What one is supposed to want, to live for, is 'gaining pleasure from the esteem and affection of others'. If not, one is a psychopath. (Laing 1967 p.53-4)

Hume would have liked this quote. It illustrates a central theme of his — the illusions that false philosophy can lead to. For it inverts truth by trying to base ordinary language on a special language — in this case the language of the boardroom. He argues that all special languages grow from ordinary language the words we learned on our mother's knee and then talking to our brothers, sisters, and friends. Secondly it claims that all desire can be subsumed under one — in this case gaining pleasure from the esteem and affection of others. Human beings however have countless desires. If I thought that this talk would get me much esteem and affection from others surely I would be grossly deluded. There are all sorts of possible responses to it, perhaps if I am lucky one or two people might give me some esteem but I should be surprised to get much affection!

Laing's insight into the importance of common sense and the ordinary is shown in much of his writing. Most importantly in his 'treatment' of schizophrenic people in small communities where the ordinary difficulties of living together can be met and discussed rather than being dealt with by well-meaning 'carers' or blotted out with drugs. So what Blankenberg (1982 &1991) has called 'the loss of natural self-evidence' — one of the fundamental defects found in schizophrenia — can be healed.

So what is the mystification of experience? How can we judge it? Experience as meant by Laing, Hume, and Montaigne, who Laing greatly admired, is not concerned with knowledge in the scientific sense but with meaning and this is mostly conveyed by stories, maxims, proverbs, etc. If something dramatic happened at this meeting you would probably go home and tell a story about it and you might add: "It was quite an experience".

Experience in this sense is incompatible with certainty and once an experience has become measurable and certain, it immediately loses its authority. There is no formulating a maxim nor telling a story where scientific law holds sway. A man of experience depends on imponderable evidence and this is difficult to teach as one has to learn correct judgments where no definite rules apply. Rather a teacher gives the right "tip" at the right time and his ability to do this shows his authority. Laing would often talk of the importance of being 'street wise' in psychotherapy.

The contempory way in psychotherapy, and much psychiatry, is of course the way of science and administration, and this conceals and mystifies experience. So no wonder psychiatrists complain of their loss of authority, for authority depends on experience whereas applied science depends on following the correct rules. When the authority lies in the rules and not the person of the psychiatrist and his/her judgment based on experience, then an administrator can easily check whether the rules have been followed or not. So authority passes from the psychiatrist to the administrator and experience is expropriated from both psychiatrist and patient.

Laing had great personal authority in his understanding of the infinitely varied forms that mental suffering presents. I think this is what made him into the effective and world famous therapist that he was.

references

Aristotle *Politics* Trans. J. Barnes 1253a7-17.

Blankenburg, W. (1982) 'A dialectical conception of anthropological proportions' in *Phenomenology and Psychiatry*. Ed. A.J.J. De Koning & F.A. Jenner. London: Academic Press.

Blankenburg, W. (1991) *Contribution a la Psychopathologie des Schizophrenies Pauci-Symptomatiques*. Trans. J.M. Azorin & Y. Totoyan. Paris: Presses Universitaires de France.

Bordieu, P. (1977) *Outline of a Theory of a Practice.* Trans. R. Nice. Cambridge University Press.

Foucault, M. (1980) *Power/Knowledge.* Ed. C. Gordon. N.Y.:Pantheon Press.

Hume, D. (1996) *Selected Essays*. Oxford University Press.

Kierkegaard, S. (1989) *The Sickness Unto Death*. Trans. A.Hannay. Penguin.

Laing, R.D. (1960) *The Divided Self*. Penguin.

Laing, R.D. (1967) *Politics of Experience*. Penguin.

Laing, R.D. (1971) *The Politics of the Family*. London: Tavistock.

Mullan, B. (1995) *Mad to be Normal*. London: Free Association Books.

Roth, M. & Krull, J. (1986) *The Reality of Mental Illness*. Cambridge University Press.

Sass, L. (1994) *The Paradoxes of Delusion*. Ithaca & London: Cornell University Press.